CULTURE, SCHOOLING, AND PSYCHOLOGICAL DEVELOPMENT

edited by

LILIANA TOLCHINSKY LANDSMANN

Tel Aviv University, Israel

Human Development, Volume 4

The Tel Aviv Annual Workshop in Human Development

Sidney Strauss, Series Editor

ABLEX PUBLISHING CORPORATION
NORWOOD, NEW JERSEY

Library of Congress Cataloging-in-Publication Data

Culture, schooling, and psychological development / edited by Liliana
    Tolchinsky Landsmann.
        p.   cm. — (Human development ; v. 4)
    Includes bibliographical references and index.
    ISBN 0-89391-529-7
    1. Educational psychology.   2. Child development.   3. Cognitive
learning.   4. Educational anthropology.   5. Education—Social
aspects.   I. Landsmann, Liliana Tolchinsky.   II. Series: Human
development (Norwood, N.J.) ; v. 4.
LB1051.C92 1990
370.15—dc20   90-49579
                                                            CIP

Ablex Publishing Corporation
355 Chestnut Street
Norwood, New Jersey 07648

Contents

Human Development:
Preface to the Series

Sidney Strauss
Series Editor

This book series is the product of annual workshops held by the Unit of Human Development and Education in the School of Education at Tel Aviv University. Whenever a new publication comes out, the person responsible for it feels compelled to answer the question: Why a new X (journal, book, book series)? I do not feel exonerated from asking and answering that question. The purpose of the series is to address topics of theory, as well as conceptual and methodological issues that reflect the diversity and complexity of human development. It aims to address four needs in our field, as they relate to edited books.

There are few attempts to deal with important developmental phenomena in a concentrated manner in most of the book series in our field. They generally contain a collection of chapters or unrelated topics. There is a need to have leading experts present their views about relatively circumscribed issues. Our books will be organized around a topic where contributors write chapters that fit into a larger picture the editor will be illuminating.

A second need in our field is to have more interdisciplinary work. We generally read books written by developmental psychologists for developmental psychologists. Restricting inquiry to the psychological realm promotes a rather narrow view of human development. The view of man as a biological entity and cultural producer and consumer as well as a psychological being has been deeply neglected, and an element that will characterize our books is the inclusion of representatives of intellectual disciplines to discuss topics we believe to be of importance for our field.

Most work in developmental psychology is published in English and written by Americans. Much of the Western and Eastern European work is unknown to the vast majority of developmental psychologists, and the same can be said with more emphasis for work being done in Latin America, Asia, and Africa. Whenever possible, we will bring leading intellectual figures from these continents to contribute to our deliberations.

The fourth need is to attend to the applied parts of developmental psychology. Some of the later books will revolve around issues relating developmental psychology and education. We chose this out of the conviction that educational issues force one to face the depth of human complexity and its development in ways that traditional academic developmental psychology often turns away from.

The topics for the books are chosen with an eye towards directions our field is taking or we think should be taking. In some instances we will have a book about a topic that has been discussed in the literature and is ripe for a summary or stocktaking. In other instances the book will be around a topic that has not been discussed at all or has only begun to be written about. In still other cases the book will be about a topic that was once a subject of inquiry and then dropped. We will publish a book around that topic if we believe it should be resurrected because of developments in the field.

The support given by Ablex Publishing Corporation, the Tel Aviv University Committee for Conferences, and different heads of the School of Education (Rina Shapira and Shimon Reshef) have made the workshops and this book series possible, and their support is gratefully acknowledged. This is especially so in light of the financial hardships in the publishing field and in Israel. Continuing support of this series is a welcome sign that despite economic adversity, there is a commitment to the intellectual pursuits that are of interest to us all.

It is the hope of the members of the Unit of Human Development and Education that this series will reflect the lively and stimulating workshops that have been held at Tel Aviv University, and that the community of developmental psychologists will find interest in the issues discussed in these pages.

Sidney Strauss
Ramat Hasharon
August 1985

Introduction

Liliana Tolchinsky Landsmann

We know very little about the process by which new ideas are generated. It seems, however, that behind any invention there is an arduous re-elaboration of old ideas: one's own old ideas and other people's's old ideas. Having access to what is already known is one of the conditions for creating something new. Some cultures have created special institutions, that is, schools, whose explicit function is to transmit what is already known. Formal education, however, is not the only way by which new members become part of the common cultural pool. Different forms of social interaction, technology, and direct participation are among the possible means of getting involved. This book deals with the nature and development of different forms of knowledge and the specific cultural, social, and educational settings that may affect their transmission.

In North America, at the turn of this century, when psychology was just starting to be delineated as an independent discipline, people believed that a scientific psychology might serve as a rational basis for education (White, Chapter 1). In the new-born Soviet Union too, young psychologists were considering a similar possibility, related to formal instruction as the main force for the development of higher psychological functions. Later on, until the 1970s, many European and American psychologists believed in the possibility of studying psychological development independently of school influences and even of cultural specifications. It is not the case that developmental psychologists were convinced that there are natural acquisitions which would occur without environmental intervention, but they preferred to make developmental studies of those behaviors where the precise role played by the environment is unspecified, rather than studying acquisitions where the role of the milieu (school, in particular) is more defined. In striving to be more experimental, universal, and objective, many developmental studies become fragmentary and artificial.

The present volume brings together several different attempts to overcome these limitations. It approaches the development of mind from a sociocultural and historical perspective and discusses the educational implication of this approach. Cross-cultural similarities and intracultural differences are brought to bear to support a fundamental distinction between cognitive structures that require minimal triggering and knowledge that in order to be transmitted requires special institutions. Two main outlooks in developmental psychology—the Piagetian and the Vygotskian—are confronted to highlight the role of social context and particular forms of social interaction in cognitive development. Specific principles, artifacts, and metaphors on which our culture is grounded are analyzed and their effect on cognition discussed. Moreover, the relationship between cultural principles, pedagogical practices, and evaluation of cognitive growth is carefully examined. The subject matters which most of the chapters deal with are those considered to be major acquisitions of childhood: reading, writing, and arithmetic—all those themes that were once supposed to be only school subjects.

In Sheldon White's chapter, we find guiding metaphors of the relationship between developmental psychology and education. They are offered in a historical perspective through the visions of three American psychologists: Hall, Thorndike, and Dewey. In their eyes, one of the psychologist's tasks should be the definition of the knowledge base educators need. Hall defines it as the study of the moods, feelings, attitudes, and automatisms that develop in the child. This would be the source of prescriptive advice for those concerned with the child's socialization and education. In Thorndike's view, psychologists should measure individual differ-ences in order to help with decisions about where and how different children should be educated. For Dewey, since school reconstructs on a symbolic level the child's personal experience, psychologists must study the role of school in society. The three agreed in their description of the child's initial state containing the seeds of complex capacities to be unfolded by personal and social experiences. They also believed in the possibility of a general learning mechanism. However, while Hall considered it possible to find fixed stages in development, Dewey believed in the power of education to change any fixed course. Both of them defended the viability of a scientifically based morality. Thorndike declared that the role of the school is to change people for the better, although it is not in the psychologist's hands to define ''the best.'' What would later become the main themes in developmental psychology are already delineated here: definition of the initial state, school modeling, learning mechanisms, value-setting, evaluation, etc.

In Atran's and Sperber's chapter, useful distinctions to understand the relationship between culture and cognition are presented. Culturally transmitted knowledge has to be distinguished from knowledge learned through instruction. It is clear that most of what we know has been learned from others, although not necessarily taught, and since it is very problematic to establish the relationship between learning and teaching in general, the authors propose to move from learning in general to learning in specific domains. The authors dissent strongly with Thorndike's connectivism and Piagetian arguments in favor of general mechanisms across domains. In their view, different concepts may require a different supporting environment and different mechanisms to be learned. Some bodies of knowledge, like color classification or taxonomies of living things, are only marginally affected by social change, while others depend for their transmission on specific institutions. However, in the process of repeated social transmission, cultural programs may come to take forms which have a good fit to the natural capacities and constraints of the human brain. Thus, when similar cultural forms are found in most societies around the world, there is a reason to search for psychological factors which could account for these similarities. The study of cultural transmission helps us to identify specific domains and to make assumptions regarding the initial state and regarding mental organization in general. Atran's and Sperber's argument and field findings show that not only sensory modalities, but also nonsensory modalities, are specific cognitive domains. Children would be assumed to come to the world equipped with an innate but specialized learning ability for which no manipulation of the learning situation (other than deprivation of relevant input) could fundamentally alter the content or development.

From a different theoretical stance, a Piagetian perspective, Bearison coincides in showing how the growing concern with the nature of sociocultural constraints has fostered the distinction between two kinds of cognitive objects: physical inanimate objects and social objects. Although early research concentrated on the evolution of children's notions of physical and mathematical objects, recent interest in Piaget's theory has extended to children's construction of social relationships. Bearison focuses on the social foundation inherent in Piaget's interpretation of cognitive development and shows very clearly that in his accounts, the objects of scientific discourse are not natural, external, or given in the environment, but are "inherently endowed with human intentionality and cultural forms." The basic unit of Piaget's developmental analysis is the interaction between subject and object.

After clarifying this basic agreement with Soviet activity theory, Bearison analyzes in a very profound manner how the two approaches differ in three fundamental issues: their conception of the features of social interaction that facilitate conceptual change; and their view of the process of internalization from social interaction to individual cognition and in the epistemological distinctions about different kinds of knowledge.

In Wertsch's chapter, we find the sociocultural approach toward these three issues—that is, the relationship between social milieu and psychological functioning, the process of internalization and the nature of knowledge. Unlike Bearison who proposes the distinction between physical and social objects, Wertsch focuses on the distinctive forms of discourse which are generated and mastered in social life to deal with any kind of object. Once he puts forward the notion of text-based reality, the form of discourse generated when dealing with natural language, he analyzes that form whose properties reflect the sociocultural category of rationality—rational text-based reality. He then suggests that children and subjects from traditional societies violate the rules of rational text-based discourse. For instance, young children "confuse" content and form of linguistic expressions. If one follows Wertsch's argument, many explanations which have been provided for similar phenomena within other theoretical backgrounds—in terms of development of metalinguistic capacities (Papandropoulu & Sinclair, 1974; Markman, 1976) or nominal realism (Piaget, 1920)—should be replaced by a sociocultural explanation. Young children respond differently because they have not yet acquired the rules of text-based reality. If the properties of this form of discourse are privileged in the child-adult zone of interaction, they will be internalized, becoming a natural way of seeing reality. The zone of interaction typically constructed in the literacy practices of the classroom has a primary function of socializing students into approaching task settings rationally.

The subject of literacy and literacy practices is taken up in two chapters (chapter 5 and 7), but with different emphasis. In my chapter, the focus is on the development of literacy before schooling, while Brown and her coworkers look at literacy activities in class contexts. Two of the Vygotyskian themes in which Wertsch's approach is grounded, that is, the need to study the origin and transformations of any knowledge in order to understand it and the notion of mediation, are taken by me to study empirically what Vygotsky called "the prehistory of written language." This specific topic is utilized to highlight Piaget's and Vygotsky's basic coincidences and divergences. They agreed in the role of assimilation and of activity in psychological development, as well as in the need to study the genesis of human behavior, both on an individual and on a social level. They disagreed on the relative importance of intra- and interpsychological interaction in development and on the limiting role of structure, as well as on the epistemological distinctions about spontaneous and scientific concepts. These convergencies and divergencies are recast further to give a specific sense to the activity construct in the teaching of reading and writing and to reject the need of pre-requisites to learn written language.

Literacy activities in school contexts are one of the subject matters utilized by Brown and her collaborators to present an experience of reciprocal teaching, one of the aspects of their work that was directly influenced by the idea of collaborative cognition and the famous Vygotskian construct—"Zone of Proximal Development." They describe the concrete strategies, the characteristics of the learning environment, and the role of the instructor used for the task of text comprehension. They also reported the impressive success of the children not only in text comprehension over time, but also in settings other than those under control. It is clear from Brown's work that the necessary knowledge base on which to find pedagogical decisions cannot be only a list of moods and feelings or even detailed cognitive abilities as depicted by previous psychological research. The knowledge base has to be constructed or at least checked for the particular didactical problem psychologists and educators are attempting to solve.

In this and the other two aspects grounded in the same ideas—child-tester interaction and mother–child interaction—they dwell extensively on one of the crucial issues raised by Bearison: the need to relate to knowledge as a process and not as a state. Bearison recalls that the shift from "fixed capacity" models of development to a more process-oriented approach constitutes a fundamental transition from describing WHAT develops to describing HOW it develops. Brown and her collaborators provide empirical evidence that only by knowing how children arrive at a response (be it wrong or right) would it be possible to get a real diagnosis and to plan effective instruction.

The goal of Damon's and Phelps's chapter is to state whether variations in forms of stimulation or social interaction make a difference to the quantity or quality of knowledge that is learned. They describe one type of social interaction as a learning context peer collaboration engagement assuming that this type is usually unavailable in most instructional relations.

This interactional setting differs from those which involve adult-child or expert-child interaction because of the fundamental symmetry—at least purported—of the relationship. In peer collaboration, a pair of children work together to solve tasks that neither could do previously. Once the vantages of this setting are advanced, empirical evidence is presented to support the conclusion that peer collaboration is an effective learning environment for tasks that require logical reasoning. The success of this strategy is explained in terms of its triggering of "sociocognitive conflict." Interaction leads to disagreements, these in turn lead to awareness of different points of view, to the need to argue (verbally) and to justify the child's own point of view. It transpires from Damon's and Phelp's description of the situation (though not so much from their interpretation), that what is acting here as a motor for improvement is not an improvement of communication skills. Thanks to the possibility of reflecting on their own actions, of the verbal rendering and of turning the procedure into an object of knowledge, children are moving toward higher levels of representation. While interacting with others, children are working internally. Doing work internally does not mean doing it in isolation. What Piaget constantly emphasizes is that development cannot be directed from outside, but has to be internally re-elaborated. It is the double dialectic—external (subject/object) and internal (relationship among ideas, hypotheses, or schemas)—that leads to cognitive change.

From Damon's and Brown's studies, it seems that both reciprocal teaching and peer engagement are equally effective contexts for learning. Nevertheless, since no comparison was made for different populations, the relative fitness of these intervention strategies for specific groups remains an open question.

Additional epistemological distinctions are presented in Strauss' chapter. They are not in terms of kind of cognitive objects, as proposed by Bearison (Chapter 2), but in terms of the Vygotskian categories of spontaneous versus school-learned knowledge. These forms of knowledge are clothed in different symbolic systems and respond to three levels of psychological reality: (1) a deep level of mental organization biologically determined, which roughly corresponds to the kind of cognitive structures that require minimal environmental triggering, according to Atran and Sperber (chapter 1), except that for Strauss, they seem general rather than domain-specific; (2) a surface level, which is very close to a description of the child's behavior; and (3) a mid-level. Educational psychologist's research should be done on mid-level spontaneous concepts to assess normative development. This is the first phase in curriculum development according to Strauss' developmental model of instruction. Further phases suggested by the model are: training research to help children overcome conceptual difficulties found in the normative development, curriculum development, and curriculum implementation and evaluation. The chapter includes a discussion of each phase and a case study on the arithmetic average to illustrate them. As in Damon's and Phelps's (Chapter 8) and Brown et al.'s (Chapter 7) chapters, in Strauss' we find a specific intervention strategy to overcome conceptual difficulties and improve cognitive growth—in this case, the use of analogy. In the presented study, children are helped to build analogies between their spontaneous knowledge clothed in a qualitative symbol system, and the school-learned knowledge, clothed in a numerical symbol system.

Up to now, reciprocal-teaching, peer-collaboration, and analogy were presented as possible ways to affect conceptual change, yet in Salomon's chapter, we encounter a theoretical exploration of five possible ways in which technologies affect the mind of the individual. These effects may vary along three interrelated dimensions: the source of the effect—whether the individual's encounter is through a cultural representation or a direct and personal one; the role of the individual in producing the effect—whether the personal engagement with technology is incidental or mindful; and their dependence from content—whether they are content-specific or content-free general skills. Following Strauss' distinction (Chapter 8), the focus is on the effect of technology on thinking frames or strategies occupying a mid-level between long-term ontogenetic developments and factual knowledge. The ways in which technology can affect the individual's mind are: (a) Creation of metaphors that turn into cultural representations, to examine and interpret other phenomena; (b) Creation of new distinctions, for instance, when computers are described as machines that think, this description challenges our notion of thinking processes and force a distinction between diverse ways of thinking; (c) Partnership with technology, direct and active contact with computers may lead to cognitive-reorganization since it redefines what we do, how we do it, and when we do it; (d) Improvement of already existing particular skills and cultivation of transferable skills. This effect cannot be attained without first-hand experience with technology and a demand to master the skill beyond the level already mastered. Mere exposure or inconsequential executed activity may not suffice; (e) Internalization of symbolic modes and tools to serve as cognitive ones. In order for a certain tool to be internalized, it must be made of the same symbolic mode, operations, or meta-operations the mind is using, and it must fit the learner's level of ontogenetic development.

Most of the chapters reflect what White defines as a "new spirit in the field" of social sensitivity and moral responsiveness. Universalistic and structuralistic developmental theories favor a nonnormative attitude. Developmentalists tend to term variances in logical thinking, as well as linguistic and dialectal variations, as "different" rather than "better" with regard to any standard logic, language, or dialect. This creates a certain divorce between developmental psychologists' standards and school standards. Teachers at school as well as traditional forms of testing used at school have continued to evaluate performance in normative terms. Alternative logics are not accepted in problem resolution and some linguistic variations are considered and evaluated better than others. Moreover, speed and accuracy are still important factors in evaluation. It is not surprising then that the theme of cultural values implicit in evaluation is approached in this volume by many of the authors.

Wertsch (Chapter 4) tries to present the category of rationality as value-free, and rational discourse as only one of the forms of cultural discourse. Although other forms may be "equally effective," rational discourse is the one privileged in our sociocultural setting and, as such, it turns out to be a key parameter in evaluating children's performance.

Brown and her collaborators (Chapter 7) reformulate the whole issue of testing from a Vygotskian perspective. Dynamic testing, as opposed to a static standardized form, is the best method to use to get an accurate picture of children's learning potential and to guide educational intervention. Taking a realistic stance, however, the authors do not suggest to replace one way of testing with the other. They rather prefer to prepare children to succeed in traditional test settings. One can conclude that through their intervention strategies they are teaching children to be more rational.

The issue of culturally valued forms does not count only for the evaluation of children's performance, but also for curriculum design. Strauss (chapter 6) reminds us that besides psychological and epistemological consideration, a cutting point for decisions about what content should appear in curricula is its cultural value. The discipline to be taught in schools is considered important for children to understand so that they can fit into and move along the general sociopolitico-economic structure of the society. According to Salomon (Chapter 9), the same counts for the appreciation of technologies. Culture determines the socially perceived status and nature of the technology, the tasks to be performed with it, and the values assigned to the encounter.

The reflections of these authors coincide with one of the general findings of cognitive anthropology, "while performance of some procedures in every culture is a matter of option or convenience, the performance of most cultural procedures is motivated by culturally learned values" (D'Andrade, 1981, p. 192). But why is it so strong? The explanation provided by D'Andrade is very revealing. "These values are a complex association of symbol and affect—that is, representation of states of affairs associated with feelings and emotions. The affective component of human information processing appears to be deeply embedded in cultural representations. By fusing fact and affective valuational reaction, cultural schemata come to have a powerful directive impact as implicit values" (D'Andrade, 1981, p. 193).

People are affectively compelled to become part of their culture. On top of this basic feeling, the amount of time, personal effort, engagement, and re-elaboration needed to learn on a personal level the increasing amount of what is already known on a social level is enormous. This may be the reason why looking for more effective ways of transmission is still a matter of scientific inquiry.

References

D'Andrade, R. G. (1981). The cultural part of cognition. *Cognitive Science, 5,* 179–195.

Markman, E. (1976). Children's difficulty with word referent differentiation. *Child Development, 47,* 742–9.

Papandropoulou, I., & Sinclair, H. (1974). What is a word? Experimental study of children's ideas on grammar. *Human development, 17,* 241–58.

Piaget, J. (1920). *The child's conception of the world.* London: Routledge & Kegan Paul.

Three Visions of a Psychology of Education

Sheldon H. White

Harvard University

In a survey of American science for the Paris Exposition of 1900, James McKeen Cattell (1900) listed three journals of education: the *Education Review* founded by Nicholas Murray Butler at Columbia University in 1891, the *Pedagogical Seminary* founded by G. Stanley Hall at Clark University in 1891, and the *School Review* founded by John Dewey at the University of Chicago later in the decade. There were other education journals in the United States in 1900, but Cattell's three were the journals published by universities and associated with science. The journals came from three places with influential visions of the way in which psychology could improve education. At Columbia there was an engineering vision, at Clark a developmental vision, and at Chicago a reconstructive vision.

The engineering vision was realized in Thorndike's *educational psychology* and was established as a fixture of American schools of education during the 20th century. The developmental vision has waxed and waned—coming to life a first time in G. Stanley Hall's child study program, dying off, coming to life a second time in the child development movement of the 1930s and 1940s, dying off again, and emerging a third time in the growth of developmental psychology in the 1960s and 1970s. A number of trends suggest that we may now be moving toward a more complete realization of Dewey's reconstructive vision in the contemporary movement of psychologists towards a more historical understanding of their discipline, toward applied work, and toward an interest in the social basis of mind.

The Pluralism Of Early Psychology

There were several psychologies of education near the turn of the century because there were several psychologies. Most historical accounts of psychology simplify its origins by conforming to a "one-big-bang" theory that says that psychology was born all at once, when philosophical questions and scientific methods were joined in Wilhelm Wundt's Leipzig laboratory in 1879. The American Psychological Association had a 100th birthday in 1979 with all members—clinical, social, experimental, physiological, personological, industrial, developmental, and educational psychologists—celebrating their presumptively common origin in Leipzig. However, not all contemporary psychology descends from Leipzig in 1879, from questions of epistemology, and from the laboratory technologies of 19th century physics and biology.

• One of the first American textbooks of the "new psychology," John Dewey's (1887/1967) *Psychology,* listed four methods of scientific psychology: (a) *the method of introspection*—the study of conscious experience; (b) the *experimental method*—with two branches: *psychophysics* and *physiological psychology;* (c) the *comparative method,* embodying four kinds of comparisons (*"Mind, as existing in the average human adult . . . compared with the consciousness (1) of animals, (2) of children in various stages, (3) of defective and disordered minds, (4) of mind as it appears in the various conditions of race, nationality, etc."*); and (d) the *objective method*—the study of things made by people, such as language, science, social and political institutions, art, religion, and so on, with these artifacts of human manufacture viewed as objectifications of the fundamental properties of the human mind (Dewey, 1887/1967, pp. 11–16).

• William James' (1890/1981) *The Principles of Psychology,* three years later, said psychology had three methods: (a) *introspective observation* (b) *the experimental method* and (c) the *comparative method.* For James, as for Dewey, introspective observation meant the study of exceptional states of consciousness. James described the comparative method in these terms:

> So it has come to pass that instincts of animals are ransacked to throw light on our own; and that the reasoning faculties of bees and ants, the minds of savages, infants, madmen, idiots, the deaf and blind, criminals, and eccentrics, are all invoked in support of this or that special theory about some part of our own mental life. The history of sciences, moral and political institutions, and languages, as types of mental product are pressed into the same service. Messrs. Darwin and Galton have set the example of circulars of questions sent out by the hundred to those supposed able to reply. The custom has spread, and it will be well for us in the next generation if such circulars be not ranked among the common pests of life. (James, 1890/1981, p. 193)

• Rand Evans (1984) has recently outlined the psychology seminar G. Stanley Hall taught at Johns Hopkins in 1886. Hall held the first American professorship in psychology and he established at Hopkins what is generally regarded as the first American brass-instruments laboratory. Nevertheless, Hall's interest in scientific psychology ranged far beyond the research work of the brass-instruments laboratory; his psychology seminar took three years, during which he dealt with the findings of experimental, abnormal, and comparative psychology.

• Danziger (1985) has surveyed the contents of eight major psychological journals between 1879 and 1898, finding evidence for three distinct traditions of psychological research which he calls the "Leipzig model," the "Paris model," and the "Clark model."

Evidence from textbooks, courses, and journals indicates that American psychology embodied several embryonic scientific programs from the beginning. Some matured earlier—generally, those that took methods and methodology from the natural sciences. The later-maturing psychologies were addressed to questions about politics, society, morality, education, human nature and character, people's capacity to change, and governance. Psychologists interested in such questions bided their time, and their psychologies were a conglomerate of essays, systematic formulations, prospectuses, mixed with diverse scientific findings. The later-maturing psychologies waited for inventions of method and methodology in order to form effective and meaningful research programs in developmental, personality, and social psychology. Evidence favors what might be called the "popcorn theory" of the birth of psychology. Historically, there have been many little "bangs," fusions of philosophical questions with empirical methods, to form a number of scientific enterprises in psychology. Indeed, psychology is still being born.

Living in a pluralistic field, the first psychologists had several visions of the way in which psychological science might be of service to education.

Psychology's Establishment And Education

It was important to link psychology to education at the beginning. Psychology did not separate from philosophy easily. There was distinguished sponsorship for the idea that psychology—all of it (Kant) or some of it (Wundt, Dilthey)—could not be approached by the methods of natural science. Many people were skeptical about psychological science. In France, Alfred Binet went to the end of a distinguished career without a professorship in a French university (Wolf, 1973). When Krohn surveyed 11 leading German universities in the 1890s, he found skepticism and resistance to the idea of a scientific psychology in several of them (Krohn, 1892a, 1892b).

As late as the 1930s, psychologists in some American universities were still struggling to establish their own freestanding departments, away from philosophers. The armchair philosophers the psychologists left behind remained, as we now know, alive and well and contentious. Nevertheless, some psychologists broke free of philosophy early. What freed them were the new teacher training colleges and schools of education being founded near the turn of the century.

Society first gave an independent place to psychologists in the expectation of benefits to education. When G. Stanley Hall went to Europe to work in Wundt's laboratory, he worried about how he would get a job with his psychological science back home. He took the precaution of touring Europe's educational facilities and, indeed, his professorship at Johns Hopkins was in psychology and pedagogy. John Dewey was head of the combined department of psychology, philosophy, and pedagogy at Chicago. The young Thorndike dreamed of a career in which he could pursue the animal studies he had begun so brilliantly in his thesis. He settled for a career as an educational psychologist at Teacher's College. Walter S. Hunter (1952) reported in an autobiographical chapter that when he completed his Ph.D. in 1917 and looked for a job in an American university, he faced the fact that the jobs were either in philosophy or in education.

Educators wanted psychologists, among others, to participate in the development of a more powerful national system of schools. School usage was changing. Each level of American education contended with problems of growth, with new demands, and with new political confrontations.

At the preschool level, kindergartens were coming into use. Kindergartening was a gathering place for feminism. Within the kindergarten movement, old-guard Froebelians contended against liberal and progressive kindergarteners. Elementary schools were growing because compulsory education laws were being passed and enforced. A coalition of social workers and organized labor moved children out of the workplace and into schools. As children of all classes and ethnicity streamed into school, there were questions about fair ways of determining the more or less academically able and about Americanizing the immigrants. At the turn of the century, high schools and colleges redesigned their requirements so that the path to college could go through the high school (rather than the traditional prep school). Both high schools and colleges experienced great growth. At both levels, proponents of the traditional classical curriculum argued with advocates of the new science curriculum, while both together contended with advocates of a more work-oriented vocationalism.

Cremin's (1964) history of progressive education examines the multiple pressures toward change that were impinging on American schools in the late 19th century. Education had to find new ideas, new management systems, and new managers to assist in the building of what would amount, in the end, to a radically new organization of American education. People sometimes say, "Nothing ever changes in American education," but there may be a tendency to underestimate the changes in education that come about because a large system of American schools, impinging on the lives of every American family, changes slowly—and, in fact, must *seem* to change slowly. But 20th-century social movements and legislation brought about many changes to American schools—see, for example, Cremin's (1964, pp. 306–308) estimate of the educational changes brought about by the progressive movement in education.

G. Stanley Hall, Edward L. Thorndike, and John Dewey were prominent figures in American discussions about education. The three men gave ideas to educational policy makers, and when you are casting about in the management of a large and imperfectly known system, trying to decide what is happening and what ought to happen, ideas are important.

• Thorndike and Woodworth's (1901) studies of transfer of training were used in arguments, against the contentions of the classicists, that Greek and Latin training are less helpful than more up-to-date subjects.

• When "liberal" and "progressive" kindergarteners contended against "conservative" Froebelians, they were building on Hall, Dewey, and Thorndike (White & Buka, 1987).

• Questions about which children should go into special educational situations—special classes, or classes for the gifted—were met by testing programs. Thorndike played a strong role in creating them.

• Should all children be given a schooling once given to the children of the well-to-do? Should schooling be redesigned to meet the new needs of industrial society? Should schooling be vocationally oriented? John Dewey was a leading figure in the progressive movement that was an important force in helping people wrestle with such questions.

Hall, Thorndike, and Dewey were significant figures in the educational deliberations and policy making of their time—as, indeed, their academic descendants have been in successive periods of active renegotiations of the social contracts in education. Beyond their work outside the universities, the three men strove to establish within the universities a programmatic body of work in psychology that would have a bearing on education—an educationally relevant psychology. They were animated by three visions of the way in which psychological research should contribute to education: Hall by a developmental vision, Thorndike by an engineering vision, and Dewey by a reconstructive vision.

The three visions all had some merit, I believe, and all were fulfilled in contemporary work on the interface of psychology and education. We will consider them here in the order in which they were set forth—Hall's first, then Thorndike's, then Dewey's—because it is convenient to discuss them in that order. But if we are talking about the fulfillment of the visions through the establishment of the programs they envisaged, then a different order of consideration is in order.

Thorndike's engineering vision was realized first; it was the basis of educational psychology programs in all colleges of education for most of this century. Hall's developmental vision had a short-lived period of influence near the turn of this century, but his program waned in the early 1900s. Still, something like his vision of an educationally relevant psychology of development had a strong influence on both psychology and education in the 1960s when Piagetian methods and theory crossed the water and had a large influence on American developmental psychology. Dewey's reconstructive vision may now be emerging in the current orientation of psychologists to the schools.

The Developmental Vision

Dorothy Ross's (1972) biography of G. Stanley Hall is subtitled "The Psychologist as Prophet," and this seems to be an incisive characterization of the role of the psychologist in education, and in society at large, as G. Stanley Hall saw it. Hall sought to address education as a new order of moral philosopher, one whose prescriptions rested on science rather than revelation.

The psychologist, in Hall's vision, would be the scientific interpreter of natural processes of human development. Child study would reveal the fundamental principles of human development, and such principles would guide parents, teachers, and others who worked with children towards effective and appropriate practices of socialization and education. Nature, properly read, would tell you what to do.

In his youth, G. Stanley Hall studied moral philosophy with Mark Hopkins at Williams College. Hall was instructed in the tradition of deism and "natural theology" which, in the early 19th century, served many people as a halfway house between religion and science, a way of accepting and harmonizing the claims of both. Deists argued that God was no longer continuously active, but that His purpose animated all processes and activities. God had wound up the clockwork of the world which now inexorably fulfilled His purposes. An interesting corollary of deism was the supposition that God's plan could be read in the book of nature. The scientist, rather than the minister, might be a privileged reader of God's will.

Hall had been introduced to developmentalism before psychology. Proponents of "natural theology"—such as Robert Chambers (1853) and Hall's teacher, Mark Hopkins (1865)—argued that what distinguishes living things from physical things is that living things *develop*. Hall, who was an ordained minister before he was a psychologist, moved during his lifetime from a developmental theology to a developmental psychology of human affairs (White, 1985). His two-volume *Adolescence* (Hall, 1904/1911) reflected his belief that the study of development can provide the basis for a scientifically grounded moral philosophy.

Hall's Adolescence

Hall's *Adolescence* is remembered but largely unread today; textbooks associate it with the slogan "ontogeny recapitulates phylogeny" but say little more about it. Hall, like others of his time, had been led towards a belief in recapitulationism by the writings of the respected embryologist, Haeckel.[1] In the preface to *Adolescence*, Hall says that he has tried to be cautious in his use of it:

> Holding that the child and the race are each keys to the other, I have constantly suggested phyletic explanations of all degrees of probability. . . . Realizing the limitations and qualifications of the recapitulation theory in the biologic field, I am now convinced that its psychogenetic applications can have a method of their own, and although the time has not yet come when any formulation of these can have much value I have done the best I could with each instance as it arose. (p. viii)

The two volumes, 1,373 pages long, contain more than an essay on recapitulationism. They offer: (a) surveys of contemporary research on child development, (b) a developmental stage theory, and (c) practical recommendations for the way schools, parents, and others in the community ought to deal with children.

The research review. The *Adolescence* volumes contain a number of long reviews of research available at the turn of the century. Volume 1 contains reviews of literatures of growth in height and weight, the growth of body parts, motor development, juvenile diseases, delinquency and crime, sexual development, phys-

---

[1] In his *Ontogeny and Phylogeny*, Stephen J. Gould (1977) gives a history of Haeckel's influence on embryological thinking. He also points out that there seems to be a lingering underground belief in recapitulationism: "I have had the same most curious experience more than twenty times: I tell a colleague that I am writing a book about parallels between ontogeny and phylogeny. He takes me aside, makes sure that no one is looking, checks for bugging devices, and admits in markedly lowered voice: 'You know, just between you, me, and that wall, I think that there really is something to it after all' " (pp. 1–2).

iological periodicities and, finally, literary treatments of adolescence. Volume 2 examines what is known about changes in the senses and the voice, adolescent feelings, adolescent love, adolescent feelings about nature, cross-cultural data on social treatments of puberty, religious conversions in adolescence, social instincts and participation in institutions, and intellectual development and education. Dealing with physical growth in the first volume, Hall writes in a measured, conservative tone. As the research literature becomes less solid—in the latter chapters of Volume 1 and in Volume 2—Hall fleshes out the literature findings with speculative argument.

Hall's developmental psychology. Weaving his analysis through the research findings, Hall sets forth a theory of stages of child development that might be called a *Social-biological* theory (White, 1990). There are biologically programmed *nascent periods.* Cognition changes from one period to the next, but the cognitive changes are part of a broader movement: changes in sentiments, will, and social attitudes that make the child able to participate in progressively more complex forms of human society. Hall's prototypical child resembles Rousseau's *Emile* (cf. White & Buka, 1987).

Hall's stages are successive epochs in child development, laid down by human evolution. In common with many people of his time, Hall believed that evolution had extended human immaturity in order to permit a longer period for education and acculturation. The most famous proponent of this view was John Fiske who argued that evolutionary increases in human intelligence had been accompanied by, and were sustained by, prolongations of early human immaturity:

> So instead of being born with a few capacities thoroughly organized, man came at last to be born with the germs of many complex capacities which were reserved to be unfolded and enhanced or checked and stifled by the incidents of personal experience in each individual. In this simple yet wonderful way there has been provided for man a long period during which his mind is plastic and malleable, and the length of the period has increased with civilization until it now covers nearly one third of our lives. (Fiske, 1883, p. 315)

Hall thought that the thinking and the behavior of very small children is dominated by instinctive feelings and automatisms. There is much about children's feelings in the *Adolescence* volumes—not the dark Freudian impulses nor the Watsonian triad of fear, rage, and love—but myriad small sensibilities, conceits, sympathies, posturings, appreciations, poutings, struttings, wants, and sensitivities. Hall's questionnaire program collected anecdotes and reminiscences associated with such feelings in childhood. The reports of Hall's respondents were, in a small way, anamneses.

The *Adolescence* volumes review the findings of the questionnaire studies concerning children's feelings about such things as: (a) boundless space and time, (b) the stars, (c) the sun and light and darkness, (d) the moon, (e) clouds, (f) wind and air, (g) heat and cold, (h) sea and water, (i) rocks and stones, (j) flowers, (k) trees, and (l) animals.

Hall searched for the pagan in the small child and there is something haunting about what he turns up. Hall felt—like Susan Langer (1967)—that mind is an essay on feeling and in a number of the questionnaire studies he sought to trace the passage from children's feelings and mythical thoughts about the world towards reasoned understanding. Some of the Hall studies were obviously antecedents of some of Piaget's early work. The Piaget work was methodologically much more sophisticated, yet one misses in his data the mythopoetic element that from time to time emerges in Hall's questionnaire data.

Feelings are one substrate of mind, automatisms another. Automatisms are "paleopsychic" fidgets and nonvolitional movements, "motor odds and ends" that increase in the kindergarten years, diminishing in the primary years as the will grows in force. Hall had an eye for the minor details in human behavior and a penchant for neverending, stamp-collecting, slightly phenomenal kinds of sentences. In one such epic sentence, he lists some childhood automatisms and makes the reader *feel* as though he confronts a room full of squirming small fry.

> licking things, clicking with the tongue, grinding the teeth, scratching, tapping, twirling a lock of hair or chewing it, biting the nails (Berillon's onychophagia), shrugging corrugations, pulling buttons or twisting garments, strings, etc., twirling pencils, thumbs, rotating, nodding and shaking the head, squinting and winking, swaying, pouting and grimacing, scraping the floor, rubbing hands, stroking, patting, flicking the fingers, wagging, snapping the fingers, snuffling, squinting, picking the face, interlacing the fingers, cracking the joints, finger plays, biting and nibbling, trotting the leg, sucking things, etc. (p. 159)

Hall felt that there was a buried adolescence, "the shores of an ancient public sea," manifesting itself at age seven in childhood, and he saw this age as a point of transition and a "stage change" in child development.

> After the critical transition age of six or seven, when the brain has achieved its adult size and weight and teething has reduced the chewing surface to its least extent, beings an unique stage of life marked by reduced growth and increased activity and power to resist both disease and fatigue which. . . suggests what was, in some just post-simian age of our race, its period of maturity. Here belong discipline in writing, reading, spelling, verbal memory, manual training, practice of instrumental technique, proper names, drawing, drill in arithmetic, foreign languages by oral methods, the correct pronunciation of which is far harder if acquired later, etc. The hand is never so near the brain. Most of the content of the mind has entered it through the senses, and the eye- and ear-gates should be open at their widest. Authority should now take precedence of reason. Children comprehend much and very rapidly if we can only refrain from explaining, but this slows down intuition, tends to make casuists and prigs and to enfeeble the ultimate vigor of reason. It is the age of little method and much matter. . .

For Hall, ages 8–12 constitute a "unique period in human life" and a first period of social maturity. The child develops a life of his own outside the home; he is "never so independent of adult influence"; but he has acute perception, and some immunity to exposure, danger, accident, as well as temptation. The child is, in short, viable for the circumstances of a simpler social life.

> Everything, in short, suggests the culmination of one stage of life as if it thus represented what was once, and for a very protracted and relatively stationary period, the age of maturity in some remote, perhaps pigmoid, stage of human evolution, when in a warm climate the young of our species once shifted for themselves independently of further parental aid. (pp. ix–x)

Adolescence, Hall believed, must be treated as a second point of initiation for socialization and education. What is missing in the psychology of the child? At age 15—the age that some today designate as "post-formal"—Hall thought there is a *beginning* of reason, true morality, religion, sympathy, love, and esthetic enjoyment. Adolescence, then, should be the occasion for a new pedagogy and a new process of socialization.

Hall's stage theory—a first consolidation of development at age seven, a second subsequently at age 15 is, when all is said and done, not terribly different in its demarcations of the early life course from the schemes of Piaget, Freud, or Vygotsky. Hall centers his attention on children's moods, feelings, and attitudes, on motor automatisms, on the will, and on the ability of the child to participate in social life. Contemporary developmental psychology needs to pay more attention to exactly these things and until we do I don't believe the *Adolescence* volumes will have been adequately mined out.

Practical Recommendations

Hall is frequently prescriptive in his *Adolescence,* moving easily and unblushingly back and forth between "is" and "ought." In his preface to the two volumes, Hall gives a brief overview of the issues of "pedagogic matter and method" he will address:

> motor education. . . and will-training. . . the pedagogy of the English literature and language, history, drawing, normal and high schools, colleges and universities, and philosophy. . . nature and the sciences. . . Menstruation and the education of girls. . . hygiene, crime and secret vice. . . social and religious training. . . and the education of the heart. (p. xix)

Hall's recommendations include the following:

Optimal period for motor specialties. "Fundamental" muscles mature before "accessory" muscles; children control large-muscle movements before small-muscle movements. Hall (1904/1911a, *I*, p. 164) argues that, from ages 4 to 8, overexercising the accessory muscles may "sow the seeds of chorea." From ages 8 to 12, overprecision, especially if fundamental activities are neglected, will bring nervous strain and be counterproductive. However, (p. 164) "motor specialties requiring exactness and grace like piano-playing, drawing, writing, pronunciation of a foreign tongue, dancing, acting, singing, and a host of virtuosities" should be begun before adolescence.

More motor activity and motor education. Exercise and motor education are essential for children (Hall 1904/1911a, *I*, p. 170). In extended sections, Hall argues for: (a) industrial education, (b) manual training, (c) gymnastics, (d) sports and play games. Hall was concerned, like many of his contemporaries, about the health of small children cooped up in school. He wrote at a time when American states were just beginning to pass laws declaring that every public school must have a playground, and that there must be physical training for all children.[2]

Juvenile justice. In a chapter on "Juvenile Faults, Immoralities, and Crimes" Hall (1904/1911a, *I*, 325-410) offers a well-researched discussion of how much and why adolescents get into trouble with the law. He discusses "bad seeds" vs. environmental theses about why children commit crimes, and the assumption that hereditary factors (*degeneration*) are a significant source of criminal behavior in society. He reviews the ages at which various societies make children liable to penalties for a crime—Roman law, 7; canon law, 7; the law of Italy, 8; Austria, Holland, and Sweden, 9; Germany, 11; England, 16—and reviews various discussions about children's sensitivity to questions of right and wrong at different ages, and the possible meanings of legal penalties to them.

Staged science education. Science education should begin in adolescence (Hall, 1904/1911a, *II*, pp. 153-154). (a) Children first respond to nature sentimentally; education should begin with the mythic and the poetic in science. (b) Education should next address popular science, finding the connections of science to the daily life of the child in home, school, and play. At this stage, there should be "abundant apparatus, models, diagrams, collections, and all aids that eye or hand can give the mind. A science building or course without these is a soulless corpse." (c) Next, utilities, machinery, and processes of manufacture should be discussed. "Contrary to common educational theory and practise, the practical, technological side of science should precede its purer forms." (d) Last and highest, pure science freed from all alloy of myth, genetic stage, or utility, and cultivated for its own sake, with no motive but love of truth, should be taught.

A radical social pedagogy. New interests in, and capacities for, social affiliation emerge in adolescence. In Chapter 15 of Volume 2, "Social Instincts and Institu-

---

[2] For an excellent historical review of this early interest in physical development of children, see Friedrich-Cofer (1986).

tions," Hall deals with a number of interrelated tendencies: (a) self-consciousness, vanity, affectation, and showing off; (b) changes in the way anger and pugnacity are dealt with; (c) fear, shock, blushing, bashfulness, modesty; (d) pity and sympathy; (e) love of home versus running away; (f) adolescents' orientations towards school and teachers vs. home and parents; (g) ideals and plans for adult life; (h) the social judgment of adolescents, their cronies; (i) spontaneous social organizations— gangs, clubs; (j) student life and organizations; (k) associations for youth guided by adults; (l) material and methods for moral and social culture of youth. The Clark University questionnaire studies come heavily into play in this chapter. Finally, Hall proposes

> a radical change of base in the pedagogy of the vernacular language, literature, and history. . . . I urge that the prime purpose in all this field which should determine every choice of matter and method is moral, viz., to so direct intelligence and will as to secure the largest measure of social service, advance altruism and reduce selfishness, and thus advance the higher cosmic order. (p. 432)

Hall is against the teaching of ethics, but he does favor involving adolescents in debate, oratory, drama, literature—particularly myths, the Bible, and history and literature. Hall's discussion of the intelligent use of social organizations and socially oriented activities is, in my view, superior to any number of the contemporary discussions of "prosocial behaviors" one finds in the research literature nowadays.

We have taken a small glance at a large body of prescriptiveness in Hall's writing.[3] The two volumes end with two chapters on special problems—one on the education of adolescent women and one on "Ethnic Psychology and Pedagogy, or Adolescent Races and their Treatment." In the former, after a sustained review of contemporary evidence and arguments, Hall takes the position that ideal institutions of higher learning for men and women should be different. In the latter, Hall argues that the genetic psychology just presented in the two volumes can be the basis of a rational training of missionaries:

> Mission work should be regarded as a part of pedagogy and be included in the work of this department in every university and college just as the psychology of the lower races should be included in every course in psychogenesis. (p. 744)[4]

Hall's Scheme
Hall's vision of a psychology of childhood saw it as a source of prescriptive advice for those concerned with the socialization and education of children.

---

[3] Seven years after *Adolescence*, Hall (1911) published two large volumes titled *Educational Problems*. These volumes give a much more complete sense of what Hall had to say about education, but *Adolescence* is of more contemporary interest because it reveals the way in which Hall's educational prescriptions grow out of his developmental theory.

[4] Hall extended his remarks on missionary training in his 1911 *Educational Problems* and it seems reasonably clear that his interest turned towards such work after, with the *Adolescence* volumes, he completed his period of interest in child study.

1. The psychologist declares both means and ends to those who rear children.
2. Child development follows a natural evolutionary sequence. Child study re-
    veals the stages of children's development, the capabilities of the child at each
    stage, and the ends and goals toward which the growth sequence directs itself.
3. There are higher and lower modes of psychological organization associated
    with higher and lower forms of human society.
4. Child development is a biological process directed toward a series of possi-
    bilities of social organization. As children grow older, they become capable of
    entering into progressively more complicated and powerful social arrange-
    ments.
5. The development of the child culminates in civility, scientific thinking, and
    morality, and participation in social arrangements that depend upon those
    qualities.

The psychology that G. Stanley Hall offered to education rested on evidence: The
two-volume *Adolescence* is compendious in its scholarship—far more so than
Thorndike's *Educational Psychology*. From his developmental theory, Hall could
derive a number of interesting ideas about the tactics and goals of education and
socialization. Of course, all the ideas were tied to one large theoretical scheme, and
in a sense all the assertions stood or fell together.

Hall's developmental psychology required a systematic method of child study.
Hall tried to develop such a method with his questionnaire studies but his questionnaire work was weak and short-lived. Without some kind of communication with a
vigorous empiricism, Hall's theory was vulnerable, and with it Hall's pedagogical
package. Hall's questionnaire method of child study lost credibility as a serious
scientific enterprise by the turn of the century, and child study had little influence on
educators after 1910 (Siegel & White, 1982).

Hall's prophetic approach would wax and wane in the 20th century. In the 1930s
and 1940s, the normative studies of the child development institutes and centers
were a source of standards for parents and teachers. The findings of the child
development studies were embodied in programs of parent education. They were
used in the development of preschool and elementary school programs, and they
were given a popular voice in the writings of Arnold Gesell and his associates. This
second surge of child study was moribund by the early 1950s. Centers and institutes
closed. Writings of the time lament the shortage of young people, research funds,
and ideas.

A decade later, child study was born again in a developmental psychology
movement that became a significant force in the compensatory education programs
of the 1960s. The developmental psychology of Jean Piaget was taught to teachers
as a broad mapping of children's cognitive development, and used to generate
curricula of early education, new approaches to high school science teaching, and
computer-based "microworlds" intended to stimulate "Piagetian learning."

The child study movement of the 1960s had much more power and depth than G.
Stanley Hall's turn-of-the-century movement. It involved a large cadre of reason-

ably sophisticated researchers. The theory and the research studies were in much richer communication with one another. People in connecting institutions—universities, schools, government, foundations—understood the possibilities and limitations of the research programs in a way that was not true at the turn of the century.

Interestingly, one paper of the 1970s is a straightforward assertion of G. Stanley Hall's old vision of developmental psychology as moral philosophy—Lawrence Kohlberg's (1971) "From Is to Ought: How to Commit the Naturalistic Fallacy and Get away With It in the Study of Moral Development." But Kohlberg's paper simply reasserts in a challenging way a use of developmental psychology to declare values that is a common practice of many producers and consumers of research in developmental psychology (Rein & White, 1977; White, 1983).

Thorndike's Engineering Vision

Edward L. Thorndike at Teachers' College outlined a program of activities for educational psychologists in his one-volume *Educational Psychology* (1903a); his *An Introduction to the Theory of Mental and Social Measurements* (1904); and his expanded, three-volume *Educational Psychology* (1913–14). The three-volume *Educational Psychology* was his most complete prospectus for scientific psychology for schools and it was followed. A useful brief statement of Thorndike's position is to be found in his lead article sending off the new *Journal of Educational Psychology* (Thorndike, 1910). Thorndike was a committed and skilled researcher and so his books focused on research programs. Some of the programs were tangible and on the ground; some were extrapolations and would require some time and some inventions to be realized.

The first volume of *Educational Psychology, The Original Nature of Man*, discusses what is scientifically understood about human inborn tendencies.

> It is a first principle of education to utilize any individual's original nature as a means to changing him for the better—to produce in him the information, habits, powers, interests and ideals which are desirable. . . . A study of the original nature of man as a species and of the original natures of individual men is therefore the primary task of human psychology. (Thorndike, 1913–14, Vol. 1, p. 4) Not only education, but any system of governance must depend upon some conception of original human nature.

> The need for an inventory of man's original nature, however is very great. It is needed as a basis, not only for educational, but also for economic, political, ethical and religious theories. (Thorndike, 1913–14, Vol. I, p. 41)

Here is a traditional philosophical issue being brought into the scientific arena. For 300 years before Thorndike, political thinkers had drawn up lists of human motives, faculties, traits, and powers and upon such lists proposed systems of government. Cofer (1986) traces this history of political philosophy that links the ancestry of psychology with the ancestry of political science. Listings of human instincts were popular in psychology books near the beginning of this century. The people who drew them up were transposing Cofer's (1986) motivological tradition into evolutionary terms; true to the tradition, they drew upon their instinct lists to make proposals about the governance of human institutions.

To initiate his exploration of the instinctive, Thorndike reproduces an inventory of 81 human instincts offered by William James (1890/1981). (James often said that humans have a *lot* of instincts, far more than the lower animals.) Wherever possible, Thorndike draws on James' book to describe an instinct as a tendency to respond in a well-defined way to a specific situation; where that is not possible, Thorndike simply gives James' name for the instinct. We arrive at a mixed list in which entries like "Envy," "Jealousy," "Secretiveness," and "Cleanliness" are mixed with entries like " 'whatever things are plastic to his hands he must'. . . 'remodel into shapes of his own'," and " 'another boy who runs provokingly near'. . . running after him" (Thorndike, 1913–14, Vol. I., pp.17-20).

Always seeking clarity, Thorndike emerges from this exercise with two questions about definition. Can we describe an original tendency so precisely that people will agree on when they have and have not seen an instance of it? What are the criteria sufficient for the decision that a function is *unlearned?*

Thorndike now makes up his own inventory of unlearned human tendencies by looking through various data and observations for situation-response connections that look as though they would meet his definitional criteria—that is, (a) be reliably observable, and (b) have qualities of universality and indifference to environmental history that an unlearned behavior ought rightly to have. His sources are: (a) baby biographies by people such as Preyer, Moore, Mrs. W.S. Hall, Shinn, Dearborn; (b) findings of G. Stanley Hall's questionnaire studies—data that have methodological problems (cf. Thorndike's criticisms on pp. 28—37) but that can be used with caution—and (c) "observations and discussions of varying degrees of merit scattered through the literature of biology, psychology, anthropology, sociology and education" (p. 37)

The book inventories innate tendencies influencing: sensory sensitivities; attention; gross bodily control; food-getting and habitation; fear, fighting, and anger; human intercourse; satisfaction and discomfort; minor bodily movements and cerebral connections; emotions and their expression; and consciousness, learning, and remembering.

The nine chapters in which the inventory passes by are frustrating. Substantively, we catch glimpses of the animal and the spiritual, the sacred and the profane, in human conduct. Motor patterns—eye fixation, grasping, retching, spitting out— mingle with rivalry, wanderlust, greed, rage, motherly behavior, teasing, bullying, dominance, display, sexual behavior, envy, constructiveness, and so on. Ideologically, all sits comfortably, if loosely, within a connectionistic framework. Methodologically, the discussion is pieced together, catch-as-catch-can. There is not even the suggestion of one or two orderly scientific programs within which the analysis can be contained and evolved.

In the end, Thorndike says that although he grouped his unlearned tendencies by response types a more useful grouping would be by eliciting situations. He calls for research that would make that possible. "There is very great need for a series of painstaking studies of man's original responses to all the important things, events, qualities and relations in his environment" (p. 207). He calls for studies of the phylogeny of unlearned behaviors as ultimately "the most scientific means of grouping and ordering original tendencies" (p. 208).

These were not programs that Thorndike was personally able or willing to set in motion. His early research papers reflect his interests in genetics, in eugenics, and in social questions thought to be related to them (Thorndike, 1903b, 1903c, 1913; Stenquist, Thorndike, & Trabue, 1915) but there were not many such papers. Probably, the research programs that Thorndike had in mind were approximated by the programs of research in ethology, behavior genetics, and psychological ecology that have arisen in the last 30 years.

Addressing *The Psychology of Learning* in Volume II, Thorndike has a respectable research literature to work with, composed of studies of what happens when people practice *functions*: telegraphy, typewriting, learning not to wink when a rubber hammer strikes a plate of glass in front of the eye, tossing shot into a glass, tracing a pencil line between the lines of a double-line maze, marking e's and t's on printed pages, writing English words in German script, adding columns of numbers, rote serial memorization, mental multiplication, and so on. We are at the historic point when American psychologists were turning towards functionalism. Thorndike is candid about the fact that neither he nor anyone else is sure about how to make a function an object of scientific inquiry:

> It may be that the chief product produced in the reader by this chapter is the conviction that the theory of describing a mental function and its degree of efficiency is in a very confused and unsatisfactory state. Such a conviction is justifiable. (p. 82)

The Psychology of Learning sets forth Thorndike's *connectionism* which, 35 years later, in the heyday of the learning theory era, Hilgard (1948) would call still the most influential learning theory in American psychology. Connectionism traveled light theoretically, and yet it had depth and reach. All cases in which situations and responses are connected together reflect the simple, powerful agency of *association*; all phenomena of human adaptation are at bottom cases in which situations and responses are connected together in some new way.

One must try to imagine how exciting it must have been for early psychologists to catch glimpses of the possible unification of a pluralistic psychology on the basis of principles of association that were, on the one hand, certified by a 200-year-old philosophical tradition and, on the other, amenable to interesting scientific research of the kind exemplified in Thorndike's brilliant thesis (Thorndike, 1898).

Thorndike's *Psychology of Learning* lays out all human learning as a matter of connection-forming. Three orders of learning are discussed: (a) "abilities that represent closely organized hierarchies of habits": telegraphy, typewriting, addition; (b) "narrow abilities of the 'formal' type": for example, number checking, the memorization of nonsense syllables; (c) "informational, appreciative, analytic and selective functions"—that is, the learning of school subjects, of interests and attitudes and tastes, and of relatively subtle forms of reasoning and judgment.

Volume II discussed critically doctrines of "transfer of training" and "mental discipline." Thorndike and Woodworth (1901) had done studies of transfer of training that seemed to speak for more currently relevant topics and against the classical disciplines in the schools. There was little else in the *Psychology of Learning* that spoke to school learning and school practices. The volume sets forth a prospectus for what, in the shorter run, would become psychology's research program on human learning and, in the longer run, would evolve to become the contemporary mixture of cognitive science and instructional psychology.

Volume III of Thorndike's *Educational Psychology* was in two parts: a first section on *Mental Work and Fatigue* and a second, longer section on *Individual Differences and Their Causes*. The section on work and fatigue discussed factors of pace and timing and workload on mental functioning and efficiency. School hygiene was a subject of considerable interest at the turn of the century when compulsory education laws were being enforced and more and more children were spending long days cooped up in schoolrooms. Thorndike (1900) had done some antecedent research suggesting that mental fatigue is not so easy to demonstrate empirically. In Volume III of *Educational Psychology*, Thorndike argues that mental work and mental fatigue must refer to activities of the "connection-system." At the same time, he argues that the *feeling* of diminished mental efficiency does not seem to be a reliable indicator of actual decline in functional capacity, and he continues to express skepticism about whether mental fatigue actually exists.

The second part of Thorndike's third volume, dealing with individual differences among children, sets forth the substance of Thorndike's first, one-volume *Educational Psychology* in 1903.

Schooling rests on a surprisingly large number of peremptory judgments about how people learn, Thorndike says.

> Schemes for individual instruction and for different rates of promotion are undertaken largely because of certain beliefs concerning the prevalence and amount of differences in mental capacity; the conduct of at least two classes out of every three is determined in great measure by the teachers' faith that mental abilities are so little specialized that improvement in any one of them will help all the rest; manual training is often introduced into schools on the strength of somebody's confidence that skill in movement is intimately connected with efficiency in thinking; the practical action with regard to coeducation has been accompanied, and doubtless influenced by, arguments about the identity or the equality of the minds of men and women; the American public school system rests on a total disregard of hereditary mental differences between the classes and the masses; curricula are planned with some speculation concerning mental development as a guide. (p.143)

"Education needs to know men as well as man," Thorndike says. He discusses the measurement of individual differences and then sex differences in ability, race

differences, familial differences, changes in mental traits with age, and questions of the relative influence of environment and heredity. This is not quite yet a volume on mental testing, but it is quite evidently a prelude to one. The volume shows an awareness of how different children are from another and its prominence in Thorndike's scheme for an educational psychology argues—here, as elsewhere, we are dealing with promissory notes—that psychologists will have a significant role in measuring such individual differences in order to help with decisions about where and how different children will be educated.

Thorndike's Scheme
Thorndike's scheme for an educational psychology was relatively modest, carefully circumscribed, and practical.

1. Psychologists would address one clientele, educators, and a limited range of practical settings—elementary schools, middle schools, and high schools.

2. They would offer educators means, not ends. Thorndike's psychologists would help educators realize their values and objectives. The psychologists might evaluate educational operations by devising and using instruments of accountability.

3. Though Thorndike's psychologists would not deal with values, they would fearlessly explore constraints on education that might have strong political or evaluative meanings for people. Educational psychology (when more appropriate and powerful research tools came along) would map out the unlearned and the instinctive in human behavior. It would measure the true extent of sex differences, race differences, and familial differences. The questions so addressed might be matters of great heat and passion to many people, but Thorndike was espousing an ideal "scientific management" held by many in his time—that dispassionate, rational, factual approaches to the burning questions would sooner or later bring about peaceful, democratic solutions to them.

4. Methodologically, Thorndike's educational psychologists would use experimental procedures, quantitative measurements, and statistical techniques of analysis and inference. They would work on selected problems. The methodological commitments of Thorndike's educational psychologists defined the grounds they would and would not enter.

5. They would be pragmatic, avoiding the conscious use of broad ideologies or systematizations.

Thorndike's scheme for an educational psychology established an administrative shell that was to endure. Within the shell, educational psychologists would devise tests and establish a methodology of "test theory." They would study rote memory when schools used much rote memorization, and they would move with schools to become more developmental and cognitive later in the century. The first educational psychologists would study "school hygiene" using at times an industrial model of school performance and at times a public health conception of the child's well being. Later educational psychologists would turn towards mental health, counseling, and personal adjustment. The early educational psychologists would try to discover universal laws of learning and learning theories. Later ones would focus on schools and school learning and try to create instructional psychologies.

Thorndike's educational psychology was a well-designed set of programs, marshalling the limited resources of a small group of psychologists and bringing them to bear on American schools. The several activities of the educational psychologists were lightly tied together practically and ideologically. As psychology developed new research instruments and as circumstances changed in American schools, educational psychology could add and drop projects.

John Dewey's Reconstructive Psychology

John Dewey was principally committed to philosophy but he had an early and strong interest in psychology, which he saw as intimately connected to philosophy. As a graduate student at John Hopkins in 1882–84, he took every course the young G. Stanley Hall offered and did some experimentation in Hall's laboratory (Dykhuizen, 1973, p. 31). One of his first published papers proclaimed the coming of "the new psychology" (Dewey, 1884/1969) and his first book, *Psychology* (Dewey, 1887/1967), put the scientific work of that new psychology together with German idealism. Dewey was a Hegelian at that time. Later, after some 40 years of work in philosophy, education, and psychology, he arrived at his call for a social psychology (Dewey, 1922).

Dewey came to the University of Chicago in 1894 to be head professor of philosophy, psychology, and pedagogy. He had chaired Michigan's philosophy department before coming to Chicago but the indications are that he welcomed his triple-barreled Chicago position as an opportunity to explore the relationships among philosophy, psychology, and education.[5]

Just as Hall's research program was child study, Dewey made educational reform projects his laboratory. Shortly after coming to Chicago, he asked President William Rainey Harper to establish a school to allow demonstration, observation, and experiment in education (Dewey, 1896/1972, p. 434). Dewey had been a high school teacher for three years before going to graduate school. At Michigan, he had been a charter member of the Michigan Schoolmasters' Club, dedicated to exploring issues of mutual interest to high schools and colleges, and he liked to talk about educational issues in philosophical and psychological terms (Dykhuizen, 1973, pp. 51, 66). Dewey gave serious thought to the place of schools in human society. He saw schools as, ideally, places where the psychological is coordinated with the social:

> The ultimate problem of all education is to co-ordinate the psychological and the social factors. The psychological requires that the individual have the free use of all his personal powers; and, therefore, must be so individually studied as to have the laws of his own structure regarded. The sociological factor requires that the individual become acquainted with the social environment in which he lives, in all its important relations,

---

[5] Dewey was a prolific writer and a respected member of several scholarly communities. C. Wright Mills (1966) once divided the journals Dewey wrote for into four groups and argued that Dewey dealt with four "publics": *social and political, technical philosophy, education,* and *student-public.*

and be disciplined to regard these relationships in his own activities. The co-ordination demands, therefore, that the child be capable of expressing *himself,* but in such a way as to realize *social* ends. (Dewey 1895/1972a, p. 224)

Dewey began his school at the University of Chicago in October 1896, with three teachers and 32 pupils aged 6 to 11. His school was a locus of research: "The conception underlying the school is that of a laboratory. It bears the same relation to the work in pedagogy that a laboratory bears to biology, physics, or chemistry" (Dewey, 1896/1972b, p. 437). The laboratory school was an extension of his thinking about school and society.

The hypothesis underlying this experiment is that of school as a social institution. Education outside the school proceeds almost wholly through participation in the social or community life of the groups of which one is a member. . . . The school is a special social community in which the too complex social environment is reduced and simplified; in which certain ideas and facts concerning this simplified social life are communicated to the child; in which, also, the child is called upon to undertake not all kinds of activity but those specially selected on the ground of peculiar adaptation to the child. (pp. 437–438)

The "Laboratory School of the University of Chicago" had a brilliant, difficult seven years of life. It grew in size and reputation each year but there was no endowment and money was a continuing problem. In the early 1900s the university proposed to merge the Laboratory School with three other schools to establish a School of Education with Dewey as director. There were prolonged negotiations, made awkward because one of the principal issues was about the employment of Mrs. Dewey (Dykhuizen, 1973, p. 108ff), and finally in 1904 Dewey was led to resign his directorship and his Chicago professorship. Teachers' College at Columbia offered him a position and he took it. The memory of his Chicago Laboratory School lived on, as one of the birthplaces of American progressive education in the 20th century. Two former teachers have described the Laboratory School, recalling that it was once called "one of the greatest experiments in education ever carried on" (Mayhew & Edwards, 1936/1965, p. 13).

The school furthered Dewey's thinking. Just as he began it, Dewey (1897/1972d) published "My Pedagogic Creed," a beautiful statement of his vision of education that still is quoted today. Two other early books on education (Dewey, 1899/1976a, 1902/1976b) reported and reflected on his ongoing work with the Laboratory School. Twelve years after leaving Chicago and the Laboratory School experience behind, Dewey (1916/1980) published what is now generally regarded as his classic work on schooling, *Democracy and Education,* reflecting his thinking about not only his own but others' experiments on education.

We will here consider *Democracy and Education* as one of a series of four books Dewey published between 1915 and 1922. *Schools of Tomorrow* (J. Dewey & E.

Dewey, 1915/1979) was a study of a number of contemporary educational experiments by Dewey and his daughter, Evelyn. Evelyn visited innovative programs and schools across the United States, and the father and the daughter wrote about what she found. *Democracy and Education* (Dewey, 1916/1980), a year later, took the title of the last chapter of *Schools of Tomorrow* and discussed the role of schools in society, the special meaning of schools in a democratic society, and how schools change in a changing society. *Reconstruction in Philosophy* (Dewey, 1920/1950), was Dewey's statement of the role that philosophy ideally ought to play in human affairs, as an activity that perpetually reconsiders and reconstitutes human morality under changing social conditions. Finally, *Human Nature and Conduct*, subtitled *An Introduction to Social Psychology* (Dewey, 1922) was a sketch of a social psychology that might serve as a moral science in the reconstruction of social conditions.

Dewey may have thought of these books as summing-up efforts. He was 63 when the fourth book was published, close to the normal retirement age. Of course, Dewey was to live to age 92, with many years before him during which he would write major works and be a prominent figure in public affairs.

Schools of To-Morrow

Schools of To-Morrow (Dewey & Dewey, 1979/1915) is a study of change in American school and the mediation of that change by philosophy. The first part of the book discusses schools following principles espoused by philosophers of education. The Deweys begin by summarizing Rousseau's argument for a natural education: learning is intrinsic to childhood, and schools should find ways to appeal to children's natural interests in learning. Mrs. Johnson's school at Fairhope, Alabama and Professor Meriam's school of the University of Missouri are described as two different implementations of Rousseau's ideas.

Pestalozzi, the Swiss educational reformer, was a follower of Rousseau and he surpassed him, the Deweys say. Pestalozzi was a teacher and he worked out teaching methods; had Rousseau been a teacher he would have invented something better than the impractical techniques he used to teach "that exemplary prig," Emile. Furthermore, Pestalozzi grasped a truth that Rousseau never saw, that the natural development of man is social development. The Deweys examine the embodiment of Pestalozzi's methods in a number of American schools: Public School 45 in Indianapolis; the Francis Parker School in Chicago; the Cottage School in Riverside, Illinois; the Phoebe Thorn Experimental School at Bryn Mawr; the boys' school in Interlaken, Indiana; the Little School in the Woods at Greenwich, Connecticut, and some others.

The Deweys next consider the Philosophy of Friedrich Froebel's *Kindergarten*, whose influence had just begun to wane at the time the book was written. (Froebel's kindergarten was, in fact, giving way at that time to new forms of kindergartening following the ideas of Dewey, Hall, and Thorndike (White & Buka, 1987).) The Deweys discuss Maria Montessori's preschool, just coming to the United States for the first time in 1915.

The first part of *Schools of To-Morrow* deals with educational implementations of philosophical conceptions. The philosopher puts forth ideas about society, human nature, and education and the educator designs a school based upon those ideas. In the second part of their book, the Deweys describe the work of contemporaries who are in a sense philosopher/educators—administrators creating new forms of schooling in response to their conceptions of changing social conditions and needs in society around them.

The central issue is the question of how intelligent, responsive change is introduced into the practices of schools. Schools must change to keep up with society's changes:

> The tremendous change in society which the application of science to industry brought about. . . effected a reconstruction[6] of nearly all the institutions of civilization, the death of a great many, and the birth of many more. The need of popular education was one of the results of the change, and with this need came the public schools. As their form did not adapt itself to the new conditions, but simply copied the schools already existing, the process of reconstruction to fit the new society is still going on, and is only just beginning to become conscious. A democratic society, dependent upon applications of science for all its prosperity and welfare, cannot hope to use with any great success a system of education which grew up for the ruling body in an autocratic society using only human power for its industries and wealth. (Dewey & Dewey, 1915/1979, pp. 316-317)

The Deweys look at the programs of Mr. Wirt, superintendent of schools in Gary, Indiana, for children of an industrial community with many foreign-born children. Mr. Valentine, principal of Public School No. 26 in Indianapolis, is representative of educators who have made their schools settlement houses, offering a wide range of services to the poor neighborhoods in which they sit. The Deweys describe programs of industrial education implemented in Gary, Chicago, and Cincinnati.

In the last chapter of *Schools of To-Morrow*, titled "Democracy and Education," the Deweys discuss what the educational experiments signify. The new programs are efforts to set forth schools appropriate for new forms of American society. Imagine schools as institutional shells—places where children 6 to 18 spend their days and prepare for adult work—remaining the same outwardly while within the shells people and requirements and rules and books and motives and emphases and arrangements with other parties all change. Families are institutional shells. Businesses are institutional shells. Things change within all the shells and cooperative changes among them have to be regularly reconsidered and reconstructed.

---

[6] The world "reconstruction" appears again and again in Dewey's writings. Dewey is generally understood to have begun his philosophical career as a Hegelian, but then to have modified his philosophy to become a pragmatist. Sidney Hook (1971), Dewey's student, says that he was never quite an orthodox Hegelian but that he was strongly drawn to certain features of Hegel's thought. It has been suggested that in the course of this transition Dewey adopted the term *reconstruction* as a translation of the Hegelian notion of a *dialectic*. I find it useful, from time to time, to look at Dewey's use of the word "reconstruction" with this in mind.

Twentieth-century schools have new roles to play in connection with children's physical welfare and health; pupils are more active, curriculum is more problem-centered and more attuned to everyday life, teachers care more about intrinsic motivation and interest-value, and, connecting all together, the system as a whole places a heightened premium on democracy and education. *Schools of To-Morrow* closes with this thought:

> The democracy which proclaims equality of opportunity as its ideal requires an education in which learning and social application, ideas and practice, work and recognition of the meaning of what is done, are united from the beginning and for all. Schools such as we have discussed in this book—are showing how the ideal of equal opportunity for all is to be transmuted into reality. (Dewey & Dewey, 1915/1979, p. 404)

Democracy and Education

Democracy and Education (Dewey, 1916/1980) picks up the title of the last chapter of *Schools of To-morrow* and extends the line of thought begun in that volume. Generally regarded as Dewey's classic work on education, *Democracy and Education* discusses what schools are and ought to be in a democratic society. Dewey once called it a major statement of his philosophy:

> Although a book called *Democracy and Education* was for many years that in which my philosophy, such as it is, was most fully expounded, I do not know that philosophic critics, as distinct from teachers, have ever had recourse to it. I have wondered whether such facts signified that philosophers in general . . . have not taken education with sufficient seriousness for it to occur to them that any rational person could actually think it possible that philosophizing should focus about education as the supreme human interest in which, moreover, other problems, cosmological, moral, logical, come to a head. (cf. Dewey, "From Absolutism to Experimentism," quoted in Hook, 1980, p. ix)

Dewey was mildly chastising his fellow philosophers for shrinking from everyday affairs. He did that from time to time in his writings. Dewey believed that philosophy ought to be an active force in social and political change, a position he was to fully express in his subsequent *Reconstruction in Philosophy*. He obviously wrote *Democracy and Education* to make a political as well as a philosophical point.

With the United States becoming an industrial society, and with more and more children moving into schools, there were efforts to broaden the curriculum of the schools to suit a broader cross-section of society. A Manual Training Movement in the 1870s was followed by enactments and appropriations for vocational education in the 1900s (Lazerson & Grubb, 1974). Dewey wrote against the scheme to establish an Illinois State Commission of Vocational Education, calling it "an undemocratic proposal" (Dewey, 1913/1974). There was a dilemma. Should schools give everyone a practical education, training some children to work with their heads and others to work with their hands, thus perpetuating and possibly deepening class divisions in American society? Or should schools give all children, the college-bound and the non-college bound, an equal education offering mixed or uncertain relevance to their adult work in society?

Dewey begins *Democracy and Education* by arguing that education is the basic human activity by which people, teaching one another, constitute a human society.

> Society not only continues to exist *by* transmission, *by* communication, but it may fairly be said to exist *in* transmission, *in* communication. There is more than a verbal tie between the words common, community, and communication, (Dewey, 1916/1980, p. 7)

Formal schooling becomes a necessity for a society when people need to communicate with another across great expanses of time and space, when communication in the here and now will not give all the experience people need.

> Roughly speaking, they [schools] come into existence when social traditions are so complex that a considerable part of the social store is committed to writing and transmitted through written symbols. . . . Consequently as soon as a community depends to any considerable extent upon what lies beyond its own territory and its own immediate generation, it must rely upon the set agency of schools to insure adequate transmission of all its resources. (Dewey, 1916/1980, pp. 23-24)

Schools teach children to consider their experience and to build knowledge about it into symbolic constructions, so that other people—and, at times, the child—may readdress previous experience and be guided by it. Dewey offers a formal definition:

> We thus reach a technical definition of education: It is that reconstruction or reorganization of experience which adds to the meaning of experience, and which increases ability to direct the course of subsequent experience. (Dewey, 1916/1980, p. 82)

Dewey's concept of *experience*, it might be noted, was subtle, complex, and central to his thinking. Scheffler (1974) offers an interesting discussion of it.

Dewey rejects the argument that education should give the child adult skills, or that it should serve child development. Education promotes growth, not development.

When we abandon the attempt to define immaturity by means of fixed comparison with adult accomplishments, we are compelled to give up thinking of it as denoting lack of desired traits. Abandoning this notion, we are also forced to surrender our habit of thinking of instruction as a method of supplying this lack by pouring knowledge into a mental and moral hole which awaits filling. Since life means growth, a living creature lives as truly and positively at one stage as at another, with the same intrinsic fullness and the same absolute claims. Hence education means the enterprise of supplying the conditions which insure growth, or adequacy of life, irrespective of age. (Dewey, 1916/1980, p. 56)

Child development is not an absolute process. We talk about stages and sequences of human development to which we must calibrate practices of parents, preschools, schools, and other social institutions. Dewey argues that there are no fixed, immutable stages of cognitive, social, emotional, or motivational development. (For an excellent recent discussion of Dewey's analysis of development, see Cahan [1987].) Indeed, children's powers are unfathomable and indeterminate outside of a social milieu.

I believe that knowledge of social conditions, of the present state of civilization, is necessary in order properly to interpret the child's powers. The child has his own instincts and tendencies, but we do not know what these mean until we can translate them into their social equivalents. We must be able to carry them back into a social past and see them as the inheritance of previous race activities. We must also be able to project them into the future to see what their outcome and education will be. (Dewey 1897/1972d, p. 85)

Dewey did not believe in a prophetic developmentalism seeking to discover immutable natural laws of child development to which human institutions must comply. Child development goes on in a human world, in an environment embodying the design, intentions, and intelligence of other people. The human world, full of objects of human design, holds out "selected and charged stimuli" that teach and develop children.

Prior human efforts have made over natural conditions. As they originally existed they were indifferent to human endeavors. Every domesticated plant and animal, every tool, every utensil, every appliance, every manufactured article, every aesthetic decoration, every work of art means a transformation of conditions once hostile or indifferent to characteristic human activities into friendly and favoring conditions. Because the activities of children to-day are controlled by these selected and charged stimuli, children are able to traverse in a short lifetime what the race has needed slow, tortured ages to attain. The dice have been loaded by all the successes which have preceded. (Dewey, 1916/1980, p. 42).

The human environment keeps changing, of course. The paths a child must follow to be a competent adult, the nature of child development, changes from one generation to the next.

The tremendous change in society which the application of science to industry brought about . . . effected a reconstruction of nearly all the institutions of civilization, the death of a great many, and the birth of many more. The need of popular education was one of the results of the change, and with this need came the public schools. . . . A democratic society, dependent upon applications of science for all its prosperity and welfare, cannot hope to use with any great success a system of education which grew up for the ruling body in an autocratic society using only human power for its industries and wealth. (Dewey, 1916/1980, pp. 316-317)

The reconstruction of philosophy, of education, and of social ideals and methods thus go hand in hand. If there is especial need of educational reconstruction at the present time, if this need makes urgent a reconsideration of the basic ideas of traditional philosophic systems, it is because of the thoroughgoing change in social life accompanying the advance of science, the industrial revolution, and the development of democracy. Such practical changes cannot take place without demanding an educational re-formation to meet them, and without leading men to ask what ideas and ideals are implicit in these social changes, and what revisions they require of the ideas and ideals which are inherited from older and unlike cultures. (Dewey, 1916/1980, p. 341)

Social change changes the way people think, bringing about a reconstruction of human experience. Dewey puts forth radical ideas in mild-mannered prose. He rejects the cornerstone of the psychology of his time: the thesis that the mind is in touch with the world of the physicist. The physical world the small child lives in today, populated by such objects as automobiles and television sets and telephones, is quite different from the physical world of the small child 100 years ago. Beyond that, what people *see,* Dewey says, are possibilities of action.

When experience is aligned with the life-process and sensations are seen to be points of readjustment, the alleged atomism of sensations totally disappears. With this disappearance is abolished the need for a synthetic faculty of super-empirical reason to connect them. Philosophy is not any longer confronted with the hopeless problem of finding a way in which separate grains of sand may be woven into a strong and coherent rope—or into the illusion and pretense of one. When the isolated and simple existences of Locke and Hume are seen not to be truly empirical at all but to answer to certain demands of their theory of mind, the necessity ceases for the elaborate Kantian and post-Kantian machinery of a priori concepts and categories to synthesize the alleged stuff of experience. The true ''stuff'' of experience is recognized to be adaptive courses of action, habits, active functions, connections of doing and undergoing; sensori-motor co-ordinations. Experience carries principles of connection and organization within itself. These principles are none the worse because they are vital and practical rather than epistemological. (Dewey, 1920/1950, pp. 85-86)

What people think about are plans or programs of action.[7] For Dewey, as for James Gibson, people live in an ecology of *affordances,* possibilities of action. In a world

---

[7] Miller Galanter, and Pribram's *Plans and the Structure of Action,* is very much an extended reassertion of John Dewey's famous paper on the reflex arc.

where behavior settings change, possibilities of action and the human mentality changes.

Dewey considers how education is to be conducted in a democracy. Democracy is a kind of perfection or idealization of the principle of a human community: If communities exist when there is communication, we optimize community as we increase the ability of each person to communicate with every other. Dewey then considers the ways in which schools should or should not be directed towards the vocations of a society in a series of chapters on educational values and substance. Schools should be redirected towards practical activities of contemporary society, Dewey says. "Both practically and philosophically, the key to the present educational situation lies in a gradual reconstruction of school materials and methods so as to utilize various forms of occupation typifying social callings, and to bring out their intellectual and moral content" (Dewey, 1916/1980, p. 325) But schools cannot be used simply to reproduce, and rigidify, the vocational roles and the social order of the past. Schools must be designed in such a way that educational reconstruction takes place along with, and in the service of, social reorganization. Societies change. Schools must allow and support the changes.

Dewey concludes *Democracy and Education* with a consideration of philosophy and education, and their work in the reconstruction of society.

> The reconstruction of philosophy, of education, and of social ideals and methods thus go hand in hand. If there is especial need of educational reconstruction at the present time, if this need makes urgent a reconsideration of the basic ideas of traditional philosophic systems, it is because of the thoroughgoing change in social life accompanying the advance of science, the industrial revolution, and the development of democracy. Such practical changes cannot take place without demanding an educational re-formation to meet them, and without leading men to ask what ideas and ideals are implicit in these social changes, and what revisions they require of the ideas and ideals which are inherited from older and unlike cultures. (Dewey, 1916/1980, p. 341)

Reconstruction in Philosophy

In the last two books we will consider here, Dewey sets forth his conception of the roles that philosophy and psychology should play in society. Morals change, Dewey says, and philosophy and psychology should be instruments in reconstructing the moral life of society to fit changing circumstances.

> No systematic efforts have as yet been made to subject the "morals" underlying old institutional customs to scientific inquiry and criticism. Here, then, lies the reconstructive work to be done by philosophy. It must undertake to do for the development of inquiry into human affairs and hence into morals what the philosophers of the last few centuries did for promotion of scientific inquiry in physical and physiological conditions and aspects of human life. (Dewey, 1920/1950, p. 33)

Dewey defines scientific research as a body of experiences designed by humans for human purposes. In societies that have scientific enterprises, people *create* events in order to explore the experiences of a changed world. There is an active conception of knowledge and nature becomes plastic, something to be subjected to human use. Some intellectuals feel obliged to stand off from everyday affairs, committing themselves only to the timeless and the universal. Dewey calls such detachment a "morally irresponsible estheticism." In a modern society, philosophy ought to change from being contemplative to operative. A philosophical epistemology in which the mind detached from objects endlessly struggles to make contact with them them makes little sense.

> [The questions of traditional epistemology] all spring from the assumption of a merely beholding mind on one side and a foreign and remote object to be viewed and noted on the other. They ask how a mind and world, subject and object, so separate and independent can by any possibility come into such relationship to each other as to make true knowledge possible. If knowing were habitually conceived of as active and operative, after the analogy of experiment guided by hypothesis, or of invention guided by the imagination of some possibility, it is not too much to say that the first effect would be to emancipate philosophy from all the epistemological puzzles which now perplex it. (Dewey, 1920/1950, pp. 106-107)

Dewey was much influenced by William James, and the philosophy he favors is a Jamesian attempt to create sense and meaning out of the flux of pure experience:

> The material out of which philosophy finally emerges is irrelevant to science and explanation. It is figurative, symbolic of fears and hopes, made of imaginations and suggestions, not significant of a world of objective fact intellectually confronted. It is poetry and drama, rather than science, and is apart from scientific truth and falsity, rationality or absurdity of fact in the same way in which poetry is independent of these things. (Dewey, 1920/1950, p. 33)

The extraction of such meaning may be a private undertaking but sooner or later it is used to constitute a publicly understood meaning and a utility for society. Dewey was intensely interested in the social role of the man of knowledge, and the responsibility carried with that role.

> Investigation has become a dominant life occupation for some persons. Only superficially, however, does this confirm the idea that theory and knowledge are ends in themselves. They are, relatively speaking, ends in themselves for some persons. But these persons represent a social division of labor; and their specialization can be trusted only when such persons are in unobstructed co-operation with other social occupations, sensitive to others' problems and transmitting results to them for wider application in action. (Dewey, 1920/1950, pp. 122-123)

We arrive, in the end, at the view that philosophy is an agent in the reconstitution of human morals under new conditions of experience.

> The conclusions of that [philosophical] inquiry by themselves would no more constitute a complete moral theory and a working science of distinctively human subject

matter than the activities of their predecessors brought the physical and physiological conditions of human existence into direct and full-fledged existence. But it would have an active share in the work of construction of a moral human science which serves as a needful precursor of reconstruction of the actual state of human life toward order and toward other conditions of a fuller life than man has yet enjoyed. (Dewey 1920/1950, p. 25)

One of the classical political arguments is about the priority of social versus psychological reforms. Can we make society better through improved social institutions or should we accept the fact that social institutions can only be as good as the people that live in them so that you have to change people—through education or therapy or eugenics—to make a better social system? The problems arise, Dewey says, when these are looked at as clear and distinct alternatives. People make social institutions and social institutions create human habits and motives. Social modifications create changed personalities. All social and political institutions are in some sense educational. Think about changing an institution and you have to think about the changes that will be brought about in the people who dwell within.

Institutions are viewed in their educative effect:—with reference to the types of individuals they foster. The interest in individual moral improvement and the social interest in objective reform of economic and political conditions are identified. (Dewey, 1920/1950, p. 154)

Instead of asking what the costs and benefits of institutional change will be (what "pains or pleasures" will be brought to people), we ought to ask in what ways the changes will release specific capacities of people and help them coordinate them into working powers. The role of philosophy in social change, ultimately, is to relate human emotions and values to the circumstances of the present existence, to help people live in a changed world.

When philosophy shall have co-operated with the course of events and made clear and coherent the meaning of the daily detail, science and emotion will interpenetrate, practice and imagination will embrace. Poetry and religious feeling will be unforced flowers of life. To further this articulation and revelation of the meanings of the current course of events is the task and problem of philosophy in days of transition. (Dewey, 1920/1950, p. 164)

One can only have a moral society, ultimately, when people believe in what they are doing, when human emotions and values are connected to and satisfied by what they do all day long. Otherwise, a faint whiff of sulfur pervades everyday human transactions. The task of philosophy is to reconstitute the interpenetration of science and emotion, practice and imagination.

Human Nature and Conduct
Dewey's lectures on human nature and conduct were given at Stanford University in 1918, just four years after the publication of Thorndike's three-volume *Educational*

Psychology, and they express a distinctly different psychology. This was Dewey's first extended statement on psychology since his *Psychology* of 1887. Dewey's (1922) publication of *Human Nature and Conduct* was subtitled *An Introduction to Social Psychology*. It presented a vision of human psychology rooted in society, and in that respect resembled the cultural psychology of Wilhelm Wundt that was failing to cross the water at just that time (Blumenthal, 1985). Presumably the same resistances that held off Wundt kept Dewey's social psychology from having a large influence on American psychology at that time.

Dewey's book followed the line of analysis in his *Reconstruction in Philosophy* and offered what might be called a politics of science. Dewey called his book an essay on morals in the tradition of David Hume, and he aspired to create a scientifically based morality.

> A morals based on study of human nature instead of upon disregard for it would find the facts of man continuous with those of the rest of nature and would thereby ally ethics with physics and biology. It would find the nature and activities of one person coterminous with those of other human beings, and therefore link ethics with the study of history, sociology, law, and economics. Such a morals would not automatically solve moral problems, nor resolve perplexities. But it would enable us to state problems in such forms that action could be courageously and intelligently directed to their solution.

The dominant psychologies of 1918 all assumed that individual minds are separate from one another and, hence, had limited access to questions about human morality.

> Social psychology is confused by the effort to render its facts in the terms characteristic of old psychology, since the distinctive thing about it is that it implies an abandonment of that psychology . . . Any moral theory which is seriously influenced by current psychological theory is bound to emphasize states of consciousness, an inner private life, at the expense of acts which have public meaning and which incorporate and exact social relationships. (Dewey, 1922, pp. 84–86)

Habits, Instincts, and Intelligence

There were three principal terms in Dewey's psychology: habits, instincts, and intelligence.

Habits. Dewey's psychology centered on *habit*, which he saw as individual outgrowths of the customs of human societies.

> The primary facts of social psychology center about collective habit, custom. In addition to the general psychology of habit—which *is* general not individual in any intelligible sense of that word—we need to find out just how different customs shape the desires, beliefs, purposes of those who are affected by them. The problem of social psychology is not how either individual or collective mind forms social groups and

customs, but how different customs, established interacting arrangements, form and nurture different minds. (Dewey, 1922, p. 68)

Dewey's habits, like Thorndike's connections, link situations to activities. But Dewey's habits were also: (a) dispositions of society, (b) units of will and compulsion, and (c) elements of the moral life.

Habits, Dewey said, are facts about societies as much as about people. That fact "brings morals to earth."

> Honesty, chastity, malice, peevishness, courage, triviality, industry, irresponsibility are not private possessions of a person. They are working adaptations of personal capacities with environing forces. All virtues and vices are habits which incorporate objective forms. (Dewey, 1922, p.16)

We usually assume that social institutions and customs are formed to fit the traits, habits, and motives of individuals, but Dewey turns this around. Behavior settings, shaping behaviors, constitute habits. Deeply grooved systems of human interaction—conventional ways of acting in stores, churches, schools, theaters— form the actions of children. "Group minds" form when people are all led to act alike, but they are not as mysterious as they seem when mind is thought of as preceding action. "It is difficult to see that collective mind means anything more than a custom brought at some point to explicit, emphatic consciousness, emotional or intellectual" (Dewey, 1922, p. 60).

Habits are something more than logical units. They motivate and, indeed, compel behaviors. "All habits are demands for certain kinds of activity; and they constitute the self. In any intelligible sense of the word will, they *are* will. . . . They are active means, means that project themselves, energetic and dominating ways of acting" (Dewey, 1922, p. 25).

In human societies the habitual tends to be the moral. What seems right is what most people do most of the time and what custom seems to dictate. "For practical purposes morals mean customs, folkways, established collective habits" (Dewey, 1922, p. 75). (At about that time, a similar linkage between the customary and the moral was stated by Franz Boas, Dewey's colleague at Columbia, as a generalization from cultural anthropology: "It would seem, therefore, that we may say in a general way that the customary action is the ethical·action, that a breach of custom is everywhere considered as generally unethical" (Boas, 1910, p. 382).

Instincts. For Dewey, instincts or impulses were a kind of capital stock of human behavior. They are innate. Human beings have a great many of them. Dewey was like William James in holding that humans have far more of the instinctive than do animals. Humans do not have the elaborate fixed action patterns, the courtship displays, and the threat of behaviors of some animal species, but we do have rudimentary precursors of mood and attitude and interest that can be selected and organized to make adaptive habits. "Man can progress as beasts cannot, precisely because he has so many 'instincts' that they cut across one another, so that the most serviceable actions must be *learned*'' (Dewey, 1922, p. 105). In infancy, through social experience, these impulses are organized into culturally appropriate habits.

> The inchoate and scattered impulses of an infant do not coordinate into serviceable powers except through social dependencies and companionships. His impulses are merely starting points for assimilation of the knowledge and skill of the more matured beings upon whom he depends. They are tentacles sent out to gather that nutrition from customs which will in time render the infant capable of independent action. They are agencies for transfer of existing social power into personal ability; they are means of reconstructive growth. Abandon an impossible individualistic psychology, and we arrive at the fact that native activities are organs of re-organization and re-adjustment. (Dewey, 1922, p. 94)

Dewey rejected argument that there is an "old Adam," or an instinctive core in human nature, that forever makes certain features of society predestined. He refused to subscribe to antireformist views that held that things like war, slavery, greed, and so on are ineradicable.

> An immense debt is due William James for the mere title of his essay: The Moral Equivalents of War. It reveals with a flash of light the true psychology. Clans, tribes, races, cities, empires, nations, states, have made war. The argument that this fact proves an ineradicable belligerent instinct which makes war forever inevitable is much more respectable than many arguments about the immutability of this and that social tradition. For it has the weight of a certain empirical generality back of it. Yet the suggestion of an *equivalent* for war calls attention to the medley of impulses which are casually bunched together under the caption of belligerent impulse; and it calls attention to the fact that the elements of this medley may be woven together into many differing types of activity, some of which may function the native impulses in much better ways than war has ever done. (Dewey, 1922, p. 112)

In an age in which instinct-listing was popular, Dewey distrusted instinctive determinisms, arguments holding that people have a fixed, given original nature to be ascertained by psychological study and to which social conditions must be adjusted. Here is Dewey, somewhat in advance of his time, on the psychoanalytic view of females:

> The treatment of sex by psycho-analysts is most instructive, for it flagrantly exhibits both the consequences of artificial simplification and the transformation of social results into psychic causes. Writers, usually male, hold forth on the psychology of woman, as if they were dealing with a Platonic universal entity, although they habitually treat men as individuals, varying with structure and environment. They treat phenomena which are peculiarly symptoms of the civilization of the West at the present time as if they were the necessary effects of fixed native impulses of human nature. (Dewey, 1922, p. 153)

Dewey sees people as possessors of a myriad of tendencies and impulses brought into coherence and given form for their participations in social organizations. We tend to type people, to characterize them as sheep and goals, but human character is "speckled." Dewey disliked the assumption that people have a fixed, simple self.

> There is no one ready-made self behind activities. There are complex, unstable, opposing attitudes, habits, impulses which gradually come to terms with one another, and assume a certain consistency of configuration, even though only by means of a distribution of inconsistencies which keeps them in water-tight compartments, giving them separate turns or tricks in action. (p. 138)

Intelligence. If habits are constituents of human organization, intelligence is that activity in humans that leads to reorganization. Habits, Dewey says, keep us going all day long. Concrete habits do all the perceiving, recognizing, recalling, judging, conceiving, and reasoning we need to get by but they do so without awareness or reflection or contemplation. We *know how* through habits, but unconsciously. What summons consciousness is an untoward impulse or a blockage of action, disturbing what was a quiet harmony between actor and environment.

With consciousness addressed to ongoing activity, there are forecasts, perceptions, and remembrances.

> The trinity of these forecasts, perceptions and remembrances form a subject-matter of discriminated and identified objects. These objects represent habits turned inside out. They exhibit both the onward tendency of habit and the objective conditions which have been incorporated within it. . . . Thus out of shock and puzzlement there gradually emerges a figured framework of objects, past, present, future. These shade off variously into a vast penumbra of vague, unfigured things, a setting which is taken for granted and not at all explicitly presented. (Dewey, 1922, HN, p. 182)

Using forecasts, perceptions, and remembrances, Dewey's thinker, like Piaget's, makes a secondary reality out of symbols. Dewey's thinker is not quite so exact and calculational; the symbolic reality blurs and darkens at the edges towards a "vast penumbra of vague, unfigured things." With intelligence, there is deliberation, a rehearsal in imagination of various possible lines of action and the consequences and moods and attitudes that might flow from them. Choice of a new line of activity occurs, Dewey says, when imagination hits upon an object that draws forth overt action. Energy and action are released. "The mind is made up, composed, unified." For Dewey, reason is not a process of bloodless calculation; it is a kind of warfare of the imagination.

> The nature of the strife of reason and passion is well stated by William James. The cue of passion, he says is effect, is to keep imagination dwelling upon those objects which are congenial to it, which feed it, and which by feeding it intensity its force, until it crowds out all thought of other subjects. An impulse or habit which is strongly emotional magnifies all objects that are congruous with it and smothers those which are opposed whenever they present themselves. (Dewey, 1922, HN, p. 195)

Deliberation is as much peacemaking as problem solving; it proceeds until a harmony is found among impulses, emotions, anticipated consequences, and so on. As one might imagine, then, Dewey sees scientific activity as involving something more than the exercise of the psychological structures of formal operational thought:

> The elaborate systems of science are born not of reason but of impulses at first slight and flickering; impulses to handle, move about, to hunt, to uncover, to mix things separated and divide things combined, to talk and to listen. Method is their effectual organization into continuous disposition, not a ready-made antecedent which can be invoked at will and set into movement. The man who would intelligently cultivate intelligence will widen, not narrow, his life of strong impulses while aiming at their happy coincidence in operation. (Dewey, 1922, p. 196)

The Reconstruction of Morals

In a changing world, morals must be reconstructed. Dewey argued that social circumstances change in human societies, challenging human intelligence to create new principles. "Morals must be a growing science if it is to be a science at all, not merely because all truth has not yet been appropriated by the mind of man, but because life is a moving affair in which old moral truth ceases to apply" (Dewey, 1922, p. 239). As social circumstances change, we observe how adherence to old principles produces unintended and possibly undesired consequences.

We can ignore the confusion of our principles by turning to the side and evoking transcendental principles of eternal morality—Paradise Lost, Paradise Regained, God in heaven, the Devil in hell. Or we can address directly the fact that our principles have floated free from our new scheme of activities; we can strive to reconnect our practices and our principles.

> Theories paint a world with a God in heaven and a Devil in hell. Moralists in short have failed to recall that a severance of moral desire and purpose from immediate actualities is an inevitable phase of activity when habits persist while the world which they have incorporated alters. Back of this failure lies the failure to recognize that in a changing world, old habits must perforce need modification no matter how good they have been. (Dewey, 1922, pp. 55-56)

We need to reconstruct human activities, to reestablish the harmony among our impulses, desires, and actions, and to reconstitute the moral order. How do we make social change? Dewey argues that the most natural and reasonable way is through education. "When customs are flexible and youth is educated as youth and not as premature adulthood, no nation grows old" (Dewey, 1922, p. 102). Our conventional view of education holds it to be *socialization*, emphasizing the reproduction of the society of the old in the society that will shortly be formed by the young. But new generations face new conditions, and no generation can reconstitute exactly the society it was born into. Dewey argues that if education can be seen as an instrument of *growth,* oncoming generations will normally and automatically accomplish the necessary reconstructions of society. The deep American commitment to education is, then, virtually a physiological necessity for American society.

> It is easy for a critic to ridicule the religious devotion to education which has characterized for example the American republic. It is easy to represent it as zeal without knowledge, fanatical faith apart from understanding. And yet the cold fact of the situation is that the chief means of continuous, graded economical improvement and social rectification lies in utilizing the opportunities of educating the young to modify prevailing types of thought and desire. (Dewey, 1922, p. 127)

Concluding Comments

At the turn of this century, when a discipline of psychology was at its very beginning, people believed that a scientific psychology might serve as a rational basis for American education. There were questions about how much psychology could be scientific, then as now, and we do not know how deep this 19th century faith went. Certainly, educators had political reasons for *wanting* to believe in such a possibility and for supporting efforts to nurture it. A scientific psychology could serve as a knowledge base for a profession of education, and a major goal of educators was to attain professionalization. In any case, this in-principle belief in a scientific psychology serving education was important in providing support for the establishment of the first professorships of psychology in American universities and in providing freestanding departments in which groups of psychologists took positions outside of philosophy departments.

It was important to develop some kind of concrete, operational, and demonstrably meaningful practice—research programs of psychologists clearly contributing to positive changes in the work of American schools. What would such research programs look like? In a pluralistic psychology, three psychologists set forth designs for research programs to provide information and guidance for educational operations. Thorndike's research program was characterized as an engineering vision, Hall's as a developmental vision, and Dewey's as a reconstructive vision.

We have characterized the three visions in part by considering direct programmatic statements by their proponents, in part by examining major works in which the three attempted to relate scientific research to education—for Thorndike, the three-volume *Educational Psychology,* in the case of Hall, his two-volume *Adolescence,* in the case of Dewey a series of works near the end of his career: *Schools of Tomorrow, Democracy and Education, Reconstruction in Philosophy,* and *Human Nature and Conduct.* These are large, complex, and subtle works. Needless to say, we have not considered all that they had to say in a chapter of this length. We have concentrated our discussion on the vision of the relationship of psychology to education that is expressed in the volumes.

The three visions came out of a pluralistic field of psychology, one that now seems to have been a mixture of "early-maturing" and "later-maturing" programs. The early-maturing psychological programs in experimental psychology and physiological psychology drew upon instruments, methods, and methodology from the natural sciences to address traditional questions in philosophical epistemology. The later-maturing psychologies addressed themselves to philosophical questions about human growth and change, about the conditions of mankind in society, about human motives and morality, about political philosophy. Devotees of such questions wrote think pieces and prospectuses, but meaningful work had to wait for inventions of research methods and new methodological conceptions appropriate for the human sciences. Developmental psychology, personality psychology, and social psychology only slowly got their research programs together in the 20th century.

In 1988, all three visions of a psychology of education seem to have had a degree of validity in the sense that all three have come to fruition in meaningful contemporary psychological work on education.

Thorndike was quickest, establishing an educational psychology that became a mainstay of American schools of education. His scheme used, for the most part, programs that were in being. He traveled light theoretically and his educational psychology was, effectively, a collection of research programs addressed to a set of operational issues in education. His educational psychology, adding and subtracting programs as issues and technological possibilities change, continues today.

Hall's prophetic developmentalism had some influence in his own time but he was unable to link his developmental theory with the Clark University child study questionnaire program in a productive way. Hall's ideas about what schools should do were tied to his theoretical investment in recapitulationism. In time, his theory and his ideas were set aside. Nevertheless, his developmental vision had some validity. When, in the 1960s, Jean Piaget's theory and research methods began to be brought over to the United States, they had a large influence on American Schools.

Dewey built his vision of a psychology of education around a social psychology that was not yet invented in his own day. It is interesting that research programs that seem to flesh out Dewey's sketch of a social psychology are emerging in developmental psychology today. If developmental psychology was dominated by work on cognitive development a decade ago, now there is more and more emphasis on social cognition, on children's ability to understand and deal with people and social conventions, and on the study of the social contexts and behavior settings within which children operate. The child is viewed as a social and historical kind rather than a natural kind. Researchers are moving into the everyday environment, studying children's behavior as it is given form by the behavior settings of the social world around the child. Applied-developmental psychologists are exploring what happens in programs in early child care, education, pediatrics, behavioral medicine, and social policy. In practice and in principle (Campbell, 1969/1988a, 1971/1988b), such work moves towards the establishment of an experimenting society.

Does developmental psychology now see itself as a moral science? Certainly, there are contemporary arguments that it can be one (Kohlberg, 1971) and that it is sometimes treated as one (Rein & White, 1977; White, 1983). Developmental psychologists have a new sensitivity about the ethical meaning of their research. Much work is directly or indirectly in the service of liberationist goals, addressing the concerns and rights of children, minorities, women, the handicapped, and the mentally ill. There is a new spirit in the field—socially sensitive, morally responsive—that seems very much in the spirit of Dewey.

References
Blumenthal, A. L. (1985). Wilhelm Wundt: Psychology as the propaedeutic science. In C. E. Buxton (Ed.), *Points of view in the modern history of psychology* (pp. 19-50). Orlando, FL: Academic Press.

Boas, F. (1987). Psychological problems in anthropology. (Lecture delivered at the celebration of the twentieth anniversary of the opening of Clark University, September, 1909). *American Journal of Psychology, XXI,* 371–384. (Original work published 1910)

Cahan, E. D. (1987). James Mark Baldwin, John Dewey, and the concept of development. Unpublished Ph.D. dissertation, Yale University, New Haven, CT.

Campbell, D. T. (1988a). Reforms as experiments. In E. S. Overman (Ed)., *Methodology and epistemology for social science: Selected Papers* (pp. 261-289). Chicago: University of Chicago Press. (Original work published 1969)

Campbell, D. T. (1988b). The experimenting society. In E. S. Overman (Ed.), *Methodology and epistemology for social science: Selected papers* (pp. 290-314). Chicago: University of Chicago Press. (Original work published 1971)

Cattell, J. McK. (1900). Scientific studies and associations. In N. M. Butler (Ed.), *Monographs on education in the United States* (Vol. 1) (Papers prepared for the United States Commission to the Paris Exposition of 1900). Albany, NY: Lyon.

Chambers, R. (1853). *Vestiges of the natural history of creation* (10th ed). London: John Churchill.

Cofer, C. N. (1986). Human nature and social policy. In L. Friedrich-Cofer (Ed.), *Human nature and public policy: Scientific views of women, children, and families* (pp. 39-96). New York: Praeger.

Cremin, L. A. (1964). *The transformation of the school: Progressivism in American education: 1876-1957.* New York: Vintage.

Danziger, K. (1985). The origins of the psychological experiment as a social institution. *American Psychologist, 40,* 133-140.

Dewey, J. (1922). *Human nature and conduct: An introduction to social psychology.* New York: Modern Library.

Dewey, J. (1950). *Reconstruction in philosophy.* New York: Mentor. (Original work published 1920)

Dewey, J. (1965). Psychology and social practice. In J. Ratner (Ed.), *John Dewey: Philosophy, psychology, and social practice.* New York: Capricorn. (Original work published 1900)

Dewey, J. (1967). *Psychology* (J. Boydston, Ed.). Carbondale and Edwardsville, IL: Southern Illinois University Press. (Original work published 1887)

Dewey, J. (1969). The new psychology. In J. Boydston (Ed.), *John Dewey: The early works, 1882-1898: Vol. 1: 1882-1888* (pp. 45-60). Carbondale and Edwardsville, IL: Southern Illinois University Press. (Original work published 1884)

Dewey, J. (1972a). Plan of organization of the university primary school. In J. Boydston (Ed.), *John Dewey: The early works, 1882-1898: 5. Early essays, 1895-1898* (pp. 224-243). Carbondale and Edwardsville IL: Southern Illinois University Press. (Original work published 1895)

Dewey, J. (1972b). The need for a laboratory school. In J. Boydston (Ed.), *John Dewey: The early works, 1882-1898: 5. Early essays, 1895-1898* (pp. 433-435). Carbondale and Edwardsville, IL: Southern Illinois University Press. (Original work published 1896)

Dewey, J. (1972c). The university school. In J. Boydston (Ed.), *John Dewey: The early works, 1882-1898: 5. Early essays, 1895-1898 (pp. 436-441).* Carbondale and Edwardsville, IL: Southern Illinois University Press. (Original work published 1896)

Dewey, J. (1972d). My pedagogic creed. In J. Boydston (Ed.), *John Dewey: The early works, 1882-1898: 5. Early essays, 1895-1898* (pp. 84-95). Carbondale and Edwardsville, IL: Southern Illinois University Press. (Original work published 1897)

Dewey, J. (1974). An undemocratic proposal. Reprinted, in part, in M. Lazerson & W. N. Grubb (Eds.), *American education and vocationalism: A documentary history, 1870-1970* (pp. 143-147). New York: Teachers College Press. (Original work published in *Vocational Education, 1913, II*, 374-377)

Dewey, J. (1976a) The school and society. In J. Boydston (Ed.), *John Dewey, The middle works, 1899-1924: 1. Essays on school and society, 1899-1901* (pp. 1-109). Carbondale and Edwardsville, IL: Southern Illinois University Press. (Original work published 1899)

Dewey, J. (1976b). The child and the curriculum. In J. Boydston (Ed.), *John Dewey: The middle works, 1899-1924: 2. Essay on logical theory, 1902-1903* (pp. 271-291). Carbondale and Edwardsville, IL: Southern Illinois University Press. (Original work published 1902)

Dewey, J., & Dewey, E. (1979). *Schools of to-morrow.* In J. Boydston (Ed.), *John Dewey: The middle works, 1899-1924: Vol. 8. Essays on education and politics, 1915* (pp. 205-404). Carbondale and Edwardsville, IL: Southern Illinois University Press. (Original work published 1915)

Dewey J. (1980). Democracy and education. In J. Boydston (Ed.), *John Dewey: The middle works, 1899-1924* (Vol. 9). Carbondale and Edwardsville, IL: Southern Illinois University Press. (Original work published 1916)

Dykhuizen, G. (1973). *The life and mind of John Dewey.* Carbondale and Edwardsville, IL: Southern Illinois University Press.

Evans, R. B. (1984). The origins of American academic psychology. In J. Brozek (Ed.), *Explorations in the history of psychology in the United States* (pp. 17-60). Lewisburg: Bucknell University Press.

Fiske, J. (1883). *Excursions of an evolutionist.* Boston: Houghton Mifflin.

Friedrich-Cofer, L. (1986). Body, mind, and morals in the framing of social policy. In L. Friedrich-Cofer (Ed.), *Human nature and public policy: Scientific views of women, children, and families* (pp. 97-174). New York: Praeger.

Gould, S. J. (1977). *Ontogeny and phylogeny.* Cambridge, MA: Belknap Press.

Hall, G. S. (1911a). *Adolescence: Its psychology and its relations to physiology, anthropology, sociology, sex, crime, religion, and education* (Vols I-II). New York: Appleton. (Original work published 1904)

Hall, G. S. (1911b). *Educational Problems* (2 Vols.). New York: D. Appleton.

Hilgard, E. L. (1948). *Theories of learning.* New York: Appleton-Century.

Hook, S. (1971). *John Dewey: An intellectual portrait.* Westport, CT: Greenwood Press.

Hook, S. (1980). Introduction. In J. Boydston (Ed.), *John Dewey: The middle works, 1899-1924.* Carbondale and Edwardsville, IL: Southern Illinois University Press.

Hopkins, M. (1865). *Lectures on moral science.* Boston: Gould and Lincoln.

Hunter, W. S. (1952). Walter S. Hunter. In E. G. Boring, H. S. Langfeld, H. Werner, & R. M. Yerkes (Eds.), *A history of psychology in autobiography* (Vol. 4, pp. 163-187). Worcester, MA: Clark University Press.

James, W. (1981). *The principles of psychology.* Cambridge, MA: Harvard University Press. (Original work published 1890)

Kohlberg, L. (1971). From is to ought: How to commit the naturalistic fallacy and get away with it in the study of moral development. In T. Mischel (Ed.), *Cognitive development and epistemology.* New York: Academic Press.

Krohn, W. O. (1892a). Facilities in experimental psychology in the various German universities. *American Journal of Psychology, 4,* 585-595.

Krohn, W. O. (1892b). The laboratory of the Psychological Institute at the University of Gottingen. *American Journal of Psychology, 5,* 282-283.

Langer, S. (1967–82). *Mind: An essay on human feeling* (3 Vols.). Baltimore: Johns Hopkins University Press.

Lazerson, M., & Grubb, W. N. (1974) Introduction. In M. Lazerson & W. N. Grubb (Eds.), *American education and vocationalism: A documentary history, 1870-1970* (pp. 1-50). New York: Teachers College Press.

Mayhew, K. C., & Edwards, A. C. (1965). *The Dewey school: The Laboratory School of the University of Chicago, 1896-1903.* New York: Atherton Press (Original work published 1936).

Mills, C. W. (1966). *Sociology and pragmatism: The higher learning in America.* New York: Oxford University Press.

Rein, M., & White, S. H. (1977). Can policy research help policy? *The Public Interest,* No. 49, 119-136.

Rein, M., & White, S. H. (1981). Knowledge for practice. *Social Service Review, 55,* 1-41.

Ross, D. (1972). *G. Stanley Hall: The psychologist as prophet.* Chicago: University of Chicago Press.

Scheffler, I. (1974). *Four pragmatists: A critical introduction to Peirce, James, Mead, and Dewey.* New York: Humanities Press.

Siegel, A. W., & White, S. H. (1982). The child study movement: Early growth and development of the symbolized child. *Advances in Child Development and Behavior, 17,* 234-285.

Stenquist, J. L., Thorndike, E. L., & Trabue, M. R. (1915). The intellectual status of children who are public charges. *Archives of Psychology,* No. 33, 52.

Thorndike, E. L. (1898). Animal intelligence: An experimental study of the associative processes in animals. *Psychological Review,* Monograph Supplement No. 8.

Thorndike, E. L. (1900). Mental fatigue. I. *Psychological Review, VII,* 466-482; II. Mental fatigue in school children. *Psychological Review, VII,* 547-579.

Thorndike, E. L. (1903a). *Educational psychology.* New York: Lemcke & Buechner.

Thorndike, E. L. (1903b, May). The decrease in the size of American families. *Popular Science Monthly,* pp. 64-70.

Thorndike, E. L. (Ed.). (1903c). Heredity, correlation, and sex differences in school abilities. *Columbia University Contributions to Philosophy, Psychology, and Education, 2,* 61.

Thorndike, E. L. (1904). *An introduction to the theory of mental and social measurements.* New York: Teachers College Press.

Thorndike, E. L. (1905). Measurements of twins. *Columbia University Contributions to Psychology and Philosophy, XIII(3),* 45.

Thorndike, E. L. (1910). The contributions of psychology to education. *Journal of Educational Psychology, 1,* 5-12

Thorndike, E. L. (1913, August). Eugenics: With special reference to intellect and character. *Popular Science Monthly,* pp. 125-138.

Thorndike, E. L. (1913-14). *Educational psychology* (3 vols.). New York: Teachers College Press.

Thorndike, E. L., & Woodworth, R. S. (1901). The influence of improvement in one mental function upon the efficiency of other functions. *Psychological Review, VIII,* 247-261, 384-395, 553-564.

Wolf, T. L. (1973). *Alfred Binet.* Chicago: University of Chicago Press.

White, S. H. (1983). The idea of development in developmental psychology. In R. M. Lerner (Ed.), *Developmental psychology: Historical and philosophical perspectives* (pp. 55-77). Hillsdale, NJ: Lawrence Erlbaum Associates.

White, S. H. (1983). Psychology as a moral science. In F. S. Kessel & A. W. Siegel (Eds.), *The child and other cultural inventions* (pp. 1-25). New York: Praeger.

White, S. H. (1985, August). Developmental psychology at the beginning. Presidential Address, Division 7. American Psychological Association Convention, Los Angeles. *Developmental Psychology Newsletter,* pp. 27-39.

White, S. H. (1990). Child study at Clark University: 1894–1904. *Journal of the History of the Behavorial Sciences, 26,* 131-150.

White, S. H., & Buka, S. (1987). Early education: Programs, traditions, and policies. *Review of Research in Education, 14,* 43-91.

2

Learning Without Teaching: Its Place In Culture*

Scott Atran
Dan Sperber
CNRS, Paris

Laymen and psychologists alike agree that some human learning takes place with the help of teaching and some takes place unhelped. Yet, as Jerome Bruner (1986) indicates, most experimental studies of "learning" ignore the role of real-life teaching and consider only the kind of drill provided in the experimental setting. This drill is usually seen as simulating repeated encounters with the evidence, rather than a deliberate teaching process.

By contrast social psychologists and educators are prone to focus almost exclusively on teacher-learner interaction and to ignore spontaneous learning. This is particularly true of L. S. Vygotsky whose pioneering work on the relations between the mental and the social is somewhat marred by his neglect of "natural" (as opposed to "cultural") development (Wertsch, 1985; cf. Fodor, 1972). As Wertsch points out:

> In his discussion of the relationship between development and instruction, (Vygotsky) argues that learning cannot be reduced to learning in instruction, yet that is precisely the interpretation that seems most compatible with his comments about the emergence of intrapsychological from interpsychological functioning. (Wertsch, 1985, p. 73)

Anthropologists, being primarily concerned with culturally transmitted knowledge, often take for granted that most learning directly or indirectly involves sustained interaction with others. But the equation, implicit in Vygotsky's work, of culturally transmitted knowledge with knowledge learned through instruction is ethnocentrically biased. In most human societies children become competent adults without the help of institutionalized teaching: There are no schools, no syllabus, no appointed teachers. Parents and other elders don't see their duty towards children as primarily one of education. They may, over the years, end up spending some time instructing the child in various skills, but actions carried out with the purpose of teaching are rare. Most learning is achieved as a by-product, in the course of interactions that have other purposes.

* Paper originally presented to the Fourth Annual Workshop on "Culture, Schooling and Psychological Development," Tel Aviv University, June 2-7, 1987.

All human life, hence all human learning, takes place in a social and cultural setting and is affected by that setting. This does not mean, however, that all human knowledge is socially transmitted: Individuals also learn from idiosyncratic experiences. Nor is all socially transmitted knowledge, properly speaking, taught: Some transmissions takes place without the help of the older generation, for instance by unencouraged imitation.[1] Transmission can even take place in spite of contrary teaching, as when parents teach one thing and practice another and are imitated rather than heard. The study of traditional societies, where rich cultures may be transmitted with very little deliberate teaching, suggests that some very basic learning abilities may need social interaction, but not teaching, in order to be effective.

In Western folk psychology, though, learning and teaching (sometimes expressed by the same word, e. g., *apprendre* in French) are considered as one and the same process seen from two complementary perspectives. When learning is achieved without apparent teaching, some kind of teaching is nevertheless assumed to have taken place. Thus we say "experience taught me. . . ," "he has taught himself. . . " These metaphorical extensions of the notion of "teaching" are carried over from ordinary language, where they are relatively harmless, into scholarly anthropology or psychology, where they beg many questions, as witnessed by the following exchange:

Papert: I would like to say something about Sperber's reference to abilities that appear in a child without having been *taught*. It is wrong to identify *teaching* with a standard situation in which a teacher stands in front of a class or a mother interacts with her child. There are much more indirect ways in which society transmits knowledge to its young. For instance we see many examples of one-to-one correspondence in our social life. The system of monogamy teaches many things; among them a precursor of arithmetic, that is, the idea of one-to-one correspondence. Is it not plausible that some forms are selected for this kind of function by some evolutionary process?

Sperber: One must distinguish between explicit, direct instruction, which in itself can account for the learning process, and objects of reflection, which can suggest to the subject a systematic development only if he has the equipment for that. An organism that constructed the one-to-one relationship from observing monogamy would not owe his learning to any kind of "teaching" but rather to his own faculties. (Piatelli-Palmarini, 1981, pp. 250-251)

---

[1] Imitation is far from the simple, unreflective phenomenon it is usually thought to be. Rochel Gelman, who was a discussant for this chapter at the Tel-Aviv workshop, plausibly suggests that imitation involves the novice (child, apprentice) "setting standards." The imitator selects a definite segment of behavior from (logically speaking, indefinitely) many possible behavioral segments, then uses that selection to further interpret and monitor the behavior of others. This allows the imitator to compare other behavior with the standard so as to master its implications. To a significant extent, therefore, even in imitation the mind may operate as a fairly autonomous mechanism that sets up and drives the use of a well-structured cognitive standard for processing behavior in the imitator's environment.

From an anthropological point of view, a social practice or an institution is characterized by the purpose the social actors attribute to it. From this viewpoint, teaching is a social practice aimed at causing learning (i.e., "education" in a broad sense). Teaching must be distinguished from other kinds of social practices that are not aimed at causing learning. Of course, the actual effects of a practice may be very different from its culturally recognized purpose. A teaching practice may, in fact, cause very little learning. Conversely, a ritual activity, say, that is not aimed at causing learning may nevertheless greatly contribute to learning because it displays a good deal of socially relevant information in an intelligible form.

Although teaching may fail in causing learning, where other institutions succeed, we expect teaching and learning to be on the whole—an in certain respects, essentially—correlated. But this correlation, which is an important anthropological and psychological topic, must be studied and not simply postulated.[2] From a psychological point of view, "learning" is a medley of problems and mysteries. The fact that learning is sometimes helped by teaching, or is dependent upon it, makes for a further problem rather than a solution.

The study of learning and its relation to teaching may be clarified by moving from a discussion of learning in general—a level at which few, if any, useful generalizations are to be expected—to learning in specific cognitive domains. The idea we want to advance is that not all concepts are equal. Different conceptual domains may require or tolerate different kinds of supporting environments. Some domains, particularly those where more or less spontaneous learning takes place, may need supporting environments with only a minimum of previous, culturally imposed structure. The environment's role would be merely to provide the physical targets that trigger the learner's attention. To say in such cases that we actually learn from the exemplars that occasion learning obviously begs the question of what may count as a legitimate datum. It is the conceptual structure of the domain that tells us what the entities are and how they are to be organized and interpreted.

But how are specific domains to be identified? Several well-known kinds of considerations can be brought to bear on the issue. Conceptual analysis can suggest domain-specificity by showing that the structures to be learned are very different, as between, say, arithmetic and color classification. The presence of much greater individual difference in performance in some fields (e.g., understanding mathematics) than in others (e.g., language comprehension) provides another source of evidence. An additional source is the study of specific cognitive losses, such as various forms of aphasia and agnosia, examples of which will be discussed later on.

---

[2] David Premack (1984) may be right in claiming that the human species has a unique pedagogic disposition. In other words, humans may well seize the chance to demonstrate or to correct performance in a way no other earthly species does. Thus, the distinction between learning *with* and learning *without* teaching may not be all that radical, with the boundary between the two being fuzzy or shifting. Even so, at this stage it seems to us more important to debunk the unreflective equation of "learning" with "being taught" by pointing to some major forms of learning without teaching and outlining the roles these play in culture.

One barely tapped source of evidence on the demarcation of cognitive domains is the study of cultural transmission: some bodies of knowledge have a life of their own, only marginally affected by social change (e.g., color classification, folktales), while other bodies of cultural knowledge (e.g., liturgy, advanced algebra) depend for their transmission, and hence for their very existence, on specific institutions. This suggests that culture should not be viewed as an integrated whole, relying for its transmission on undifferentiated human cognitive abilities. Rather, it seems that human cognitive resources are involved in different ways in the many more or less autonomous psychological subsystems that go into the making of culture.

With a few examples, let us illustrate how this simultaneously cognitive and anthropological approach might help demarcate those specific cognitive domains where spontaneous learning takes place.

Spontaneous Learning

Until recently, in anthropology as in education theory and developmental psychology generally, all human knowledge was assumed to be acquired essentially in the same way. Learning was seen to derive from a unitary system of cognitive structure, with some complexity in its organization over time, but not in its procedures at any given stage (Leach, 1964; Inhelder & Piaget, 1964; Vygotsky, 1965). Pathology aside, individual and cultural differences presumably owed to differences in the particular experiences the developing system was intended to interpret. By manipulating individual and collective experiences, then, people might be led to acquire different bodies of knowledge. Teaching could reasonably be seen as a deliberate manipulation of that kind, potentially effective in all domains.

There is now a good deal of plausible speculation and empirical evidence against such views. Work in theoretical linguistics and experimental psycholinguistics posed the first, and still the most significant, challenge to the idea of a single unspecialized learning ability (Chomsky, 1965, 1986; Pinker, 1984). For the first time in the study of the human mind, formally integrated and highly articulated systems of principles were proposed to account of significant aspects of human linguistic competence and for its development in the individual. No other psychological domain appears to reflect the peculiar kinds of empirical regularities that might suggest a wider operation of these linguistic principles in human cognition.

Furthermore, it takes extremely severe pathology or total deprivation of human interaction to prevent linguistic development. So far as we know, absence of language teaching (understood, in the widest reasonable sense, as interaction specifically aimed at helping language learning) is no hindrance at all. What role language teaching may play (when it actually occurs) is, as we have already suggested, very unclear. In a society with many social dialects, it may ensure that a socially more valued dialect is being learned. It may bring about a marginal difference in linguistic proficiency which, in a very competitive society, may turn out to be of real social significance. Other linguistic niceties are probably favored by some kind of language teaching. But basic linguistic abilities seem to develop spontaneously, given a modicum of ordinary linguistic interaction. This constitutes strong evidence not just for the innate, but also for the specialized, character of human language learning ability.

While language may provide the best and richest example of a specialized learning mechanism, it is not the only one. Take the case of color. Until the 1970s the dominant view of color categorization was that advanced in linguistics by Saussure (1916/1972), in anthropology by Benjamin Whorf (1956), and in philosophy by Willard Quine (1960). According to that view, innate human abilities impose no particular organization on the color continuum. Each culture apprehends this continuum and divides it into named zones as it wishes. Hence, there should be no universals in color categorizations—a prediction corroborated by a superficial look at color terms across languages.

To the contrary, more recent, methodologically sounder cross-cultural studies of color categories have indicated that basic color foci are perceptually invariable across cultures (Berlin & Kay, 1969; Heider, 1972; Kay & McDaniel, 1978). Thus, we find that in all languages having at least three basic color terms, there is one term whose meaning is best instantiated by focal red (a small region of the spectrum definable as a particular combination of hue, saturation, and brightness), and essentially the same holds for all basic colors. Moreover, variations in identifying the best instance of, say, "red" are individual rather than cultural.

Taken together, the cross-cultural and developmental evidence suggest that deliberate manipulation of the learning situation (other than deprivation of relevant input) could not fundamentally alter the content or development of color categorization. In other words, teaching is largely irrelevant to the learning of this very basic cognitive ability. In particular, different color terminologies, far from determining different color categorizations, all accommodate to the existing universal one. They differ merely in providing richer or poorer means of verbally encoding preexisting basic color categories. To be sure, what takes place once we move beyond *basic* color categories and look at elaborate terminologies linked to special uses of color (e.g., dyeing or painting) largely remains an open empirical question. In this regard, it would not be surprising if we found important cultural differences together with a regular involvement of teaching in transmission.

Nowadays cognitive scientists often take for granted the specific and spontaneous character of language learning abilities and are willing to acknowledge the cognitive specificity of each sensory modality. At the same time, there is still a widespread tendency to consider that our nonmodality-specific concepts are all learned and processed in the same way. In particular, it is often assumed in the cognitive literature that a single semantic theory uniformly holds for all terms, however much the kinds of objects or events they denote might differ. For instance, it is generally taken as

[a] working assumption . . . that in the domains of both man-made and biological objects, there occur information rich bundles of attributes that form natural discon-

tinuities [and] these bundles are both perceptual and functional. (Rosch & Mervis, 1975, p. 586; see also Smith & Medin, 1981)

Consequently, when interesting results are found for, say, living kinds, as a matter of course they are extended to, say, artifacts. This not only applies to the adult's conceptual system. Because the initial mental state associated with concept formation is assumed to be uniform across domains, theories of cognitive development may conflate analyses of different domains (e.g., Anglin 1977; Markman & Hutchinson, 1984).

If we look at the anthropological evidence, however, we find cross-cultural regularities within domains and domain differences within cultures. In the next section we illustrate the point in detail with the case of living kinds, and signal in a more cursory manner some interesting psychological findings about this domain and others.

An Example: The Classification of Living Kinds

Two decades of intensive cross-cultural study in ethnobiology seem to reveal that people's ordinary knowledge of living kinds is spontaneously ordered as a taxonomy whose structure is unique to the domain. Lay taxonomy, it appears, is universally and primarily composed of three transitively tiered levels, which are absolutely distinct ranks: the levels of *unique beginner, basic taxa,* and *life-form* (cf. Berlin, Breedlove, & Raven, 1973).

The unique beginner refers to the ontological category of plants or animals. Some cultures use a specific marker for the unique beginner, like the numerical classifier *tehk* for plants, as with the Tzeltal Maya (Berlin, Breedlove, & Raven, 1974). Others use a descriptive phrase, such as ''the hairs of the earth'' (*muk gobul nor*) for the Bunaq of Timor (Friedberg, 1984). Yet others have no word or ready-made phrase for *plant* or *animal,* although from an early age all humans seem to distinguish these categories conceptually, as indicated by studies of young Mayan (Stross, 1973) and American children (Dougherty, 1979; Macnamara, 1982), New Guinea highlanders (Hays, 1983), Indonesian natives (Taylor, 1984), and so on.

The basic level is logically subordinate, but psychologically prior, to the life-form level. Ideally it is constituted as a *relational* partitioning: an exhaustive and mutually exclusive segregation of the local flora and fauna into well-bounded morpho-behavorial gestalts (which visual aspect is readily perceptible at a glance) (Hunn, 1976). For the most part, taxa at this level correspond, within predictable limits, to the species distinguished by the modern field biologist in the local environment.

This basic folk kind also generally conforms to the modern conception of the genus, being immediately recognizable both ecologically and morphologically. In fact, the scientific distinction between genus and species is largely irrelevant in any local area since most local genera are represented by a single species. This is why the confused and seemingly inexhaustible controversy over whether the genus (Bartlett, 1940; Berlin, 1972) or the species (Diamond, 1966; Bulmer & Tyler, 1968) constitutes the psychologically and historically primitive grouping has remained inconclusive. In fact, the basic folk-biological kind may be properly designated "generic-specieme" (Atran, 1987a).

The life-form level further assembles generic-speciemes into larger exclusive groups (tree, grass, moss, quadruped, bird, fish, insect, etc.). Life forms appear to partition plants and animals into a contrastive lexical field: a pre-theoretical *division* of positive features that are opposed along one or more perceptible dimensions (size, stem habit, mode of locomotion, skin covering, etc.) (cf. Brown, 1984). By and large, plant life forms do not correspond to scientific taxa, while animal life-forms approximate modern classes, save the phenomenally "residual" invertebrate groups ("bugs," "worms," etc.).

A consequence of division and ranking at the life-form level is that phenomenally and ecologically marginal groups may assume the status of monogeneric life forms. The phenomenally peculiar (though taxonomically regular) characteristic of monogeneric life forms is that they have intuited aspects of both generic-speciemes and life forms. As generic-speciemes their facies are readily perceptible at a glance. As life forms they occupy a distinctive role in the economy of nature. Because they are so distinctive, they may be easily marked off by characters chosen from dimensions spanning other life forms: For example, "cactus" for many American and French folk, as well as for the Aguaruna of Peru *(ikamas),* can be segregated from "tree," "grass," and the like by a rather simple set of diagnostic oppositions (Atran, 1985; cf. Sperber, 1975a).

Taxonomic ranking of living kinds is apparently peculiar to that domain. The field structure for artifacts, while often confounded with that of living kinds, is quite different. For one thing, that taxa of the same category are disjoint precludes artifact groupings entering into ranked taxonomies. There can be no absolute artifact *ranks:* Not only can artifactual items belong to more than one "taxon" within an inclusion series (a wheelchair as both "furniture" and "vehicle") but a given item may belong to different series (the same item as a crate for packing furniture or as a table used as furniture). It would also be senseless to think in terms of "monogeneric" artifact categories.

Talk of artifact "natures" is idle as well. For example, one and the same item can literally *be* an instance of "wastepaper basket" in one context and "stool" in another if oriented differently (cf. Dougherty & Keller, 1985). It is the fact that artifacts are defined by the functions they serve, rather than by any inherent perceptual properties, that allows a given (morphologically self-same) item to belong to different categories of artifacts in different circumstances (cf. Miller, 1978). But, for example, a dog is always a dog.[3]

---

[3] Still, according to Rosch (1973, p. 111), just as "some colors to which English speakers apply the word 'red' or 'redder' than others[,] some breeds of 'dog' (such as the retriever) are more representative of the 'meaning' of dog [than a Pekinese]." But the analogy with color is untenable. If a Pekinese is not

The transitive structure of groupings ranked according to their presumed underlying natures thus hardly applies to artifacts. For example, "carseat" may be judged varities of "chair," but not of "furniture," even though "chair" is normally thought of as a type of "furniture" (cf. Hampton, 1982). By contrast, although for ancient and modern Greek folk some instances of herbaceous mallow might resemble trees and some stunted oaks might not look like trees at all, tall-growing mallow would not be classified under "tree" while stunted oaks would be (cf. Theophrastus, 1916). Similarly, among the Tobelo of Indonesia (as most other cultures), "one hears of a particular small sapling. . . 'this weed (*o rurubu*) is a tree (*o gota*) . . . or of the same sapling . . . 'this is not a (member of the) herbaceous weed class, it is a tree' (*o rurubu* here contrasts with *o gota*" (Taylor, 1979, p. 224).

The claim for universal principles of folk-biological taxonomy is not for the universal status of particular *taxa,* only for taxonomic *categories.* The categories of generic-specieme and life form are universal. The delimitation and placement of particular taxa is not. To claim that life forms are fundamentally pragmatic notions (Randall & Hunn, 1984) is belied by obvious fact; for instance, children—be they 3-year-old Americans (Dougherty, 1979) or Mayans (Stross, 1973)—certainly don't learn "wood-use" when they learn "tree" (Atran, 1987c). Also, claims as to any "universal principles" governing the sequence in which life forms appear in the language of any given society (Brown, 1984), whether or not such principles are related to societal complexity, may have little to do with *taxonomic* principles. A persistent empiricist bias confounds the a priori nature of abstract taxonomic schema with substantive patterns derived from experience. Categories as such have no historical dimension, even though particular sorts of taxa may.

Linked to the cross-cultural stability of the living kind conceptual domain, we find that the learning of ordinary living kind terms is remarkably easy and needs no teaching. At a limit, one need only once point to an animal (even in a zoo or book) and name it to have young children immediately classify and relationally segregate

---

properly, or only peripherally, a dog, what other kind could it be confused with? It may be difficult to decide where "red" ends and "orange" starts, or where "cup" leaves off and "bowl" begins (cf. Labov, 1973; Kempton, 1978); however, this is certainly not so for "dog," "oak," or any other such living kind. Perhaps there is a lesser degree of confidence in the judgment (especially the child's judgment) that a Pekinese or Boston terrier is a dog and not another basic kind such as a cat, than in the judgment that a retriever or German shepherd is a dog rather than a cat. But Pekinese and Boston terriers cannot *be* anything but dogs.

The reason is that members of a living kind, but not an artifactual kind, are presumed to have the same essential underlying natures regardless of the extent to which those members actually differ in physical appearance. This presumption underpins the taxonomic stability of ordinary types of living kinds despite obvious token variation among exemplars (Atran, 1987b; cf. Sperber, 1975a). It is why, for example, legless tigers may still be classed with animals defined as "quadrupeds by nature." Note, however, that it is senseless to say of a beanbag chair that it lacks "its" legs, or of a legless table suspended from a ceiling that it lacks "its." For the "legs" of a tiger advert necessarily to the tiger's presumed underlying nature. By contrast, those of a table or chair are merely plausible or likely—not necessary—means for those artifacts to realize their defining functions.

it from all other taxa. The naming might, of course, be done (and in a zoo is likely to be done) with pedagogic intent ("this, children, is a sheep"); however, it may just as well occur in an utterance not at all aimed at teaching ("let's feed this sheep") and provide the required input. Such basic human knowledge of living kinds does not depend on teaching, nor is it gradually abstracted from experience. It is spontaneously acquired in accordance with innate expectation about the organization of the everyday biological world.

Appreciation of artifacts, too, might be governed by innate expectations: "Even preschoolers clearly believe that artifacts tend to be human made and that natural kinds are not" (Gelman, 1988, p. 88; cf. Keil, 1986). Although, for lack of systematic analysis, the character of these expectations is wide open to speculation, it seems that in this domain as well humans are able to categorize fragmented experiences and, with little or no "trial and error," extend the resulting categories to an indefinitely large set of complexly related experiences. As in any other area of cognitive endeavor, it is difficult to imagine how such spontaneous learning could succeed without a powerful set of innate organizing principles.

A bit more evidence is at hand regarding initial expectations about three-dimensional rigid bodies, and the spatiotemporally contiguous relations of physical causality between them (Bower, 1982; Spelke, 1987) and for intentional causality in animate beings (Gelman & Spelke, 1981; Gelman, Spelke, & Meck, 1983). In important respects, then, it appears that in addition to innate expectations governing the spontaneous learning of language and such basic perceptual categories as colors, humans are also endowed with the means to spontaneously develop concepts and views in accordance with "naive" theories of biology, psychology, and physics. It seems likely that the list of distinct, innately determined cognitive domains will turn out to be longer.[4]

Evidence for Domain-Specificity

Let us now return to the issue of what sorts of evidence might be brought to bear on the delimitation of basic cognitive domains. Thus far, we have relied chiefly on conceptual analysis: showing that a given domain is universally present and structured in a specific way that differs radically from the ways other domains are structured. In particular, anthropological and psychological findings clearly suggest that the mind organizes the domain of living kinds in a very different way from that of artifacts, no matter what the culture.

But the argument for universal, domain-specific cognitions does not depend exclusively, or even necessarily, on cross-cultural pervasiveness (e.g., cultural

---

[4] Hirschfeld (1988) argues for the domain-specificity of certain aspects of children's knowledge of social relations. Gelman (1982) suggests that counting skills are acquired early on in any society without schooling; moreover, even preverbal infants show an appreciation of the one-to-one correspondence relations that such skills require (Starkey, Spelke, & Gelman, 1983).

"universals" in the sense of Levi-Strauss, 1969). The social subordination of women, for example, appears to characterize all known cultures. It could even be argued that there is some biological grounding for this condition. There is no reason, however, to attribute the varied ways people psychologically process this pervasive social phenomenon to some universal cognitive mechanism. Conversely, the ability to develop and understand mathematics may be rooted in some fairly specific cognitive mechanisms, which human beings are innately endowed with (cf. Chomsky, 1988). But if so, many cultures do not require that people use this ability. Nor is it occasioned by every environment. Mathematics does not spontaneously arise irrespective of social context, but seems to require a richer and more sustained sequence of experience and instruction in order to flourish than, say, basic grammatical knowledge, color perception, or appreciation of living kinds (cf. Rosskopf, Steffe, & Taback, 1971).

A more revealing indication of basic, domain-specific knowledge comes from study of cultural transmission. Admittedly, the acquisition of all cultural knowledge depends upon its mode of transmission. But the acquisition of certain basic forms of knowledge does not seem much influenced by the sequence in which it is communicated; that is, *what* is learned does not much depend on *how* it is passed along. Taxonomic knowledge of living kinds, for instance, is roughly comparable across similar physical environments regardless of whether it is "ideologically formless' in one society or has a "high rhetorical profile" in another. Thus, the Hanunóo of the Philippines possess detailed basic botanical knowledge that they take every occasion to demonstrate and pontificate upon (Conklin, 1954); but the Zafimaniry of Madagascar, whose tropical environment and swidden technology are rather similar to that of the Hanunóo, appear to pass on their equally detailed basic botanical knowledge quite informally and with scarce commentary (Bloch, 1988).[5]

An additional source of evidence for domain-specificity stems from developmental psychology. For it is logical to suppose that the basic structures of human cognition are those which severely constrain, and therefore greatly facilitate, the rapid acquisition of cultural knowledge. Experiments in the field indicate accordingly that young children—be they American (Keil, 1986) or Yoruba (Jeyifous, 1985)—categorically distinguish *artifacts* from *living things,* and come to presume that only the latter constitute "natural kinds" with underlying essences.

Concerning notions of underlying nature, more recent studies by Keil (1988) and his colleagues show that even preschoolers have some presumptions, however rudimentary. In other words, the youngsters clearly "have some beliefs about what are not likely to be biologically relevant properties, regardless of salient characteristics." Thus, most of the kindergartners tested did not allow temporary and intermit-

---

[5] This is not to deny that Hanunoo eloquence on general botanical matters, like specialized Zafimaniry concern with wood, relies on complex modes of transmission governing social "wisdom." Neither is it to suggest that such complex notions as "wisdom"—which comprise the traditional bread and butter of anthropologists—can be studied exclusively with the techniques typically employed by cognitive psychologists. It does suggest, however, that basic psychological analysis is pertinent to understanding the cognitive foundations of even these more traditional concerns of anthropology.

tent alterations (e.g., paint that wears off a tigerized lion) to signal changes in kindhood, and even 3-year-olds tended not to admit costume change (e.g., putting a horse in a zebra outfit) as a change of identity.

In short, the youngest children tested to date evince some knowledge that animals of a kind share properties that are not readily apparent. Moreover, earlier studies by Keil (1979) in two cultures also suggest that preschoolers are apt to categorically restrict certain predicates, such as "grow," to plants and animals only (the children thought it did not make sense to say, for example, that rocks grow). This intimates that at least some concepts are constrained to the category *living kind*, however underdifferentiated the underlying biological "theory" that unifies conceptions of animals with those of plants.[6]

Selective cerebral impairment and selective preservation of certain cognitive categories can provide further clues for domain-specificity (Warrington & McCarthy, 1983; Hart, Berndt, & Caramazza, 1985). There is an increasing body of literature in neuropsychology that refers to "category-specific" deficits in brain-damaged patients. In particular, there is considerable evidence not only for a distinct "gnostic field" of living kinds (Konorski, 1967), but also for "modality specific semantic systems" that involve both visual and verbal understanding of artifacts versus living kinds (Warrington & Shallice, 1984). More specifically, Sartori and Job (1988) describe impairments that differentially affect the basic and superordinate levels of living kind taxonomy (cf. McCarthy & Warrington, 1988)[7]

---

[6] Carey (1985), however, argues that an overriding notion of *living thing* that causally links all and only plants and animals in terms of "natural kinds" is acquired only with (informal or formal) instruction in biological theory. But it seems more likely that people's knowledge of the biological domain becomes "theory-driven" because they have prior presumptions of underlying organic natures than the other way around (see Atran, 1987b, 1988, for discussions of this point). Indeed, the islanders of West Futuna (Polynesia), for example, manifestly attach a notion of "material essence" (*hkano*) to "living things" (*ne mauri*); yet there appears to be no lawfully consistent theory about the underlying biology (or cosmology) of all and only living kinds (Dougherty, 1983; Keller & Lehman, 1988).

[7] Warrington and Shallice experimented with four patients affected by herpes simplex encephalitis. They performed very poorly on visual and verbal identification tasks for "animals" (e. g., deer, wasp, ostrich), "plants" (e. g., palm) and "food" (e. g., grapefruit, cabbage, egg), but as well as normal controls for "inanimate" objects, that is, artifacts: "We would suggest that identification of an inanimate object crucially depends on determination of its functional significance, but that this is irrelevant for identification of living things. We would therefore speculate that a semantic system based on functional specifications might have evolved for the identification of inanimate objects" (1984, p. 849).

Now, foods are not living kinds *per se*. Indeed, appreciation of foods clearly depends on functional distinctions, as with artifacts (cf. Wierzbicka, 1984). Thus, although preschoolers may experience similar difficulties in imposing consistent hierarchical relations on foods and artifacts (cf. Rosch, Mervis, Gray, Johnson, & Boyes-Braem, 1976), they seem much better at biological taxonomies (cf. Waxman, 1985). But like living kinds and unlike artifacts, foods also have nonfunctional, perceptible defining characteristics. One might thus expect that *both* category-specific impairments for living kinds and for artifacts would affect appreciation of foods. Indeed, Nielson (1946) mentions an impairment with "inanimate" objects, including foods, but not living things.

Sartori and Job (1988) report on a patient whose appreciation of taxonomic structure remains intact but who has difficulty processing basic kinds: "He adds fins to fishes, wings to birds and horns to certain

In sum, it is logically impossible that humans are able to conceptually generalize from limited experience without a priori structures that govern the projection of finite instances to their infinitely extendable classes. It is an entirely empirical question whether or not these principles cross domains, and, if they do, which domains they cross. No a priori assumption in the matter is justified. The implication for research strategies is clear: In the absence of sufficient further evidence, results from a potentially autonomous cognitive domain should not be extended to other domains. We should be prepared to discover that, after all, the structure of human concepts is a motley rather than a monolith.

The Place of Spontaneous Learning in Culture

What we have suggested so far is that some abilities, concepts, and beliefs are easily acquired, without the help of teaching, and on the basis of ordinary interactions with others and the environment. What makes this acquisition easy is an innate readiness that takes different forms for different domains, or, in other terms, a set of domain-specific cognitive dispositions. The existence of such dispositions is, of course, neither more nor less mysterious than that of any adaptive aspect of the species' genetic endowment.

Innate cognitive dispositions determine a core of spontaneously learnable representations that are highly similar across cultures. Cultures develop—with greater diversity—beyond this core. They include systems of representations that are not spontaneously learnable. On the contrary, these systems require deliberate and often long and difficult learning, which may greatly benefit from adequate teaching.

We will now consider, briefly and in a very simplified way, two types of such systems of representations, science and religion; let us see how they depart from the cultural core while nevertheless remaining rooted in it.

Core concepts and beliefs are easily acquired and tend to be adequate for ordinary dealings with the social and natural environment. Yet they are restricted to some cognitive domains and are rather rigid. Other, harder-to-learn representations may be less limited in their domain of application and less rigid. They involve different cognitive abilities, in particular, the typically human ability of forming representations of representations. This metarepresentational ability (closely linked to linguistic communication: see Sperber & Wilson, 1986) allows people to retain information that they only partly understand and to work on it in order to understand

---

mammals, but he has great problems in distinguishing e. g. the horn of a rhinoceros from the antlers of a deer" or in discriminating real from unreal creatures (task 15). Also, "accuracy for vegetables was poor although somewhat better than for animals" (task 18). The "somewhat better," however, may owe to the fact that vegetables, unlike animal and plant kinds as such, also generally involve functional attributes whose appreciation is not impaired. Still, the impairment does seem restricted to only living things without regard to typicality; that is, the patient's performance on typical versus atypical items was "not significant . . . which is the opposite direction of what would be predicted" if living kind categories were prototypically based (task 6).

it better. Such processing of half-understood information over time is typical of deliberate efforts to learn counterintuitive ideas, and is found in both science and religion.

A major difference between spontaneous and nonspontaneous, or sophisticated, learning is that only in the former case are the individual's newly acquired thoughts directly about the objects of the new knowledge: for example, about physical properties or animals. As for sophisticated learning, the individual's newly acquired thoughts are initially about the knowledge itself: for example, about notions and ideas in physics or in biology. Only if and when these notions and ideas become fully assimilated may the knowledge cease to be non- or even counterintuitive and become direct knowledge of, say, physical or biological facts. The passage from representation of knowledge to assimilation of knowledge is often difficult, as in the sciences. Sometimes it is not even possible, so that some forms of knowledge, such as religious ideas, remain forever metarepresentational.

In the case of the sciences, what makes this counterintuitive ideas understandable at all is that they remain rooted in common sense intuitions, however remotely (see Atran, 1986). The history of science, for instance, suggests that the breakthroughs that characterize modern theories followed a conscientious probe of the scope and limits of common sense "givens" in the corresponding naive theories. Consider evolutionary theory: Darwin (1883, p. 426) rejects the essences of species as "merely artificial combinations made for convenience"; yet the argument for natural selection would fail, in Darwin's eyes, if it failed to be a solution to the problem of the origin of species, a problem whose formulation presupposed that the term had its customary reference (Wallace, 1901, p. 1; cf. Hodge, 1987). Evolutionary biology today has gone even further against the grain of intuition in rejecting the common sense view of species as classes of organisms and substituting the notion of the species as a "logical individual" (Ghiselin, 1981). But even those axiomatizations of evolutionary theory (Williams, 1985) that treat species communities as individual spatiotemporal wholes implicitly appeal to a notion of the "nondimensional" species that closely approximates the lay conception (Mayr, 1969, p. 27).

In practice, the field biologist who is initially unfamiliar with a terrain can usually rely on local folk to provide a fairly accurate first approximation of the scientific distribution of the local flora and fauna (at least for vertebrates and flowering plants). True, genetics and molecular biology have little recourse to folk intuitions, but in these fields as well generalizations depend on the acceptance of taxonomic inferences that do make use of notions like species.

Plainly, the learning of the sciences need not recapitulate the historic process of discovery. It seems, however, that understanding at least some central notions of a science presupposes understanding the corresponding "naive" notions and relating the two appropriately. This throws some light on the role of quality of teaching in cases of sophisticated learning: The role of the teacher is not merely to present, however soundly and clearly, the scientific notions and theories; it is also to help students relate these to common-sense experience and knowledge.

In the case of religious beliefs, we take the view that they never become fully assimilated to basic knowledge. They retain an element of mystery not just for outsiders but also, though differently, for the believers themselves. In cognitive terms, this means that religious beliefs are held metarepresentationally (see Sperber, 1975b, 1985a). In sociological terms, they are displayed, taught, discussed, and reinterpreted as doctrines, dogmas, or sacred texts. The fact that religious beliefs do not lend themselves to any kind of clear and final comprehension allows their learning, their teaching, and their exegeses to go on forever.

Religious beliefs, however, are not unconnected to common-sense knowledge. They are generally inconsistent with common sense knowledge, but not at random: rather, they dramatically contradict basic common sense assumptions (see Atran, 1986). For instance, they include beliefs about invisible creatures, beliefs about creatures who can transform themselves at will or who can perceive events that are distant in time or space (see Sperber, 1975b). This flatly contradicts factual, common-sense assumptions about physical, biological, and psychological phenomena. Such dramatic contradictions contribute to making religious beliefs particularly attention-arresting and memorable. As a result, these beliefs are more likely to be retained and transmitted in a human group than random departures from common sense, and thus to become part of the group's culture (see Sperber, 1985b).

In brief, religious beliefs, too, are rooted in basic beliefs, albeit in a "dialectical" way. Thus, within a given religious text or tradition, one might "predict that the likelihood of a transformation from one thing into another should decrease as the distance . . . between the [common-sense ontological] categories of these two things increases" (Kelly & Keil, 1985). For instance, the metamorphosis of humans into animals and animals into plants may be more common than that of humans or animals into artifacts. To the extent such violations of category distinctions shake basic notions of ontology, they are attention-arresting, hence memorable. But only to the degree that the resultant impossible worlds remain bridged to the everyday world can information about them be stored and evoked in plausible grades.

Our metaphorical talk about a core of spontaneously learnable knowledge, and a periphery of further knowledge that requires deliberate learning and teaching not only suggests that the one is more stable and central than the other; it also indicates that they are functionally related: The very existence of the periphery is made possible by the core. Sophisticated knowledge elaborates or challenges common-sense knowledge but never develops in society or the individual without reference to basic common-sense knowledge. This implies that the study of spontaneous learning, of obvious interest in itself, is also a prerequisite to enhanced understanding of deliberate and sophisticated learning, and of the role teaching plays, in the acquisition of complex cultural knowledge.

References

Anglin, J. (1977). *Word, object, and conceptual development.* New York: Norton.

Atran, S. (1985). The nature of folkbotanical life-forms. *American Anthropologist, 87,* 298-315.

Atran, S. (1986). *Fondements de l'histoire naturelle.* Brussels: Complexe.

Atran, S. (1987a). Origin of the species and genus concepts. *Journal of the History of Biology, 20,* 195-279.

Atran, S. (1987b). Ordinary constraints on the semantics of living kinds: A common sense alternative to recent treatments of natural-object terms. *Mind and Language, 2,* 27-63.

Atran, S. (1987c). The essence of folkbiology: A response to Randall and Hunn. *American Anthropologist, 88,* 149-151.

Atran, S. (1988, March 22-24). Whither the "New Ethnography"? Paper presented to the King's College Research Centre Conference on "The Representation of Complex Cultural Categories." Cambridge University, Cambridge, England.

Bartlett, H. (1940). History of the generic concept in botany. *Bulletin of the Torrey Botanical Club, 47,* 319-62.

Berlin, B. (1972). Speculations on the growth of ethnobotanical nomenclature. *Language and Society, 1,* 63-98.

Berlin, B., Breedlove, D., & Raven, P. (1973). General principles of classification and nomenclature in folk biology. *American Anthropologist, 75,* 214-42

Berlin, B., Breedlove, D., & Raven, P. (1974). *Principles of Tzeltal plant classification.* New York: Academic Press.

Berlin, B., & Kay, P. (1969). *Basic color terms: Their universality and growth.* Berkeley, CA: University of California Press.

Bloch, M. (1988, March 22-24). *The concept of "wisdom" in Madagascar and elsewhere.* Working Paper presented to the King's College Research Centre Conference on "The Representation of Complex Cultural Categories," Cambridge University, Cambridge, England.

Bower, T. (1982). *Development in infancy* (2nd ed.). San Francisco, CA: Freeman.

Brown, C. (1984). *Language and living things.* East Brunswick, NJ: Rutgers University Press.

Bruner, J. (1986). *Actual minds, possible worlds.* Cambridge, MA: Harvard University Press.

Bulmer, R., & Tyler, M. (1968). Karam classification of frogs. *Journal of the Polynesian Society, 77,* 333-85.

Carey, S. (1985). *Conceptual change in childhood.* Cambridge, MA: MIT Press.

Chomsky, N. (1965). *Aspects of the theory of syntax.* Cambridge, MA: MIT Press.

Chomsky, N. (1986). *Knowledge of language.* New York: Praeger.

Chomsky, N. (1988). *Language and problems of knowledge.* Cambridge, MA: MIT Press.

Conklin, H. (1954). *The relation of Hanunóo culture to the plant world.* Unpublished Ph.D. dissertation, Yale University, New Haven, CT.

Darwin, C. (1883). *On the origins of species by means of natural selection* (6th ed.). Appleton.

Diamond, J. (1966). Zoological classification system of a primitive people. *Science, 15,* 1102-04.

Dougherty, J. (1979). Learning names for plants and plants for names. *Anthropological Linguistics, 21,* 298-315.

Doughtery, J. (1983). West Futuna-Aniwa: An introduction to a Polynesian outlier language. *University of California Publications in Linguistics, 102.*

Dougherty, J., & Keller, C. (1985). Taskonomy. In J. Dougherty (Ed.), *Directions in cognitive anthropology.* Urbana, IL: University of Illinois Press.

Fodor, J. (1972). Some reflections on L. S. Vygotsky's "Thought and Language." *Cognition, 1,* 83-95.

Friedberg, C. (1984). Les Bunaq de Timor et les plantes, tome 4. Thèse de Doctorat d'Etat, Université de Paris V. Paris, France.

Gelman, R. (1982). Basic numeral abilities. In R. Sternbeg (Ed.), *Advances in the psychology of human intelligence,* Hillsdale, NJ: Erlbaum.

Gelman, R., & Spelke, E. (1981). The development of thoughts about animate and inanimate objects. In J. Flavell & L. Ross (Eds.), *Social cognitive development.* Cambridge, England: Cambridge University Press.

Gelman, S. (1988). The development of induction within natural kind and artifact categories. *Cognitive Psychology, 20,* 65-95.

Gelman, S., Spelke, E., & Meck, E. (1983). What preschoolers know about animate and inanimate objects. In D. Rogers & J. Sloboda (Eds.), *The acquisition of symbolic skills.* New York: Plenum.

Ghiselin, M. (1981). Categories, life, and thinking. *The Behavioral and Brain Sciences, 4*, 269-313.

Hampton, J. (1982). A demonstration of intransitivity in natural categories. *Cognition, 12*, 151-164.

Hart, J., Berndt, R., & Caramazza, A. (1985). Category-specific naming deficit following cerebral infarction. *Nature, 316*, 439.

Hays, T. (1983). Ndumba folk biology. *American Anthropologist, 85*, 592-611.

Heider, E. (1972). Universals in color naming. *Journal of Experimental Psychology, 93*, 10-20.

Hirschfeld, L. (1988). On acquiring social categories. *Man, 23*, 611-38.

Hodge, M. J. S. (1987). Darwin, species and the theory of natural selection. In *Histoire du concept d'espéce dans les sciences de la vie*. Paris: Editions de la Fondation Singer-Polignac.

Hunn, E. (1976). Toward a perceptual model of folk biological classification. *American Ethnologist, 3*, 508-24.

Inhelder, B., & Piaget, J. (1964). *The early growth of logic in the child*. London: Routledge & Kegan Paul.

Jeyifous, S., (1985). *Atimodemo: Semantic conceptual development among the Yoruba*. Unpublished Ph.D. dissertation, Cornell University, Ithaca, NY.

Kay, P. & McDaniel, C. (1978). The linguistic significance of the meaning of basic color terms. *Language, 54*, 610-46.

Keil, F. (1979). *Semantic and conceptual development*. Cambridge, MA: Harvard University Press.

Keil, F. (1986). The acquisition of natural kind and artifact terms. In A. Marrar & W. Demopoulos (Ed.), *Conceptual change*, Norwood, NJ: Ablex.

Keil, F. (1988). *Intuitive belief systems and informal reasoning in cognitive development* (Working Paper). Ithaca, NY: Department of Psychology, Cornell University.

Keller, J., & Lehman, F. (1988, March 22-24). *Complex concepts*. Working Paper presented to King's College Research Centre Conference on "The Representation of Complex Cultural Categories," Cambridge University, Cambridge, England.

Kelly, M., & Keil, F. (1985). The more things change. . .: Metamorphoses and conceptual structure. *Cognitive Science, 9*, 403-416.

Kempton, W. (1978). Category grading and taxonomic relations: A mug is a sort of cup. *American Ethnologist, 5*, 44-65.

Konorski, J. (1967). *Integrative activity of the brain: an interdisciplinary approach*. Chicago, IL: University of Chicago Press.

Labov, W. (1973). The boundaries of words and their meanings. In C. Bailey & R. Shuy (Eds.), *New ways of analyzing variations in English*. Washington, DC: Georgetown University Press.

Leach, E. (1964). Anthropological aspects of language: Animal categories and verbal abuse. In E. Lennenberg (Ed.), *New directions in the study of language*. Cambridge, MA: MIT Press.

Levi-Strauss, C. (1969). *The elementary structures of kinship*. Boston: Beacon Press.

McCarthy, A., & Warrington, E. (1988). Evidence for modality-specific meaning systems in the brain. *Nature, 88*, 428-29.

Macnamara, J. (1982). *Names for things: A study of human learning*. Cambridge, MA: MIT Press.

Markman, E., & Hutchinson, J. (1984). Children's sensitivity to constraints on word meaning: Taxonomic versus thematic relations. *Cognitive Psychology, 16*, 1-27.

Mayr, E. (1969). *Principles of systematic zoology*. New York: McGraw-Hill.

Miller, G. (1978). Practical and lexical knowledge. In E. Rosch & B. Lloyd (Eds.), *Cognition and categorization*. Hillsdale, NJ: Erlbaum.

Nielsen, J. (1946). *Agnosia, apraxia, aphasia. Their value in cerebral localization*. New York: Hoeber.

Piatelli-Palmirini, M. (1981 [1980]) *Language and learning: the debate between Jean Piaget and Noam Chomsky* (2nd printing [part of the passage quoted was mistranslated in the original 1980 printing]). Cambridge, MA: Harvard University Press.

Pinker, S. (1984). *Language learnability and language development*. Cambridge, MA: Harvard University Press.

Premack, D. (1984). Pedagogy and aesthetics as sources of culture. In M. Gazzaniga (Ed.), *Handbook of cognitive neurosciences*, New York: Plenum.

Quine, W. (1960). *Word and object*. Cambridge, MA: Harvard University Press.

Randall, R., & Hunn, E. (1984). Do life forms evolve or do uses for life? Some doubts about Brown's universal hypothesis. *American Ethnologist, 11*, 329-349.

Rosch, E. (1973). On the internal structure of perceptual and semantic categories. In T. Moore (Ed.), *Cognitive development and the acquisition of language* (pp. 1-20). New York: Academic Press.

Rosch, E., & Mervis, C. (1975). Family resemblances: Studies in the internal structure of natural categories. *Cognitive Psychology, 8*, 382-439.

Rosch, E., Mervis, C., Gray, W., Johnson, D., & Boyes-Braem, P. (1976). Basic objects in natural categories. *Cognitive Psychology, 8*, 382-439.

Rosskopf, M., Steffe, L., & Taback, S. (1971). *Piagetian cognitive development research in mathematical education.* Washington, DC: National Council of Teachers of Mathematics.

Sartori, G., & Job, R. (1988). The oyster with four legs: A neuropsychological study on the interaction of visual and semantic information. *Cognitive Neuropsychology, 5*, 105-132.

Saussure, F. (1972). *Cours de linguistique générale.* Paris: Payot. (Original work published 1916)

Smith, E., & Medin, D. (1981). *Categories and concepts.* Cambridge, MA: Harvard University Press.

Spelke, E. (1987, April 3-6). *The origins of physical knowledge.* Paper presented at the Fyssen Symposium, "Thought Without Language." Versailles, France.

Sperber, D. (1975a). Pourquoi les animaux parfaits, les hybrides et les monstres sont-ils bons á penser symboliquement? *L'Homme, 15*, 3-34.

Sperber, D. (1975b). *Rethinking symbolism.* Cambridge, England: Cambridge University Press.

Sperber, D. (1985a). *On anthropological knowledge.* Cambridge, England: Cambridge University Press.

Sperber, D. (1985b). Anthropology and psychology: Towards an epidemiology of representations. *Man, 20*, 73-89.

Sperber, D., & Wilson, D. (1986). *Relevance.* Oxford: Blackwell.

Starkey, P., Spelke, E., & Gelman, R. (1983). Detection of 1-1 correspondences in human infants. *Science, 222*, 79-81.

Stross, B. (1973). Acquisition of botanical terminology by Tzeltal children. In M. Edmonson (Ed.), *Meaning in Mayan languages.* Hawthorne, NY: Mouton.

Taylor, P. (1979). Preliminary report on the ethnobiology of the Tobelorese of Hamalhera, North Moluccas. *Majalah Ilmu-ilmu Sastra Indonesia, 8*, 215-229.

Taylor, P. (1984). "Covert categories" reconsidered: Identifying unlabeled classes in Tobelo folk biological classification. *Journal of Ethnobiology, 4*, 105-22.

Theophrastus. (1916). *Enquiry into plants [Historia plantarum]* (trans. A. Hort). London: Heinemann.

Vygotsky, L. (1965). *Thought and language.* Cambridge, MA: MIT Press.

Wallace, A. (1901). *Darwinism.* London: Macmillan.

Warrington, E., & McCarthy, R. (1983). Category-specific access dysphasia. *Brain, 106*, 859-878.

Warrington, E., & Shallice, T. (1984). Category-specific impairments. *Brain, 107*, 829-854.

Waxman, S. (1985). *Hierarchies in classification and language: Evidence from preschool children.* Unpublished Ph.D. dissertation, University of Pennsylvania, Philadelphia, PA.

Wertsch, J. (1985). *Vygotsky and the social formation of mind.* Cambridge, MA: Harvard University Press.

Whorf, B. (1956). *Language, thought, and reality.* Cambridge, MA: MIT Press.

Wierzbicka, A. (1984). Apples are not a "kind of fruit": The semantics of human categorization. *American Ethnologist, 11*, 313-328.

Williams, M. (1985). Species are individuals: Theoretical foundations for the claim. *Philosophy of Science, 52*, 578-90.

3

Interactional Contexts of Cognitive Development: Piagetian Approaches to Sociogenesis*

David J. Bearison

The Graduate School and University Center of the City University of New York and The Hebrew University of Jerusalem

> There are many unnecessary problems arising from the fact that some have committed themselves from the outset to a dichotomy ''individual or society'' while forgetting that there is a relational perspective according to which there exist only interactions. . . (Piaget, 1966, p. 249)

Developmental theories often are characterized by opposing stances on fundamental issues regarding basic cognitive processes, such as continuous or discontinuous kinds of changes, environmental or maturational sources of change, atomistic or holistic units of change analysis, and the relative primacies of learning and development, thought and emotion, or self and other. These stances serve as convenient analytic tools for comparing and distinguishing one theory from another and, although the practice of stance taking may be appropriate for such purposes (e.g., Reese & Overton, 1970; Kuhn, 1978), it inevitably entails the risk of fragmenting a theory in the certain way in which it treats its objects of inquiry and constitutive realities and thereby distorting it. In the case of Piaget's theory, mutually contradictory stances have been invoked relative to the theoretical perspectives and biases of different interpreters. For example, behaviorist social learning theorists have characterized the theory as mentalistic with a heavy emphasis on maturational factors accounting for developmental transitions, while neonativists have described the theory as being environmentally based (Bringuier, 1980). Admittedly, there are certain ambiguities within Piaget's theory that invite multiple, and sometimes even conflicting interpretations, however, in most cases the theory transcends these selective analytic stances and, thereby, more fully captures the

---

* This chapter was prepared while the author was a Lady Davis Fellow and Visiting Professor of Developmental Psychology in the Department of Psychology of the Hebrew University of Jerusalem and was supported by the Lady Davis Foundation, Jerusalem, Israel. I am grateful for discussions I had regarding some of the ideas herein with members of the Study Group on Human Development at the Tel Aviv University. Author's current address: Ph.D. Program in Developmental Psychology, The Graduate School and University Center of the City University of New York, 33 West 42nd Street, New York, NY, 10036.

integrity and manifold complexity of its objects of inquiry; in Piaget's terms, there is coordination of opposing centrations.

Today, increasing concern with the social and historical contexts of higher mental processes, prompted in part by the growing interest in Vygotsky's work and Soviet activity theory, and by the increasing appreciation of sociohistorical constraints on all forms of scientific inquiries, has yielded another set of analytic stance polarities: individual versus social determinants of cognition. Soviet psychology, in line with Marx and Lenin, maintains that social forms of human activity (i.e., labor organization and modes of production), determine the course of human development. Individuals develop in environments created by social and historical forces mediated by semiotic systems that serve to organize and categorize known realities. Thinking, in this sense, is a distinctly sociohistorical process (Luria, 1976; Scribner, 1985).

Within this socially and historically contexted account, Piaget's theory has been interpreted as emphasizing individual development to the regretful exclusion of sociocultural constraints. The focus of this chapter, however, is to betray this recent and particular form of analytic stance taking, individual versus social, by considering the social foundations of cognitive development inherent in Piaget's program and, thereby, to establish its affinities with Soviet activity theory. Although substantive differences exist between them, they do not arise simply from opposing stances regarding that which is primary in development, the individual or society, or whether knowledge is individually constructed or socially mediated. Both theories acknowledge the social contexts of development but yield different approaches to understanding how they influence individual development. Such differences reflect Piaget's and Vygotsky's respective recognition of the facilitating features of social interaction (sociocognitive conflicts versus intersubjective regulations), the process of internalization from the social to the individual plane of cognition (structural isomorphism versus semiotic mediation), and epistemological assumptions regarding the nature of knowledge (idealistic versus materialistic epistemologies, e.g., Descartes and Kant versus Hegel and Marx) that, in turn, yield different methodologies (form-function relationships versus material continuities).

Despite such differences, a rapprochement between a social psychology of cognitive development and a cognitive psychology of social development (i.e., a social theory of knowledge) can be approached by theoretically redefining the discipline of social cognition so that its proper object of inquiry is the change in individual behavior brought about by interaction with others in socially, historically, and culturally embedded contexts. Although cognitive developmental psychology has mapped useful dimensions of change and recent studies have begun to test and explain the effects of social interaction on these change variables (e.g., Bearison, Magzamen, & Filardo, 1986; see also Chapters 4 and 8, respectively), we have yet to acknowledge in an empirically meaningful and systematic way the effects of social contexts as they are revealed in the cognitive activities of interpersonal engagement. In other words, somewhere in the enterprise, the process of social engagement must be acknowledged and the socially and historically constituted nature of cognitive development must be reflected in the units of developmental analysis (Bearison, 1986). By so doing, the study of social cognition will be more fully in accord with the principles of social psychology (Doise, 1978).

The Social Context of Knowing

The social foundations of cognition can be articulated at various levels of analysis which, in effect, are embedded versions of the same issues. At the most general level, there is no such thing as a natural object of inquiry or scientific discourse because all knowledge presupposes a social-historical context (Vygotsky, 1978; Hamlyn, 1982). All scientific inquiries ''are shot through with conscious or unconscious construals that reflect social, historical, and even political interests or outright ideological prejudices'' (Wartofsky, 1983, p. 192). Thus, even if it was somehow possible to arrive at a universal conception of development based on cultural and historical invariants, it would be bereft of any psychological meaning; the developing individual would be reduced to a biological speciation in phylogenesis. From this perspective, developmental cognitive psychology begins where the evolution of biological instincts and hereditary programing leave off and where cultural artifacts, social conventions, interpersonal transactions, and semiotic systems function as culturally evolved vehicles for the transmission from one generation to the next of modes of thinking and feeling (Piaget, 1971a; Wartofsky, 1983). These vehicles are products of cognitive praxis (cultural activities) that represent, express, and transform our constructed realities. Thus, the objects of scientific discourse, psychological or otherwise, are not natural, external, or given in the environment but are inherently endowed with human intentionality and cultural forms.

Such a sociogenetic view of knowledge has its roots in the work of Durkheim and the French school of sociology which maintained that ''the first logical categories were social categories'' and that objects were categorized according to ''their place in society which determined their place in nature'' (Durkheim & Mauss, 1963, p. 83). This theme has been further elaborated by psychologists including Mead, Baldwin, Piaget, Vygotsky, and Luria. Sociogenesis, as employed by these theorists, doesn't imply a direct, substantial, and reductionist relationship of mind from society but instead a mediated, functional, and developmental relationship.

For Piaget, the social foundations of knowing have been a consistent, if not always explicit, theme in all of his theoretical discussions. For example, in considering the relationship between ''biology and knowledge'' Piaget (1971a) distinguished the metabolic mode of organic adaptation from the cognitive mode in terms of the latter's potential for sociocultural forces to influence the course of cognitive adaptation. Accordingly, cognitive evolution is possible only because instinctual regulations are subplanted by phenotypic operatory regulations and these kinds of regulations are developmentally dependent upon ''interindividual or social interactions.''

Social and Individual Cognition

In order to appreciate Piaget's uses of sociogenesis, we need to consider more inclusive and fundamental categories in the theory than the stance specifications of individual versus social cognition. This brings us to the basic unit of Piaget's developmental analysis, the interaction between subject and object. In the general framework of Piagetian theory, cognitive development constitutes a dialectical interaction between the knower and the known such that they are inextricably interpenetrated in a fashion that makes it impossible to disentangle the object of cognitive inquiry from the inquirer. Elaborating upon and revising the agenetic and fixed categories of Kantian epistemology, Piaget considered knowledge as "neither arising from objects nor from the subjects, but from the interaction between subject and object (self and other)" (Piaget, 1970, p. 704).

The interaction between subject and object, knower and known, is a transformational, self-regulating activity that constitutes the fundamental unit in Piaget's program; it accounts for the motive force of development, the genesis of cognitive structures, and knowledge itself. "The proper mode of intelligence is not, in effect, contemplation, but transformation, and its mechanism is essentially operatory" (Piaget, 1970, p. 84). The qualitative form and logical coordination of such activity, how it evolves from sensorimotor acts to operatory schemes (i.e., reversible mental activities), and how it transforms objects of knowing increasingly have become the locus of interest among many "neo-Piagetians" who have become more concerned with problems of cognitive processes (i.e., equilibrations) and contextual constraints (e.g., Kuhn, 1983; Cole, 1983; Feldman, 1980) than normative assumptions regarding sequentially invariant and universal stages of development. This shift from a "fixed capacity" model of development to a more process oriented (Glick, 1983) or functionalist approach constitutes a fundamental transition in hypothesis testing from issues emphasizing *what* is developing to *how* it is developing (Flavell & Wohlwill, 1969; Nielson & Dockrell, 1982) and is consistent with the last phase of Piaget's own efforts at theory building (e.g., Piaget, 1975/1985). It has led to new kinds of theoretical questions and methodologies that are more context oriented and sensitive to conditions that selectively inhibit or facilitate the deployment in practice of cognitive and metacognitive capacities. This also has led to new kinds of questions regarding the utility of cross-cultural studies of cognitive growth. There is less concern with establishing cultural universals and greater concern with the manifold integrity of cultural differences and ethnocentric biases in conceptual organization.

Growing concern with the nature of sociocultural constraints has fostered a distinction between two general classes of cognitive objects and the kinds of cognitive activities associated with them. On the one hand, there are physical, inanimate, impersonal objects associated with the cognition of space, time, number, mass, and physical causality and, on the other hand, there are social objects associated with the cognition of self, others, and interpersonal relationships. Early interest in Piaget's theory focused primarily on children's construction of physical relationships while recent interest has extended to children's construction of social relationships. This is a curious reversal of the temporal sequence of Piaget's own interests. Some of his earliest studies of children's interpersonal communicative competence (1928) and moral reasoning (1932) raised issues of childhood egocentrism as a primarily social form of cognitive centration and it was only later that he began to systematically formulate his main line of interest in the more strictly mathematical and physical domains of intelligence.

Piaget's early interests in the social domain frequently have been cited as establishing the foundations of social cognition as a subdiscipline within Piagetian psychology. However, in retrospect, it appears that attempts to define and map the conceptual boundaries and methodologies of social cognition were misguided in that they implied that social knowledge is somehow predicated on different kinds of cognitive activities than physical knowledge because people are inherently different (e.g., more complex, less predictable, etc.) than objects. According to Hoffman (1981), for example, people have psychological perspectives consisting of feelings, thoughts, needs, and intentions that are lacking in objects so that interpersonal interactions reflect the reciprocity of mutual intentions that are realized through the logical coordination of perspectives (i.e., role taking). These kinds of interactions yield knowledge of the distinctly social properties of the environment while the reflective abstractions of individuals in social isolation acting on objects yield knowledge of physical relations. In other words, physical and social knowledge can be distinguished in terms of the kinds of constraints that they impose on the accommodative pole of cognitive adaptation. Physical knowledge is dependent on universal constraints provided in the laws of physics that, for practical purposes, transcend particular time, space, social, and cultural conditions. Being universal, physical knowledge is amenable to construction through individual reflection. Social knowledge, on the other hand, is dependent upon more arbitrary kinds of constraints that reflect particular sociocultural groups at particular times in particular places. Consequently, it is amenable to construction through social interactive contexts (Glick, 1985).

However, despite this dubious distinction between physical and social knowledge and the kinds of cognitive activities commensurate with each, early studies within this emerging subdiscipline in the 1960s were designed with the implicit assumption that translating cognitive tasks into social contexts would necessarily obscure the underlying "pure" cognitive activities (Glick, 1981). Accordingly, investigators adapted experimental paradigms from the already established domain of physical cognition. Subjects were individually interviewed by experimenters who asked them to resolve various kinds of social dilemmas involving people and the kinds of social relationships that people construct and maintain for themselves. However, the presentation of others, as social agents in these dilemmas, was in the form of hypothetical individuals interacting in hypothetical social contexts that lacked compelling immediacy and subjective meaning for the knower. Subjects' social cognitive operations were assessed independently of their conditions of deployment. Rather than recognizing the social relational quality of cognitive operations in Piaget's theory as being particularly relevant to the development of social concepts, theoretical explanations of social cognitive development were made to fit existing ideologies that favored the study of cognitive processes as individualized, asocial, and transcendental phenomena (Youniss, 1981).

Such a categorical distinction between objects of knowing (i.e., physical vs. social) as well as knowing activities (i.e., individual vs. interactive) belies Piaget's premise that all forms of knowing, social and physical, are structured by a common core of cognitive operations. Because there are not two structural systems, one for individual cognition and one for social cognition, there cannot exist different cognitive processes or even different cognitive contexts by which such categories of knowing are constructed. All cognition is inherently social as well as individual since the coordination of activities (i.e., schemes) that constrain the construction of physical knowledge obey the same laws as social cognitive activities and, in the course of development, yield structurally isomorphic forms of knowing. Thus, "the reaction of intelligence . . . to the social environment is exactly parallel to the reaction to the physical environment . . . " (Piaget, 1963b, p. 160).

By proposing a common cognitive-structural system, Piaget denies a dichotomy between individual and social modes of knowing. One cannot be conceptually prior to the other because each presupposes the logical operations of the other. Hence, for Piaget, arguments for the primacy of one against the other "is a problem just like that of deciding which comes first, the chicken or the egg" (Piaget, 1971, p. 368) because " . . . individual operations of the intelligence and operations making for exchanges in cognitive cooperation are one and the same thing, the 'general coordination of actions' . . . being an interindividual as well as intraindividual coordination . . . " (Piaget, 1971, p. 360). Because operational equilibration is simultaneously individual and social, the social logic of interindividual coordinations and the individual logic of intraindividual coordinations constitute inseparable and structurally isomorphic aspects of a singular reality reflecting the interpenetration of mind and society (Piaget, 1968). In other words, there is a structure to social contexts that is isomorphic with the structure of knowledge derived within those contexts, and, therefore, the coordination of actions of individuals obeys the same operatory laws as interindividual coordinations. This isomorphism should not be surprising since social structures are products of knowing systems that are themselves cognitively structured (Bearison, 1982).

Critics of the currently pervasive cognitivist orientation in the social sciences in general, and in Piaget's theory in particular (e.g., Sampson, 1981; Riegel, 1979), have argued that such an orientation is a form of "individualistic reductionism" and "subjective mentalism" in that the construction of reality rests solely on the logic of individually derived operations. However, Piaget does not consider logic as a form of natural thought, to be a strictly individual construction open to any and all conclusions that follow logically consistent derivations and verifications (i.e., a "system of free operations"), nor does he consider the properties of natural thought to be solely equivalent to the properties of formal logical systems. The logical operations proper to natural thought, unlike formal logic, bear essentially upon the content of actions and verifications that are socially and historically derived whereas formal logical systems are contentless and, thus, lack the power to generate any conclusions reflecting human values and social relevancies. According to Piaget (1950), logic, as "a psychological process . . . expresses itself as a complex of states of awareness, intellectual feelings and responses, all of which are characterized by certain obligations whose social character is difficult to deny, be it primary or derived. Considered from this angle, logic requires common rules or norms; it is a morality of thinking imposed and sanctioned by others" (p. 163).

While the principle of structural isomorphism explains the social context of operatory intelligence, what about preoperatory intelligence? How is it constrained by sociocultural contexts? The preoperational infant and child, lacking the benefit of operational structures, is not yet able to actively participate in cooperative social functions (i.e., mutual reciprocity of intentions) so that from the infant's cognitive perspective, "the social environment is not essentially distinct from the physical environment" (Piaget, 1963b, p. 158). However, the infant is still subject to a variety of social influences which profoundly affect the objects of sensorimotor activities and which dynamically constrain the quality of such activities. For example, from the first few weeks of life, infants participate with others in a highly limited yet intersubjective dialogue of gestures and body movements (Trevarthen, 1977) that are precursors to developmentally more advanced forms of intelligence. The advent of language further allows the infant to enter socially and historically constructed realities and regulations.

The interpenetration of social forces on individual cognition also exists in the kinds of sociocultural constraints that parents and others impose upon a child in terms of the kinds of opportunities to have intellectually challenging experiences that lead to cognitive growth of a kind that is culturally valued. Parents contribute to the social distribution of knowledge by selectively choosing, shaping, and valuing certain kinds of cognitive activities over others. Even the seemingly natural physical objects with which a child might individually act upon are defined, categorized, valued, and made available in particular ways by adults who serve as cultural transmitters (Glick, 1985; Newman, Riel, & Martin, 1983; Nelson, 1981).

The subtle yet profound ways in which social and historical forces are prefigured in the child's cognitive environment are described by Wartofsky (1983) in his argument for greater recognition of "social, linguistic and historically variable praxis" in Piaget's concept of activity: "The world of objects is largely a world of social artifacts that bear the impact of our intentionality, our needs and purposes, our social and technical skills and structures. What the child learns to see, to touch, to move around, to throw is a range of artifacts that already has a human significance for even the very young child. What is more, these objects of child actions are manipulated in the company of others and by the example of others, in contexts of approval and disapproval, and in the framework of questions, descriptions, and instructions which all bring the sociality of language into the situation. The coordination of actions and the development of operative structures all take place, as Piaget agrees, in an environment where adult thought and norms play a large part in defining what is to be learned'' (p. 13). In addition, the products of knowing so constructed by the child as a function of his or her socially organized modes of acting on socially defined and culturally available objects is selectively valued by the culture and imbued with varying degrees of sociocultural relevance and meaning.

Because Piaget's own research program did not emphasize the interrelatedness of social and individual factors in development but instead focused on the child's construction of physical knowledge of impersonal environments, and because findings from these studies were used to define the conceptual boundaries of the stages of cognitive development, studies of social cognition often were treated as an attempt to restore a perceived imbalance in the theory by introducing constructs borrowed from more socially mediated accounts of cognitive development (Chandler, 1977). Such approaches, however, reflected a confusion between the core elements of the theory (i.e., the process of change and development through praxis; cf. Beilin, 1985) and particular instances of hypothesis testing and research techniques.

Piaget's contributions can be dichotomized into substantive and methodological ones and, tenuous as such a distinction might be, it reminds us that substantively ''the theory . . . was never intended as a restricted account of the private contemplations of individuals working in social isolation'' (Chandler, 1977, p. 96). Indeed, Piaget's earliest psychological works reflected his theoretical commitment to the social foundations of cognitive processes in terms of the development of social cooperation in peer groups, interpersonal communication, the social exchange of satisfactions, affective valuations, normative thinking in moral and justice reasoning, as well as the epistemological reflection of science on its own historical foundations. Furthermore, Piaget's references to social factors in intellectual development revealed a socially contexted approach (e.g., ''social interaction is a *necessary* condition for the development of logic'' [emphasis added, 1976, p. 80, cited in Doise & Mugny, 1984]). Piaget often described cognition in ways that are strikingly similar to such social dialogical positions as those advanced by Mead (1934) and Vygotsky (1962): ''Logical reasoning is an argument which we have with ourselves, and which reproduces internally the features of a real argument'' (Piaget, 1928, p. 204). Such passages reveal, as we will elaborate further, that intelligence for Piaget is not only an individual process, but also a relational one between individuals organizing their activities in socially relevant contexts through the logic of interindividual coordinations.

Aspects of Internalization

Given the sociohistorical contexts of knowledge and the knowing process, the essential and persistent problem in all theories of development is to account for how knowledge is thereby constructed in individuals because it cannot be constructed independently of them. It is in the matter of the internalization of thought (i.e., what, if anything, is internalized from the social to the individual plane and how is it accomplished) that critical differences exist among such different developmental programs as Piaget's, Vygotsky's, and Freud's. Thus, Vygtosky accounted for internalization through the mechanism of ''semiotic mediation'' and Freud, through such mechanisms as introjection, identification, and incorporation. These mechanisms yield inner regulations that replace regulations that have taken place in interaction with others (see Wertsch and Stone, 1985, and Schafer, 1968, respectively, for discussions of Vygotsky's and Freuds' concepts of internalization).

Piaget's view regarding internalization often has been misunderstood because of confusion about his notions regarding relationships among representation, symbol formation, language, and thinking (Furth, 1969). Piaget posits no intervening system of mediation between the social and individual planes of knowing because the organization of activity in both planes is structurally isomorphic. Thus, interindividual coordinations obey the same laws of operatory logic and verification as intraindividual coordinations. In this sense, Piaget is unique in dispensing with the mediational function of language and other symbol systems that other theorists (particularly Vygotsky) have assigned to the process of internalizing socially derived regulations. Although language, as such, is not a constitutive component or causal source of operativity in that the structure of knowledge is not derived from linguistic structures, language serves a significant role in interindividual coordinations because it is a conventionally socialized vehicle for the expression and transmission of ideas (cognitive perspectives). Music and art, for example, also can serve such purposes, but they are less conventional and socially accessible than language. Language, therefore, serves an educative function in the process of interindividual equilibration (Piaget, 1963a) while intraindividual cognition is served by more idiosyncratic forms of representation (Werner & Kaplan, 1963). Thus, the function of language and the "semiotic function" from which all representational systems derive is to formulate the products of knowing and its verifications, either for others or for the self, but the operative activity of knowing, either individually or interactively, is not constituted through language (Piaget, 1951). From this perspective, the role of semiotic mediation that Vygotsky (1962) assigns to language (and speech) in the internalization from other- to self-regulations in social transactions is an artifact or distillate of the knowing activity.

Social Conflicts and Peer Interaction

What then is the activity of knowing for Piaget and how is it necessarily served by social interaction? The activity of knowing in its most fundamental sense is regulated by a dynamic process of equilibration, disequilibration, and reequilibration between organismic and environmental effects. Each successive disequilibration of an equilibrated cognitive state leads to compensatory reactions which yield higher levels of cognitive development either through the construction of new cognitive schemes or the extension and coordination of existing schemes within a hierarchically organized cognitive system (i.e., reciprocal assimilation; Piaget, 1985). A necessary, but not sufficient, condition for disequilibration is a perturbation to the knowing system. Such perturbations are subjectively experienced (consciously or unconsciously) as cognitive conflicts that "force the subject to go beyond his (or her) current state and strike out in new directions . . . " (Piaget, 1985, pp. 10–11).

Conflicts arise from asymmetries between assimilations and accommodations, between affirmations and negations in the evolving adaptation between subject and environment. Conflicts are necessary but not sufficient for requilibration because not all conflicts have the potential to upset an equilibrated system. The reason for this has to do with the developmental level of the organism and its "adaptive reach" (Piaget, 1980; see Walker, 1980, for a methodological illustration regarding procedures to empirically confirm a "necessary but not sufficient" relationship in cognitive development).

The role of social cognitive conflict in motivating cognitive development is illustrated in numerous Piagetian "training-type" studies. In such studies experimenters intervene in children's spontaneous levels of reasoning about given problems with explicit expectations (hypotheses) that their interventions will promote more advanced levels of reasoning. Although not commonly acknowledged as such, these interventions constitute a form of socially induced conflicts in the interaction between subjects and experimenters (Donaldson, 1978; Light, Buckingham, & Robbins, 1979). For example, in a study designed to explain the cognitive mechanisms affecting the transition from preoperational to concrete-operational levels of reasoning within the domain of conserving quantities, Bearison (1969) had subjects repeatedly count equal units of small beakers of liquids as they poured them into different-shaped larger beakers. This kind of numerical iteration induced a conflict between subjects' existing perceptually-based schemes for judging relative amounts of liquids and their deployment of existing counting schemes for the same purpose but yielding contradictory conclusions. By having subjects successively reason back and forth between these two mutually contradictory schemes (i.e., perceptual activity = different amounts; iterative correspondence = same amounts) most of them resolved the contradiction on a higher cognitive plane. Thus a conflict which was interindividually constituted was overcome intraindividually through a reequilibration of operatory schemes as evidenced by the extent of subjects' task transfer and temporal stability of conservation responses and logical justifications on traditionally constituted conservation problems. The intervention established a kind of interaction between successive schemes which the subjects, although capable of deploying individually in different problem contexts, were not prone to bring into successive interaction within the same context. Once so induced, however, they were able to decenter from the perceptual immediacy of the context and internally coordinate these schemes deriving from incompatible viewpoints (subjects' and experimenter's) into a more equilibrated structure.

There are two kinds of structurally isomorphic interactions at work here: an internal interaction occurring individually which, in turn, is derived from a social interaction between subject and experimenter. Bearison's particular type of intervention is but one of numerous kinds that have been empirically verified as an effective means of promoting conservation attainment. A case can be made that all such successful interventions have in common the creation of socially induced conflicts of some sort between subjects' existing schemes for making sense of the task and the schemes for making sense of the experimenter's intervening manipulation of the task. That so many different kinds of intervention procedures should lead to conservation attainment (see Beilin, 1978, for a review) is evidence that what promotes development is not the specific learning effects of any particular kind of cognitive activity, but the underlying conflict and felt need to resolve it that is commonly induced in all successful intervention techniques. The fecundity of any given intervention is a function of the perturbation or conflict it engenders relative to the extent of the underlying schemes for conservation. Such conflicts, therefore, do not function in an absolute sense independent of a subject's existing schemes but only at certain developmental levels (Inhelder, Sinclair, & Bovet, 1974). Hence, they are not sufficient conditions for development.

The operatory regulations by which conflicts moderate reasoning are the same whether the conflicts arise intraindividually in the course of solitary reflections on objects of knowing or whether they arise interindividually in the course of social interactions. The interchange of thought with others in an interactive context obeys the same principles of equilibration (i.e., the logical coordination of operations) as does intraindividual thought. Hence, social cognition is an interactive process in which there is a coordination of operations or activities emanating from different individuals, while individual cognition is a coordination of operations or activities arising within the individual. Although the source of generative cognitive conflicts might differ structurally, social cognition is simply an externalization of individual cognition and, conversely, individual cognition is simply an internalization of social cognition. Consequently, cognitive interactions have the potential to reveal to experimental observation conflicts and resistances that are not apparent in individual cognitive activities (Bearison, 1982; Damon, 1983).

The structural morphisms between individual and social thought raise the inevitable developmental question regarding priorities in ontogenesis: Is one the cause of the other? Does the development of operational thought in the individual presuppose the formation of cooperative social functions, or on the other hand, is the formation of social cooperation a causal determinant of the individual's capacity to attain reversible operational structures? We will maintain, consistent with Piaget's reasoning, that there are certain conditions inherent in interpersonal cognitive activities prior to the attainment of fully operational structures in ontogenesis that are absent in intrapersonal cognitive activities that give credence to Vygotsky's (1962) claim that "what the child can do in cooperation today, he can do alone tomorrow" (p. 104). However, once fully operational structures are attained in ontogenesis, this issue regarding developmental priorities between social and individual cognition becomes moot as they are completely reversible; social forms of cognition can be internalized (i.e., cognitively reconstructed) for purposes of reflective interpretation and individual forms of cognition, externalized for social communication and consensual verification.

Peer Interactions and Adult–Child Interactions

In considering the effects of social interaction on developing cognition, Piaget proposes a critical distinction between adult-child types of interactions and interactions among peers or equals. As discussed earlier, adults provide the child with socially and historically constituted environments upon which to act, and they constrain the quality of such actions consistent with cultural norms. However, adults' interactions with children are usually characterized by asymmetrical constraints and authority relations founded on principles of unilateral respect of the child for his or her parents. In contrast, peer relations are founded on the principle of bilateral respect and thus allow the possibility of negotiating mutually reciprocal intentions based upon differing points of views. According to Piaget, cooperation among equals "leads to the recognition of the principles of formal logic in so far as these normative laws are necessary to a common search for truth. It leads, above all to a conscious realization of the logic of relations, since reciprocity on the intellectual plane necessarily involves the elaboration of those laws of perspective which we find in the operations distinctive of systems of relations" (1932, p. 403). Thus, we see that the reciprocal coordination of relations that the child experiences on the social plane through the mutual regulations and coordinations inherent in egalitarian interactions among peers presupposes such coordinations on the reflective plane. The fundamental difference, then, between constraint and cooperation is that only the latter is a source of contradiction, criticism, and conflicting perspectives born of discussions regulated by the logic of reciprocal interaction that parallels the logic of reflective cognition. "Cooperation (among equals) alone will therefore accomplish what intellectual constraint failed to bring about" (Piaget, 1932, p. 402).

Piaget's ideas regarding the critical significance of peer interactions and egalitarian discourse for the ontogenetic construction of operational logic is analogous to the "standards of rationality" in sociopolitical and scientific discourse. Accordingly, "all decisions are supposed to be made equally dependent on a consensus arrived at in discussion free from domination. . . . Here the principle of public discourse is supposed to eliminate all forms other than that of the better argument . . . only reason should have force" (Habermas, 1970, p. 7).

The relationship between social interaction and individual structures in cognitive development rests on the ideas of contradiction and verification of thought. Because preoperational or intuitive thought is phenomenalistic and centered from moment to moment on perceptual appearances and immediate desires, the preoperational child sees no incompatibility between thoughts that are contradictory from one context to another. Hence, the child fails to see the need to verify the reasoning that underlies such contradictions. While consistently maintaining the primacy of his or her own point of view (or blindly conceding to the practical consequences of the points of view of authority figures), the child successively maintains at different times, relative to changing intuitive desires and practical goals, contradictory points of view (Piaget, 1980). Unless the child is able to bring incompatible schemes into simultaneous interaction within given cognitive contexts, he or she remains ignorant of his or her own subjectivity (i.e., egocentrism) and intuitive centrations. The reequilibrative force of cognitive conflicts, therefore, arise from the child's felt obligation not to contradict himself or herself. It is in the interchange of thought with others who are one's equals that contradictions between self and others are initially recognized in ontogenesis along with the social obligation to resolve them (either completely or partially; Smedslund, 1966). In other words, the child initially seeks to avoid contradicting himself or herself when he or she is in the presence of others who contradict his or her own way of thinking so that "only under the pressure of argument and opposition will he (or she) seek to justify himself (or herself) in the eyes of others and thus acquire the habit of watching himself (or herself) think, i.e., of constantly detecting the motives which are guiding him (or her) in the direction he (or she) is pursuing" (Piaget, 1959, p. 137).

Thus, the obligation to resolve contradictions comes from the establishment of common rules or norms of thought derived from the social consequences inherent in sharing thoughts with others, communicating one's own thoughts with success, and verifying one's own reasoning in relation to the reasoning of others. Therefore, "the obligation not to contradict oneself is not simply a conditional necessity (a 'hypothetical imperative') for anybody who accepts the exigencies of operational activity; it is also a more 'categorical' imperative, in as much as it is indispensable for intellectual interaction and cooperation" (Piaget, 1963b, p. 163).

Hence, the resolution of contradictions stemming from opposing centrations is ontogenetically first a social phenomenon because in social interactions contradictory centrations can arise simultaneously, and, as Doise and Mugny (1984) have noted, these "cannot be as easily denied as a conflict resulting from successive and alternating individual centrations" (p. 28). Also, children are more capable of recognizing cognitive discrepancies in the thinking of others (including self vs. others) before they are aware of them in their own thinking (Gelman & Meck, 1983). The key, then, to the social foundations of cognitive development is in the social origins of decentration as they arise from mutually conflicting interpersonal centrations which are more explicit, synchronous, and, hence, demanding of verification and reconciliation in accordance with the basic principles of cognitive consistency. In Piaget's words (1950), "it is precisely by a constant interchange of thought with others that we are able to decentralize ourselves . . . to coordinate internally relations deriving from different viewpoints" (p. 164).

References

Bearison, D. J. (1969). The role of measurement operations in the acquisition of conversation. *Developmental Psychology, 1,* 653–660.
Bearison, D. J. (1982). New directions in studies of social interaction and cognitive growth. In F. Serafica (Ed.), *Social cognitive development in context* (pp. 199–221). New York: Guilford Press.
Bearison, D. J. (1986). Transactional cognition in context: New models of social understanding. In D. Bearison & H. Zimiles (Eds.), *Thought and emotion: Developmental perspectives* (pp. 129–146). Hillsdale, NJ: Erlbaum.
Bearison, D. J., Magzamen, S., & Filardo, E. (1986). Socio-cognitive conflict and cognitive growth in young children. *Merrill-Palmer Quarterly, 32,* 51–72.
Beilin, H. (1978). Inducing conservation through training. In G. Steiner (Ed.), *Psychology of the 20th century, Vol. 7, Piaget and beyond.* Zurich: Kindler.
Beilin, H. (1985). Dispensable and core elements in Piaget's research program. *The Genetic Epistemologist, 13,* 1–16.
Bringuier, J. (1980). *Conversations with Jean Piaget.* Chicago: University of Chicago Press.

Chandler, M. (1977). Social cognition: A selective review of current research. In W. Overton & J. Gallagher (Eds.), *Knowledge and development* (pp. 93–147). New York: Plenum.

Cole, M. (1983). Society, mind and development. In F. S. Kessel & A. W. Siegel (Eds.), *The child and other cultural inventions*. New York: Praeger.

Damon, W. (1983). The nature of social-cognitive change in the developing child. In W. Overton (Ed.), *The relationship between social and cognitive development*. Hillsdale, NJ: Erlbaum.

Doise, W. (1978). *Groups and individuals*. Cambridge, England: Cambridge University Press.

Doise, W., & Mugny, G. (1984). *The social development of the intellect*. Oxford, England: Pergamon Press.

Donaldson, M. (1978). *Children's minds*. London: Fantana.

Durkheim, E., & Mauss, M. (1963). *Primitive classification*. Chicago: University of Chicago Press.

Feldman, D. (1980). *Beyond universals in cognitive development*. Norwood, NJ: Ablex.

Flavell, J., & Wohlwill, J. (1969). Formal and functional aspects of cognitive development. In D. Elkind & J. Flavell (Eds.), *Studies in cognitive development: Essays in honor of Jean Piaget* (pp. 67–120). London: Oxford University Press.

Furth, H. G. (1969). *Piaget and knowledge: Theoretical foundations*. Englewood Cliffs, NJ: Prentice-Hall.

Gelman, R., & Meck, A. (1983). Preschoolers counting: Principles before skill. *Cognition, 13,* 343–359.

Glick, J. (1981). Functional and structural aspects of rationality. In I. Sigel, D. Brodzinsky, & R. Golinkoff (Eds.), *New directions in Piagetian theory and practice*. Hillsdale, NJ: Erlbaum.

Glick, J. (1983). Piaget, Vygotsky and Werner. In S. Wapner & B. Kaplan (Eds.), *Towards an holistic developmental psychology* (pp. 35–52). Hillsdale, NJ: Erlbaum.

Glick, J. (1985). Culture and cognition revisited. In E. Niemark, R. DeLisi, & J. Newman (Eds.), *Moderators of competence*. Hillsdale, NJ: Erlbaum.

Habermas, J. (1970). *Toward a rational society*. Boston: Beacon Press.

Hamlyn, D. (1982). What exactly is social about the origins of understanding. In G. Butterworth & P. Light (Eds.), *Social cognition: Studies of the development of understanding*. Chicago: University of Chicago Press.

Hoffman, M. L. (1981). Perspectives on the difference between understanding people and understanding things. In J. Flavell & L. Ross (Eds.), *New directions in the study of social-cognitive development*. New York: Cambridge University Press.

Inhelder, I., Sinclair, H., & Bovet, M. (1974). *Learning and development of cognition*. London: Routledge & Kegan Paul.

Kuhn, D. (1978). Mechanisms of cognitive and social development: One psychology or two. *Human Development, 21,* 92–118.

Light, P. H., Buckingham, N., & Robbins, A. H. (1979). The conservation task as an interactional setting. *British Journal of Educational Psychology, 49,* 304–310.

Luria, A. R. (1976). *Cognitive development: Its cultural and social foundations*. Cambridge, MA: Harvard University Press.

Mead, G. H. (1934). *Mind, self, and society*. Chicago: University of Chicago Press.

Nelson, K. (1981). Social cognition in a script framework. In J. Flavell & L. Ross (Eds.), *The development of social cognition in childhood*. New York: Cambridge University Press.

Newman, D., Riel, M., & Martin, L. (1983). Cultural practices and Piagetian theory: The impact of a cross-cultural research program. In D. Kuhn & J. Meacham (Eds.), *On the development of developmental psychology* (pp. 135–154). Basel: S. Karger.

Nielson, I., & Dockrell, J. (1982). Cognitive tasks as interactional settings. In G. Butterworth & P. Light (Eds.), *Social cognition: Studies of the development of understanding* (pp. 213–237). Chicago: University of Chicago Press.

Piaget, J. (1928). *Judgment and reasoning in the child*. New York: Harcourt Brace.

Piaget, J. (1932). *The moral judgment of the child*. London: Routledge & Kegan Paul.

Piaget, J. (1950). *The psychology of intelligence*. London: Routledge & Kegan Paul.

Piaget, J. (1951). *Play, dreams and imitation in childhood*. New York: Norton.

Piaget, J. (1959). *Judgment and reasoning in the child.* Paterson, NJ: Littlefield Adams.

Piaget, J. (1963a). La language et les opérations intellectuelles. In *Problèmes de psycholinguistique: Symposium de l'association de psycholgie scientifique de langue francaise* (pp. 51–61). Paris: Presses Universitaries de France. (Reprinted in English in H. G. Furth (1969). *Piaget and knowledge: Theoretical foundations.* Englewood Cliffs, NJ: Prentice-Hall.)

Piaget, J. (1963b). *The psychology of intelligence.* Paterson, NJ: Littlefield, Adams.

Piaget, J. (1966). La psychologie, les relations interdisciplinaires et le système de sciences. *Bulletin de Psychologie, 254,* 242–254.

Piaget, J. (1968). *Six psychological studies.* New York: Random House.

Piaget, J. (1970). Piaget's theory. In P. H. Mussen (Ed.), *Carmichael's manual of child psychology* (Vol. 1, pp. 703–732). New York: Wiley.

Piaget, J. (1971). *Biology and knowledge.* Chicago: University of Chicago Press.

Piaget, J. (1976). *Postscript. Archives de psychologie.* Paris: Gonthier.

Piaget, J. (1980). *Adaptation and intelligence.* Chicago: University of Chicago Press.

Piaget, J. (1985). *The equilibration of cognitive structures.* Chicago: University of Chicago Press. (Originally published as L'equilibration des structures cognitives; Problem central du developpement, 1975.)

Reese, H., & Overton, W. (1970). Models of development and theories of development. In L. R. Goulet & P. Baltes (Eds.), *Life-span developmental psychology: Research and theory.* New York: Academic Press.

Riegel, K. (1979). *Foundations of dialectical psychology.* New York: Academic Press.

Sampson, E. (1981). Cognitive psychology as ideology. *American Psychologist, 36,* 730–743.

Schafer, R. (1968). *Aspects of internalization.* New York: International Universities Press.

Scribner, S. (1985). Vygotsky's uses of history. In J. Wertsch (Ed.), *Culture communication and cognition.* Cambridge, England: Cambridge University Press.

Smedslund, J. (1966). Les origenes sociales de la décentration. In F. Bresson & H. de Montmollin (Eds.), *Psychologie et épistèmologie génétiques: Thèmes Piagétiens.* Paris: Dunod.

Travarthen, C. (1977). Descriptive analyses of infant communicative behavior. In H. R. Schaffer (Ed.), *Studies in mother-infant interaction.* New York: Academic Press.

Vygotsky, L. S. (1962). *Thought and language.* Cambridge, MA: MIT Press.

Vygotsky, L. S. (1978). *Mind in society: The development of higher mental processes.* Cambridge, MA: Harvard University Press.

Walker, L. J. (1980). Cognitive and perspective-taking prerequisites for moral development. *Child Development, 51,* 131–139.

Wartofsky, M. (1983). From genetic epistemology to historical epistemology: Kant, Marx, and Piaget. In L. S. Liben (Ed.), *Piaget and the foundation of knowledge* (pp. 1–18). Hillsdale, NJ: Erlbaum.

Werner, H., & Kaplan, B. (1963). *Symbol formation.* New York: Wiley.

Wertsch, J. V., & Stone, C. A. (1985). The concept of internalization in Vygotsky's account of the genesis of higher mental functions. In J. V. Wertsch (Ed.), *Culture, communication and cognition.* Cambridge, MA: Cambridge University Press.

Youniss, J. (1981). A revised interpretation of Piaget (1932). In I. Sigel, D. Brodzinsky, & R. Golinkoff (Eds.), *New directions in Piagetian theory and practice.* Hillsdale, NJ: Erlbaum.

4

Sociocultural Setting and the Zone of Proximal Development: The Problem of Text-Based Realities*

James V. Wertsch

Department of Psychology
Clark University

The fundamental goal of a sociocultural[1] analysis of mind is to explicate the historical, institutional, and cultural specificity of human psychological processes. Instead of focusing on aspects of human mental functioning that are assumed to be constant across history, institutional settings, and cultures, such an analysis seeks to identify ways in which mind reflects and constitutes a specific sociocultural setting. For example, it might be concerned with ways in which people participating in different institutional settings in Soviet Central Asia in the 1930s differ in their cognitive skills (Luria, 1976), or it might be concerned with the cognitive correlates of different types of literacy in Liberia in the 1970s (Scribner & Cole, 1981). Or it might be concerned with ways in which subjects in either of these studies differ from twentieth century Europeans and Americans.

Studies concerned with a sociocultural perspective have typically involved subjects from traditional societies and have relied on cross-cultural comparisons. To qualify as a sociocultural analysis of mind, however, research need not meet either of these criteria. The only general criterion it must meet is that it examine some tie between sociocultural milieu and psychological functioning. In this connection, I would like to examine the psychological aspects of a fundamental category that social theorists building on the ideas of figures such as Weber and Marx have used to analyze modern technological societies. This is the category of rationality.

Rationality and the associated notion of rationalization (the process whereby rationality emerges in a society during modernization) are constructs that social

*Revised version of a paper presented at the Tel-Aviv Annual Workshop in Human Development: "Culture, Schooling and Psychological Development" (Tel Aviv University, June, 1987). The author is grateful for the comments of the participants of the workshop, especially those provided by Gavriel Salomon and Liliana Tolchinsky Landsmann. The research reported in this chapter was assisted by the Spencer Foundation. The data presented, the statements made, and the views expressed are solely the responsibility of the author.

[1] I use the term "sociocultural" rather than "sociohistorical" because in English the latter is commonly interpreted as having little to do with some of the cultural phenomena that I wish to address. I use "sociocultural" rather than "cultural-historical" (cf. Smirnov, 1975) because I am attempting to deal with sociological as well as cultural forces.

theorists have used primarily to analyze economic and bureaucratic aspects of society. In summarizing Weber's ideas on rationalization, Habermas (1970) writes:

> Rationalization means, first of all, the extension of the areas of society subject to the criteria of rational decision. Second, social labor is industrialized, with the result that criteria of instrumental action also penetrate into other areas of life (urbanization of the mode of life, technification of transport and communication). Both trends exemplify the type of purposive-rational action, which refers to either the organization of means or choice between alternatives. Planning can be regarded as purposive-rational action of the second order. It aims at the establishment, improvement, or expansion of systems of purposive-rational action themselves.
>
> The progressive "rationalization" of society is linked to the institutionalization of scientific and technical development. To the extent that technology and science permeate social institutions and thus transform them, old legitimations are destroyed. The secularization and "disenchantment" of action-orienting worldviews, of cultural tradition as a whole, is the obverse of the growing "rationality" of social action. (p. 81)

Like Weber, other social theorists utilizing his ideas and the ideas of Marx (e.g., Habermas, 1970, 1984; Lukacs, 1971) have focused primarily on sociological and political economic issues such as modern economic activity and bureaucratic authority. However, they have also touched on the psychological aspects of rationality, usually in the form of claims about consciousness. For example, in an examination of "reification and the consciousness of the proletariat," Lukacs (1971) outlined some of the ways that commodification is tied to the history of philosophical thought.

There have been major problems, however, in social theorists' attempts to create a serious, detailed psychology. These problems stem from several sources. On the side of social theorists there has been a tendency to assume that once the social or economic forces in a social formation such as capitalism were spelled out, the concrete psychological aspects would be obvious (i.e., in little need of detailed study). On the part of psychologists there has been a tendency to ignore the issues typically raised in social theory. This is reflected in the universalistic assumptions that underlie so many psychological models. These universalistic assumptions are often grounded in the very positivistic and instrumental rationalist claims that are the object of social theorists' critique. Because of this, contemporary psychological theories have often produced models of mind that have no way of "coming into contact" with constructs from sociology or anthropology.

In what follows, I shall use a Vygotskian sociocultural approach to the study of mind (cf. Vygotsky, 1934, 1978; Wertsch, 1985) in an attempt to find a way out of this incompatibility between the study of social processes and the study of psychological functioning. The basic tenet of my argument is that the key to coordinating the study of the sociocultural context of modernity and its psychological correlates is the discourse which is generated and mastered in social life. At this general level my approach is similar to Habermas's (1979, 1984) recent claims about the role of communicative action in the rationalization of society, and it has some parallels with the claims of authors such as Bellah, Madsen, Sullivan, Swidler, and Tipton (1985) who argue that various "languages" are involved in the creation of socioculturally specific aspects of consciousness. However, because my argument is grounded in Vygotsky's ideas, the approach outlined here has several aspects that are not necessarily a part of other analyses of discourse in social and psychological processes.

Vygotsky's approach is based on three general themes. The first of these is the reliance on a "genetic method." This method assumes that mental functioning can be understood only by understanding its origins and the transformations it undergoes. As I have outlined elsewhere (Wertsch, 1985), Vygotsky attempted to carry out such an analysis in each of several "genetic domains" (e.g., phylogenesis, social history). In what I shall have to say here, however, the focus will be on the genetic domain he examined in most detail—ontogenesis. The second theme in Vygotsky's work is his claim that uniquely human (i.e., "higher") mental functioning has its origins in social action. Vygotsky's clearest single statement of this point can be found in his formulation of the "general genetic law of cultural development."

> Any function in the child's cultural development appears twice, or on two planes. First it appears on the social plane, and then on the psychological plane. First it appears between people as an interpsychological category, and then within the child as an intrapsychological category. This is equally true with regard to voluntary attention, logical memory, the formation of concepts, and the development of volition. (1981, p. 163)

Many of the specific constructs in Vygotsky's writings (e.g., about inner speech or about the zone of proximal development) are concrete instantiations of the general genetic law of cultural development.

The third general theme that runs throughout Vygotsky's writings is the claim that human activity is mediated by technological tools and by signs ("psychological tools"). Since the focus here is on signs, I shall term this the "semiotic mediation" theme. The basic claim here is that human social and mental functioning is mediated, and hence shaped by signs systems such as natural language. As I have noted elsewhere (Wertsch, 1985), this is the most important and unique contribution Vygotsky made in his account of human mental processes. It is in connection with the theme of semiotic mediation that I shall examine the forms of discourse connected with rationality in the social institutional sphere and its psychological aspects.

Rationality and Text-Based Realities

One of the major features of rationality is that it produces outcomes that come to be viewed as necessary and natural. What are in fact socially constructed aspects of reality come to be seen as part of the way the world naturally is organized. To see the world in this way reflects mastery of a particular form of action (what Habermas, 1970, variously terms "purposive-rational," "instrumental," or "strategic" action). When approaching a situation from the perspective of instrumental action, certain basic assumptions are made about the claims that can be made and the ways in which they can be defended. I shall outline these assumptions and examine the ways in which they come into play in formal schooling by introducing the notion of a "text-based reality."

A text-based reality is a special sort of "problem-space" (Karmiloff-Smith, 1979) or object upon which one can operate. As the term implies, the fundamental property of text-based realities is that they are created and maintained through textual[2], or semiotic means. Instead of using language and other sign systems to refer to, describe, and operate on independently existing realities, text-based realities are grounded in the possibility of constituting and manipulating problem spaces through semiotic means alone. As authors such as Hickmann (1985) have demonstrated, this form of linguistic activity is ubiquitous and is not tied to any special forms of activity such as conscious metalinguistic reflection. However, this use of language plays a particularly important role in the context of formal schooling.

The power of rationality as a social institutional force means that the employment of text-based realities occupies a privileged position in the speaking and thinking of modern societies. This is a claim similar to one made by Olson and Bruner (1974) when they wrote that "a scientific and technological culture like our own has put a premium on translation into a few symbolic systems—written language as in literature and explanations, in logical and mathematical statements, and in spatial systems such as maps, models, graphs, and geometry" (p. 145).

The major purpose of this chapter is to outline the concrete properties of text-based realities and to examine how children are socialized into mastering discourse structured in accordance with them. The properties I shall enumerate are: *depersonalization, boundedness, conscious reflection,* and *systematicity*. The first two characterize all text-based realities, whereas the second two do not. However, conscious reflection and systematicity play such important roles in much of the discourse found in formal schooling that they will be given special consideration here.

Depersonalization

The notion of depersonalization is tied to what is often termed "objectivity." The idea here is that something is objective if it is not tied to the subjective, personal perspective of particular individuals. Habermas (1984) deals with what I am terming depersonalization in several places in his recent writings on communicative action. For example, in dealing with "communicative rationality," he writes:

---

[2] I am using the notion of "text" in a broader sense than is often found in the psychological literature. Unlike Olson (1977), for example, my understanding of this notion does not limit the term to written texts.

This concept of communicative rationality carries with it connotations based ultimately on the central experience of the unconstrained, unifying, consensus-bringing force of argumentative speech, in which different participants overcome their merely subjective views and, owing to the mutuality of rationally motivated conviction, assure themselves of both the unity of the objective world and the intersubjectivity of their lifeworld. (p. 10)

When dealing with communicative rationality, Habermas has several complex issues in mind. For my purposes, the main point is that in order to participate in text-based realities, it is necessary to understand that discourse is to be grounded in a publicly accessible (i.e., "objective") reality rather than a personal, subjective one.

As Rommetveit (1979) has noted, the "pure intersubjectivity" that Habermas envisions in his account of objectivity and emancipated human communication is unattainable and therefore must be viewed as a theoretical fiction. Nonetheless, it can be a useful fiction when trying to understand the ways in which rationality shapes human activity on the interpsychological and intrapsychological planes identified by Vygotsky. For my purposes, the main point is that by agreeing to act in accordance with the dictates of communicative rationality, participants in discourse enter into a depersonalized system of speech and thinking. It is depersonalized in the sense that by entering into it, one deemphasizes the personal, subjective perspectives on reality to which one has access. In their place, one agrees to enter into an activity (either social or individual) on the basis of a publicly accessible and ratified reality.

Ideas closely related to what I am terming "depersonalization" have been used from time to time in analyses of discourse in socialization settings. For example, in his account of the "universal orders of meaning" associated with an "elaborated code" Bernstein (1975) was dealing with this issue. More recently, Michaels (1983, 1985) has examined a related phenomenon in her analyses of the classroom activity of "sharing time." In these analyses, she has outlined some of the ways in which teachers' and students' understanding of the sharing time speech situation differ and how teachers try to shape students' speech production as part of "oral preparation for literacy."

One of Michaels's central claims is that the teacher-student interaction in this context operates in quite different ways for different students. In particular, she has identified differences in teachers' interaction with middle-class white students and working-class black students. A major characteristic of one of the teachers' interactions with a working-class black student was that the teacher viewed the student's sharing time contributions as "long and rambling, moving from one thing to the next." As Michaels notes, the problem for the teacher here was that connections between the various topics introduced by the student were not made clear or explicit in a way that would make the text count as coherent for the teacher. Instead of being "topic-centered," these texts are constructed from "topic associating" turns. In the terms I am using, the text produced by the child does not meet the criterion of depersonalization for the teacher—it is not structured in such a way that its meaning is publicly accessible and objective by the standards of classroom discourse.

An additional fact reported by Michaels (1983) is extremely interesting in this connection. She notes that several adult black subjects, unlike adult white subjects, found texts constructed of topic-associating turns actually to be superior to texts produced by white middle-class children. They judged the texts to be "well-formed, easy to understand, and interesting, 'with lots of detail and description' " (p. 33). Furthermore, by examining a set of detailed linguistic and paralinguistic markers, Michaels was able to identify a quite complex and coherent structure to the texts produced by the black children. These facts indicate that depersonalization may be an ideal of a certain sort associated with text-based realities rather than a property of texts which makes them more advanced or superior in some absolute sense. This ideal is manifested in the phenomenon of "privileging," which I shall examine below.

Boundedness

The boundedness of text-based realities is tied to their depersonalization. It is concerned with the fact that once one agrees to operate within an objectively identifiable text-based reality, one implicitly agrees to stay within the boundaries of its "space." This space is defined by the text; it is not allowable to introduce information that is not included in or directly inferable from this text. Attempts to do so in the classroom are typically met with negative sanctions from the teacher. This is not to say that it is always easy to follow the dictates of boundedness. Examples of the difficulties encountered in this respect can be found in research on syllogistic reasoning (e.g., Luria, 1976; Scribner, 1977; Wason & Johnson-Laird, 1972). Syllogisms are one form of a text-based reality; the space they create is depersonalized and bounded. One of the primary findings of studies on syllogistic reasoning is that subjects carrying out the tasks often go beyond the information provided in the premises by incorporating information from other sources in deriving a conclusion. This is true even for subjects who have had extensive experience with formal reasoning tasks. Such findings reflect the difficulties involved in staying within the boundaries of a publicly accessible text when trying to derive a rational conclusion.

As an example of boundedness from classroom discourse, consider the following teacher-student interchange in a first grade classroom.[3] The focus of this interchange is an exercise in remembering the words used in a poem read by the teacher. This exercise is carried out by the teacher with six students sitting in a semicircle of chairs facing her.

T: I'm going to read you a little poem called "Surprises," and I want you to tell me one thing in that poem about surprises that you can tell me about surprises. You have to listen to know about it. "Surprises" by Jean Conger Sole. That's her name. Now we're going to read the poem.

---

[3] This example comes from a larger study that is being conducted by Norris Minick and myself.

Surprises are round or long and tallish,
Surprises are square or flat and smallish,
Surprises are wrapped in paper and bow,
And hidden in closets where secrets don't show.
Surprises are often good things to eat,
A get-well toy or a birthday treat,
Surprises come in such interesting sizes,
I like surprises.

Now I want you to tell me something about surprises you heard in that poem. The last person I ask is going to have the hardest job. Matt?
C: I like surprises.
T: I like surprises. OK.
T: What are surprises like?
C: Big and small. . . .
C: Colors.
T: Colors? OK, let's see if there's anything in there that talks about colors. (T looks at the written text.) It didn't say in the poem about colors. They *could* be colors though. . . .
C: Clothes.
T: Clothes? They can be clothes? (T looks at the written text.) Well, I don't think it said they could be clothes. They certainly *could* be clothes. You're right.

In this interaction the last two answers were judged to be incorrect by the teacher. In both cases she affirmed that their answer made sense by saying that surprises "*could*" be colors or clothes. However, she also made it clear that even though these answers could make sense based on students' personal experience, they fell outside the bounds of the text accessible to the entire group and hence outside the boundaries of the objective, text-based reality at issue.

Conscious Reflection

This property of text-based realities has been raised by many investigators concerned with the effects of schooling (e.g., Donaldson, 1978). The major point here is that the form and content of semiotic systems such as natural language may be taken as objects of reflection in text-based realities. This contrasts with the practice of using language in a nonconscious, nonreflective way. Vygotsky was so concerned with this phenomenon that he viewed conscious reflection, or intellectualization, as one of the general defining criteria for all forms of higher (i.e., uniquely human) mental functioning. He made this point particularly clear with regard to the development he saw occurring in formal schooling contexts.

At the center of development during the school age is the transition from lower functions of attention and memory to higher functions of voluntary attention and logical memory . . . the intellectualization of functions and their mastery represent two moments of one and the same process—the transition to higher psychological functions. We master a function to the degree that it is intellectualized. The voluntariness in the activity of a function is always the other side of its conscious realization. (1934, p. 189)

As Wertsch and Youniss (1987) have noted, Vygotsky's focus on conscious realization reflects his concern with formal schooling, a concern that grew out of his desire to contribute to the nation building underway in the USSR in the 1920s and 1930s. In some cases this concern came to dominate Vygotsky's thinking about what were supposedly more general claims about mental functioning. This seems to be one of these cases. From other aspects of his writings, it is clear that conscious reflection does not characterize all forms of higher mental functioning; it is characteristic of "advanced higher mental functioning" only (cf. Wertsch, 1985). Regardless of how conscious reflection fits into Vygotsky's account of higher mental functioning, however, it is a major aspect of many text-based realities that teachers and children create and operate on in formal schooling settings.

Under the heading of conscious reflection, at least two distinctions can be made. These distinctions concern the objects upon which conscious reflection is focused. The first distinction is between reflecting on sign tokens and reflecting on sign types. That is, one can speak and think about concrete, contextualized signs such as words and more extended utterances, or one can speak and think about signs in such a way that the reflections apply regardless of context. The context at issue here is the speech event context in which sign tokens (Lyons, 1977; Silverstein, 1976) appear. Sign types, in contrast, are abstract (i.e., decontextualized) entities that are defined as the class of all tokens. When one speaks generally of "the letter 'w' " or "the word 'computer'," one is speaking of a sign type; when one speaks of a particular instance (i.e., a unique speech event in a unique spatiotemporal and social context) of a letter or a word, one is speaking of sign tokens. Consider the case of example (1).

(1) I am working on this computer now.

When considered as a unique, concrete speech event, (1) is an utterance or sign token which, among other things, is used to pick out specific referents in time and space. The context-dependence of the referring expressions in this example is reflected by the fact that the referents of expressions such as "this computer" and "now" may change depending on when and where they appear.

When considered as a sign type, this sentence does not have reference; it has "denotation" and "sense" in the terminology employed by Lyons (1977). The relationship between (1) considered as a type and (1) considered as a token involves the notion of "instantiation" (Lyons, 1977): tokens of the type (1) can be instantiated in many different contexts.

The second distinction needed to enumerate the various kinds of objects upon which conscious reflection may focus differentiates between the form and the meaning of signs. When considered as forms there are many things that can be said about sign types. For example, one can say that the sign type (1) includes seven words or 27 letters. Such statements are true independently of when and where (1) might be instantiated as a token utterance. In addition to focusing on the form, one can focus on the meaning of a sign type. For example, one can focus on the senses (Lyons, 1977) of the lexemes involved. Thus in (1) one can define "computer" as "a device that calculates or computes." This definition is an equivalence relationship or a "metasemantic relationship" (Silverstein, 1985) that exists between the meanings of two sign types. Because sign types are involved, it holds independently of context (i.e., it is decontextualized).

In addition to such definitional equivalence relationships, other relationships between sign types' meanings exist and are commonly employed in the text-based realities found in classrooms. For example, one can focus on synonymy, antonymy, or hyponymy. Under the heading of hyponymy one finds instances in which the focus might be on the fact that "hammer," "saw," and "ax" are all instances of "tool," whereas an "apple" is not. Again this kind of hierarchical relationship exists among sign types and hence is independent of context. The text-based realities concerned with sense are grounded in decontextualized relationships into which sign types can enter, not the reference or other context specific properties of token instantiation of these types. Among other things, this means that referents of signs (in this case actual, physical hammers, saws, axes, and apples) are not at issue; they lie outside the boundaries defined by the sense relationships. Thus, when dealing with text-based realities that involve conscious reflection (remembering that all text based realities need not involve this property), one can reflect on sign types or sign tokens. Furthermore, within each of these two categories, one can reflect on the form or the meaning of the signs involved.

The various objects of reflection specified by these two distinctions frequently appear in the rational discourse of schooling. For example, in the teacher–student interaction from the first-grade classroom examined earlier, the teacher's questions had to do with whether certain words had been used in an earlier utterance (the poem). Hence, the exercise was one that encouraged children to reflect on sign tokens. In addition to the depersonalization and boundedness involved in this text-based reality, then, students were being encouraged to reflect on the precise forms of the sign tokens that appeared.

Other examples from the same classroom illustrate other possibilities for conscious reflection. Consider first an exercise the teacher carried out with a group of eight children on "opposites." In this exercise the teacher provided a word such as "laugh" or "fast," and a child was to provide the opposite. This is a clear example of an exercise concerned with sense relations. Specifically, it involves the relation of antonymy. Such exercises deal with the meaning of decontextualized sign types (namely, lexemes). In another exercise, children were asked to think of words that begin with "the 'th' sound." In this case sign types are still involved, but now the focus is again on the form of the signs rather than their meaning. The fact that all of these, as well as several similar examples, occurred within the space of 30 minutes of classroom interaction suggests that in the rational discourse of formal schooling children are encouraged to shift frequently from one kind of object of reflection to another. Such frequent shifts indicate that one of the goals of formal instruction may be a kind of facility in dealing with text-based realities of several different kinds.

Systematicity

The final property of text-based realities I shall outline is systematicity. Like conscious reflection, this property does not characterize all text-based realities. At issue here is the fact that in many cases a text-based reality does not consist of a random set of components. Instead, the components are interconnected or inter-defining. As a result, once one is "in" a text-based reality one can perform a set of operations on one object in order to define another. In this connection, consider an example from arithmetic (a prototypical case of sign types). One of the basic points of arithmetic exercises is that the number system is just that—a system, which means that various components and operations can be defined in terms of others. For example, the number one can be defined in various ways: Any number subtracted from the next larger number, any number divided by itself, and so forth.

In general, some of the best illustrations of systematicity in the text-based realities of classroom discourse can be found in arithmetic exercises. For instance, when children are asked to use a number line to add, they are often encouraged to use it to subtract as well. The purpose of such activity is typically to demonstrate that addition and subtraction are not isolated, unrelated operations; instead they are represented in terms of the systematic interconnection that exists between them.

The four properties of text-based realities I have outlined do not appear in ideal form in all instances one can find in the classroom or anywhere else. For example, in many cases, it is difficult to specify clearly whether or not conscious reflection is involved. Furthermore, as I mentioned at the outset, only depersonalization and boundedness characterize all text-based realities; the other two appear in some, but not all cases. A cursory examination of classroom discourse, however, reveals that a great deal of time is spent in creating and operating within text-based realities. As with other aspects of cognitive socialization, a mechanism whereby this occurs is what Vygotsky termed the "zone of proximal development."

Text-Based Realities and the Zone of Proximal Development

The zone of proximal development is a construct that Vygotsky introduced in connection with two interrelated issues that concerned him a great deal—instruction and mental testing. The former is of primary interest here. In both cases he was concerned with "those functions that have not yet matured but are in the process of maturation, functions that will mature tomorrow but are currently in an embryonic state. These functions could be termed the 'buds' or 'flowers' of development rather than the 'fruits' of development" (1978, p. 86). Not surprisingly, Vygotsky viewed the buds or flowers of development as appearing on the interpsychological plane of functioning mentioned in the general genetic law of cultural development. Indeed, from Vygotsky's perspective the zone of proximal development is only one of several concrete instantiations of the broader set of issues he identified in the general genetic law of cultural development.

Vygotsky defined the zone of proximal development as the distance between a child's "*actual developmental level as determined by independent problem solv-*

ing" and the higher level of *"potential development as determined through problem solving under adult guidance or in collaboration with more capable peers"* (Vygotsky, 1978, p. 86).[4]

I have noted elsewhere (Wertsch, 1984) that the zone of proximal development can be understood only by taking into consideration assumptions about "definitions of situation," that is, assumptions about the ways in which participants in a task setting define the objects and events involved. The term "define" here reflects an emphasis on the contribution made by active cognitive agents. Instead of viewing a static, preexisting context as controlling agents, the focus is on how agents actively represent (i.e., create) and manipulate situations in accordance with the dictates of goal-directed actions.

The range of objects and events that needs to be examined in any complete account of situation definition is quite extensive. For example, participants' expectations, attributions, intentions, and perceptions of each other and of the social setting more generally may be taken into account. If this is done, one can address issues such as whether the participants in a task setting understand it as a setting in which they are to have fun, as a setting in which they are under pressure to demonstrate their intellectual competence, and so forth. It is issues such as these that have concerned researchers interested in when and where children invoke various types of skills. For example, Salomon and Globerson (1987) has dealt with this under the heading of "mindfulness."

For now, I focus on a more restricted aspect of situation definition, an aspect that can be termed "problem definition." Such an approach makes certain assumptions about participants' underlying views of each other and of the social situation more generally, and focuses on how they represent and deal with the objects that are the specific concern of the problem-solving task. Even when one restricts the focus in this way, it is clear that the notion of the zone of proximal development is virtually meaningless unless it is taken into account. This is so because it is impossible to assess the actual and potential developmental levels without specifying how participants in a task setting define the objects and events in that setting.

As an example of this consider a case in which an adult and child are working together on an arithmetic problem. In such a setting an adult can regulate a child's performance in any of several different ways. For example, the adult could guide the child's performance by instructing him or her to write down certain numbers in particular places on a page, or the adult could regulate the child's performance by posing complex questions about arithmetic operations, sums, and so forth. In both of these cases the "same" outcome may be produced and hence the "same" level

---

[4] Although it is often overlooked, most of Vygotsky's comments about the zone of proximal development were made in the context of discussions of formal instruction. For example, in *Thinking and Speech* (1934), they appeared in his chapter on the development of scientific concepts in childhood, and in *Mind in Society* they appeared in a chapter about the interaction between development and learning, or instruction. In both cases Vygotsky's concern was with the kind of rational communicative action found in classrooms.

of potential development may be identified, but there is clearly something that distinguishes them. They differ in what is required of the child. In one case he or she is asked to define the objects and operations simply in terms of symbols that are to be written down somewhere on a page, whereas in the other case she or he is asked to function in a problem setting defined in terms of complex arithmetic concepts. It is just this sort of difference that cannot be accounted for in an analysis of the zone of proximal development which does not take into consideration the notion of problem definition.

This example touches on a general property of how problem definitions function in the zone of proximal development. The interpsychological functioning involved in this zone is typically such that, at least at the outset, the tutor and tutee have quite different definitions of the objects and events involved. This results in relatively low levels of "intersubjectivity" (Rommetveit, 1979) between them. The task for the tutor is to enter into interpsychological functioning with the tutee in spite of this barrier—something that is often accomplished by grounding discourse in a shared referential context which does not require the tutee to define objects in the same way as the tutor (cf. Wertsch, 1985). For example, to extend the illustration used above, a tutor might use a directive such as "Put a three underneath this line" because he or she knows that the tutee can respond appropriately without understanding how that behavior fits into a problem definition grounded in the complex operations of mathematics (e.g., what "this line" is and why a three goes underneath it). If a higher degree of intersubjectivity with the tutee exists, the tutor might use an interrogative directive such as "What is eight minus five?" The two directives are geared to two quite different levels of tutees' definitions of the objects and behaviors in the problem setting.

In creating this intersubjectivity in the zone of proximal development tutors of course do not lose sight of how they think the objects and events in the context should be defined. Instead, they typically retain their representation of what the objects and events "really" are and try to encourage the tutee to accept this representation by continually posing "semiotic challenges" (Wertsch, 1985) to them. This is apparently done with the goal of encouraging tutees to change the way they define objects and behaviors in the problem setting. If tutors were satisfied to establish and maintain intersubjectivity on tutees' grounds, there would be little reason for the latter to go through the problem "redefinitions" (Wertsch, 1984) that characterize change in the zone of proximal development.

As many studies (e.g., Wood & Middleton, 1975) have demonstrated, tutees cannot simply redefine the objects and events in a problem setting in any way imaginable; they are capable of making only certain transition in their understanding of the behaviors and objects in a setting. It is for this reason that instruction must be appropriate for the developmental level of the tutee. If it is geared at a level too far advanced for the tutee, it will not be understood and hence cannot act as an appropriate semiotic challenge. In Vygotsky's words, the child can operate "only within certain limits that are strictly fixed by the state of the child's developmental and intellectual possibilities" (1934, p. 219).

Vygotsky made this point in his discussion of the interaction between development and instruction. In actuality, however, his descriptions of concrete research procedures and results indicate that he often viewed development as little more than the product of instruction. As I have argued elsewhere (Wertsch, 1985) an account of developmental processes that are genuinely distinct from instruction is lacking in Vygotsky's approach. It is a point where "Vygotsky the methodologist" and "Vygotsky the psychologist" (Davydov & Radzikhovskii, 1985) are not in complete agreement.

To recognize this limitation in Vygotsky's account, however, is not to say that the form interpsychological functioning takes in the zone of proximal development is determined solely by some sort of preestablished developmental level or readiness on the part of tutees. The approach I am proposing here suggests that sociocultural forces often will play a role as well. This is a point similar to that made by McCarthy (1979) when he argues that an agent's definition of situation

is not solely a matter of subjective motivations. [Instead], The meanings to which social action is oriented are primarily intersubjective meanings constitutive of the sociocultural matrix in which individuals find themselves and act: inherited values and world views, institutionalized roles and social norms, and so on. (p. xi)

Thus for McCarthy and Habermas as well as for the view outlined here, the way in which a particular problem and situation more generally are defined will not always or solely depend on what is most effective for the immediate task at hand. To a great extent it may depend on the forms of discourse that for other reasons are "privileged" (Wertsch, 1987) in particular settings.

In formal schooling settings, the use of text-based realities is a privileged form of discourse. This means that the forms of rational discourse and the situation definitions associated with them will be preferred despite the fact that other forms of discourse and other situation definitions are imaginable and may be equally effective for dealing with the task confronting a child in a particular setting. My use of the notion of privileging reflects a view that is sometimes termed the "tool kit" approach to culture (cf. Schudson, 1987). In this view culture offers people a variety of tools for dealing with task settings. This does not mean that individuals consciously choose among a set of alternatives when approaching a task, but it does mean that culture often provides more than one way of defining a situation. While the options are sometimes recognized, the notion of privileging is introduced here to deal with the tendency to view one alternative or situation definition as the obvious or natural one. This means that a particular situation definition will be used unless some, often effortful, attempt is made to recognize and employ an alternative.

By introducing the notion of privileging one can avoid some of the dead ends that arise when one accepts the widespread implicit assumption that one form of discourse is inherently more sophisticated, powerful, or appropriate than others. Authors, such as Shweder (1984), have noted that this assumption underlies a great deal of cross-cultural research on cognitive processes; instead of viewing rational discourse as one of several different means for approaching a task (a means that is privileged in our sociocultural context), researchers have tended to view it as naturally occupying a higher, more adaptive position under all circumstances. Therefore, when children or subjects from traditional societies do not approach a task in a rational way, they are often assessed as being deficient on some absolute scale. Instead of falling into this trap Shweder notes that in many cases there are no absolute or a priori criteria that can specify why a rational approach to a task is preferred over a nonrational (not irrational) one. Indeed, in some cases a rational approach is clearly less relevant or efficacious for the task at hand. Yet schooling contexts are such that rationality continues to be a privileged form of discourse.

The notion of privileging has major implications for the zones of proximal development typically constructed in the "literacy practice" (Scribner & Cole, 1981) of the classroom. Specifically, it suggests that a primary function of the zone of proximal development is to socialize students into approaching task settings with a particular type of problem and situation definition, namely a definition grounded in the rational discourse of text-based realities. This approach may be encouraged even though other approaches might serve equally well or be locally advantageous for organizing the problem solving or pedagogical effort at hand.

If we turn to the issue of why one kind of situation definition is privileged over others, we are led back to the issues I raised at the outset of this chapter. There I outlined briefly some of the ways that rationality has come to permeate all spheres of life in modern technological societies. In this picture of bureaucratic and economic forces, formal educational institutions became one of many settings in which rationality is a dominant form of discourse. The specific way that this is manifested in practices found in classrooms is to be found in the forms of interpsychological functioning found in the zone of proximal development. In this functioning rational discourse in the form of text-based realities occupies a privileged position. It seems that just as important as teaching children specific skills, the lesson teachers convey in such interpsychological functioning is that one should define as many task settings as possible in terms of rational procedures.

Thus when examining the role of text-based realities in the zone of proximal development, we are examining a phenomenon whose explanation cannot be grounded solely in psychological or even microsociological processes. To paraphrase Cole (1985), we are examining a case where sociocultural forces and cognition create each other.

References

Bellah, R. N., Madsen, R., Sullivan, W. M., Swidler, A., & Tipton, S. M. (1985). *Habits of the heart: Individualism and commitment in American life*. New York: Harper and Row.

Bernstein, B. (1975). *Class, codes and control: Theoretical studies towards a sociology of language*. New York: Schocken Books.

Cole, M. (1985). The zone of proximal development: Where culture and cognition create each other. In J. V. Wertsch (Ed.), *Culture, communication, and cognition: Vygotskian perspectives*. New York: Cambridge University Press.

Davydov, V. V., & Radzikhovskii, L. A. (1985). Vygotsky's theory and the activity-oriented approach to psychology. In J. V. Wertsch (Ed.), *Culture, communication, and cognition: Vygotskian perspectives.* New York: Cambridge University Press.

Donaldson, M. (1978). *Children's minds.* Glasgow: Fontana.

Habermas, J. (1970). *Toward a rational society: Student protest, science, and politics.* Boston: Beacon Press.

Habermas, J. (1979). *Communication and the evolution of society.* Boston: Beacon Press.

Habermas, J. (1984). *The theory of communicative action. Volume one: Reason and the rationalization of society.* Boston: Beacon Press.

Hickmann, M. (1985). The implications of discourse skills in Vygotsky's developmental theory. In J. V. Wertsch (Ed.), *Culture, communication, and cognition: Vygotskian perspectives.* New York: Cambridge University Press.

Karmiloff-Smith, A. (1979). *Language as a formal problem-space for children.* Paper presented at the MPG/NIAS Conference on "Beyond description in child language." Nijmegen, Holland.

Lukacs, G. (1971). *History and class consciousness: Studies in Marxists dialectics.* Cambridge, MA: MIT Press.

Luria, A. R. (1976). *Cognitive development: Its cultural and social foundations.* Cambridge, MA: Harvard University Press.

Lyons, J. (1977). *Semantics* (Vol. 1). Cambridge: Cambridge University Press.

McCarthy, T. (1979). Translator's introduction to J. Habermas. *Communication and the evolution of society.* Boston: Beacon Press.

Michaels, S. (1985). Hearing the connections in children's oral and written discourse. *Journal of Education, 167,* 1.

Michaels, S. (1983). Influences on children's narratives. *The Quarterly Newsletter of the Laboratory of Comparative Human Cognition, 5,* 2.

Olson, D. R. (1977). From utterance to text: The bias of language in speech and writing. *Harvard Educational Review,* pp. 257–281.

Olson, D. R., & Bruner, J. S. (1974). Learning through experience and learning through media. In D. R. Olson (Ed.), *Media and symbols: The forms of expression, communication, and education.* (National Society for the Study of Education Yearbook, vol. 33, Part 1). Chicago: National Society for the Study of Education.

Rommetveit, R. (1979). On the architecture of intersubjectivity. In R. Rommetveit & R. Blakar (Eds.), *Studies of language, thought, and verbal communication.* London: Academic Press.

Salomon, G., & Globerson, T. (1987). Skill is not enough: The role of mindfulness in learning and transfer. *International journal of educational research, 11,* 623–637.

Schudson, M. (1987). *How culture works: Information and reminder in social life.* Unpublished paper, Department of Communication, University of California, San Diego.

Scribner, S. (1977). Modes of thinking and ways of speaking. In P. N. Johnson-Laird & P. C. Wason (Eds.), *Thinking: Readings in cognitive science.* New York: Cambridge University Press.

Scribner, S., & Cole, M. (1981). *The psychological consequences of literacy.* Cambridge, MA: Harvard University Press.

Shweder, R. A. (1984). A colloquy of culture theorists. In R. A. Shweder & R. A. Levine (Eds.), *Culture theory: Essays on mind, self, and emotion.* Cambridge: Cambridge University Press.

Silverstein, M. (1976). Shifters, linguistic categories, and cultural description. In K. Basso & H. Selby (Eds.), *Meaning in anthropology.* Albuquerque: University of New Mexico Press.

Silverstein, M. (1985). The functional stratification of language and ontogenesis. In J. V. Wertsch (Ed.), *Culture, communication, and cognition: Vygotskian perspectives.* New York: Cambridge University Press.

Smirnov, A. N. (1975). *Razvitie i sovremennoe sostoyanie psikhologicheskoi nauki v SSSR* [The development and present status of psychology in the USSR]. Moscow: Izdatel'stvo Pedagogika.

Vygotsky, L. S. (1934). *Myshlenie i rech': Psikhologicheskie issledovaniya* [Thinking and speech: Psychological investigations]. Moscow and Leningrad: Gosudarstvennoe Sotsial'no-Ekonomicheskoe Izdatel'stvo.

Vygotsky, L. S. (1978). *Mind in society: The development of higher psychological processes.* Cambridge, MA: Harvard University Press.

Vygotsky, L. S. (1981). The genesis of higher mental functions. In J. V. Wertsch (Ed.), *The concept of activity in Soviet psychology.* Armonk, NY: M. E. Sharpe.

Wason, P. C., & Johnson-Laird, P. N. (1972). *Psychology and reasoning: Structure and content.* Cambridge, MA: Harvard University Press.

Wertsch, J. V. (1987). Modes of discourse in the nuclear arms debate. *Current Research on Peace and Violence,* pp. 2–3.

Wertsch, J. V. (1985). *Vygotsky and the social formation of mind.* Cambridge, MA: Harvard University Press.

Wertsch, J. V. (1984). The zone of proximal development: Some conceptual issues. In B. Rogoff & J. V. Wertsch (Eds.), *Children's learning in the "zone of proximal development," New directions for child development* (no. 23, 7–18). San Francisco: Jossey-Bass.

Wertsch, J. V., & Youniss, J. (1987). Contextualizing the investigator: The case of developmental psychology. *Human Development, 30*(1), 18–31.

Wood, D., & Middleton, D. (1975). A study of assisted problem solving. *British Journal of Psychology, 66,* 181–191.

5

*The Conceptualization of Writing in the Confluence of Interactive Models of Development**

Liliana Tolchinsky Landsmann

Tel Aviv University

Our topic is basically Vygotskian in that we deal with the acquisition of a semiotic system. As did Vygotsky, we aim "to reveal the prehistory of children's written language, to show what leads children to writing, through what important points this prehistorical development passes, and in what relationship it stands to school learning" (Vygotsky, 1978, p. 107). We used one of Vygotsky's preferred techniques: We set tasks before the child that exceeded his expertise and abilities, in order to discover the onset of a new knowledge. We asked young children to write or to identify words and sentences, thus disclosing to us their understanding of the nature of graphic symbolism. In so doing, we found clear examples of what Vygotsky defined as mediated knowledge, that is, an active modification of some of the features of the written language as part of the process of responding to it. Even the line of research from which our own work stems can be viewed as Vygotskian in its motivation. This line of research was born within the endemic illiteracy of South America, illiteracy that persisted even in children who had attended school for three or four years. It was motivated by the need to understand the roots of the mismatch between school achievements and children's capacities. It started among Spanish-speaking children (Ferreiro & Teberosky, 1979), but after several years, found its way into different languages, including Hebrew (Tolchinsky Landsmann & Levin, 1985, 1986).

At the theoretical source of our approach to literacy, however, are two of Piaget's core ideas: First, even when the child has to incorporate knowledge of a conventional kind from his membership in a social community (e.g., through language) he must make that knowledge his own and reconstruct it in his own terms (Beilin, 1985). Second, no knowledge begins from zero but rather all knowledge has a developmental history. Accordingly, we should differentiate between written language acquisition and written language teaching and study the former from a very early age. Moreover, any pedagogical proposal, in order to be successful,

---

* This is Working Paper Number 66 of the Tel Aviv University Unit of Human Development and Education. It was prepared for presentation at the annual Tel Aviv University Workshop on Human Development: "Culture, Schooling and Psychological Development," June 2–7, 1987. Thanks are extended to Ann Brown and Sidney Strauss for their most helpful comments.

should be based on this process of acquisition because a child's mode of understanding is always stronger than any teaching effort.

In the first part of this chapter we sketch the process of written language acquisition as it appears in a series of studies conducted in Hebrew. We will see that children produce many transformations on the rules and the semiotic function of the written system, in order to better understand its nature. We shall see, moreover, that these transformations are in every case a reinterpretation of the features of the written system in the children's own terms. In the second part of the chapter we argue that the study of written language acquisition highlights both a meeting and a divergent point between Piaget and Vygotsky.

Our aim is to show that whenever we focus on the interactions of the individual and any part of his environment, we shall find a dialectical relationship between private meanings and thoughts and publicly available means of expression (Glick, 1983). This argument constitutes, in our view and in spite of Zebroski (Zebroski, 1982), the most Piagetian aspect of Vygotsky or the most Vygotskian aspect of Piaget.

Singling Out a Notational System

Written texts, road signs, drawings, and pictures are part of children's environment from the day they are born. They are inserted into the physical context and in the web of social interactions. How do children differentiate iconic and non-iconic graphic materials, between writing and other noniconic materials that are not writing? Do children learn spontaneously to draw and only later learn to write under formal tutoring, as assumed by most lay "psychologists"? How early can children's productions be defined as writing?

With these questions in mind, we conducted a study in which 3- to 5-year-old Hebrew speakers were asked to draw and then write various statements. By analyzing the differences between the productions elicited by the request to write and those elicited by the request to draw, we could extract the graphic features that distinguish these two activities from the child's point of view. There were very few children, and those only from the youngest age group, who produced writings and drawings that were graphically indistinguishable, as seen in Figure 5.1.

By the age of 4, children's writing already appears as a linearly arranged string of distinctive units separated by regular blanks. By the age of 5, children use Hebrew letters almost exclusively.

The figure shows drawing and writing samples of two children. Dana's writing and drawing are almost indistinguishable. Just as her writing lacks the superordinate or ordinate features of the written system, so her drawing lacks the figurative features of a "realistic" representation. Ronen's writing in contrast, though not yet linear, appears as a string of distinctive units separated by more or less regular blanks. His writing becomes writing as his drawing becomes drawing.

Three main conclusions can be drawn from this study: First, drawing and writing become differentiated in children's graphic responses long before formal teaching.

Figure 5.1. Graphic Differentiation Between Drawing and Writing.

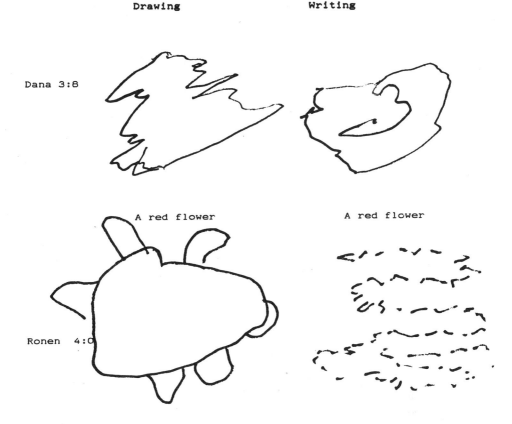

Second, drawing does not seem to precede writing in the sequence of graphic behaviors children master but rather both seem to emerge from a sort of undifferentiated graphic response. And third, features of writing become part of children's graphic expression very early on. These conclusions are supported by many studies carried out with English-speaking children and seem to be independent of race, socioeconomic status, or microcultural milieu (Bissex, 1980; Clay, 1982; Goodman, 1982; Harste, Burke, & Woodward, 1984). Other studies showed, however, that the features of writing are a sort of raw material for the children to work out their own constraints with. Ferreiro (1982a, 1982b, 1982c) followed up a group of 3-, 4-, and 5-year-old Spanish speakers in a number of experimental situations and illustrated how children worked out the two main conditions that a string of marks has to fulfill in order to be something readable or something written: It must be limited in number and variety. Single letters will be rejected as impossible to read because "they are not enough" to mean something. In the same vein, long strings containing the same repeated letter will also be rejected because "it says the same thing all the time.'' The constraints are initially imposed on the string as a whole rather than on the particular features of its components. Hence, strings of letters of different written systems will be included in the category ''readable'' if they fulfill the conditions of being limited in number and variety. Similar ''rules'' are also evident in children's production of written messages. When asked to note diverse utterances they tend to write strings of about three marks that do not repeat themselves in the same string. These constraints seem to be resistant across orthographies (Tolchinsky Landsmann, 1986).

Sometimes a definite piece of socially transmitted information, such as the child's name, becomes the raw material with which children work out the rules of limited number and variety. In those cases the child's name becomes a sort of ''repository'' from which he extracts the elements necessary to note any other word. Sometimes the role of ''repository'' is taken over by another word that a big brother, a road sign, or an adult has transmitted, as seen in Figure 5.2.

The figure shows the written samples of three children. Each child resorts to a different repository that acts as an ''alphabet'' from which they build every word or sentence they are asked to write. All of them produce written displays containing almost the same number of marks, without repeating of adjacent marks. Doron (4:8) utilizes an almost fixed number of idiosyncratic pseudoletters that he reiterates in different combinations. Orit (5:3) regulates her writing according to the same constraints of number and variety of signs, but utilizing her name's letter. Although Guy (5:6) uses more letters when writing the sentence than when writing the words, he uses only the letters of the word *hatul*/'cat' in different combinations.

In any case, we see that children set a limit to the number of possible graphic forms. Not every number of marks and not every succession of marks are legal in the child's view. In spite of these limitations, children succeed in producing different notations for different utterances. Singling out writing from drawing, producing strings of marks that look like writing or even drawing conventional letters does not mean knowing how to write. The questions that follows are obligatory: What is the meaning children attribute to writing, in general, and to their written productions, specifically? Do children put together strings of letters haphazardly? Do they combine or modify the number of letters they use according to some criteria? This constituted the main concern of our second study (Levin & Tolchinsky Landsmann, in 1990).

Defining a Semiotic Function

The sine qua non condition of a conventional system of notation is the finitude of its graphic forms. Children begin to regulate their written productions precisely according to this condition. The difference between iconic and written representation does not only reside in the graphic organization of the signifiers. It lies in the figurative similarity there is between the iconic signifier and the signified in contrast to the arbitrary relationship existing between the written forms and their meaning. It also lies in the fact that written signifiers stand for linguistic forms that can be

Figure 5.2. The Utilization of Limited Number and Variety of Signs with Different "Alphabets."

bayt (A house)	perach adom (A red flower)	yeled mesahek bekadur (A child playing with a ball)	Own name

Doron (4:8)

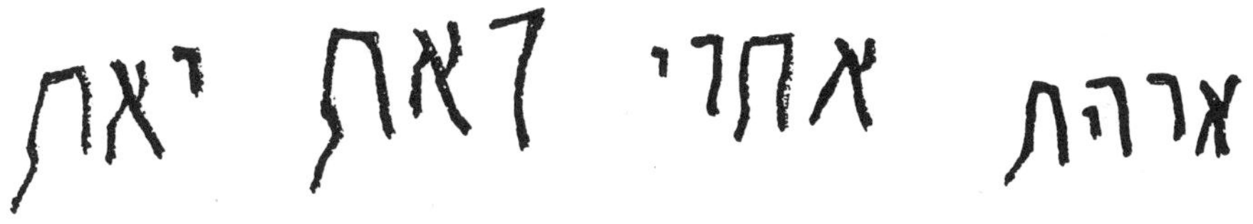

Orit (5:3)

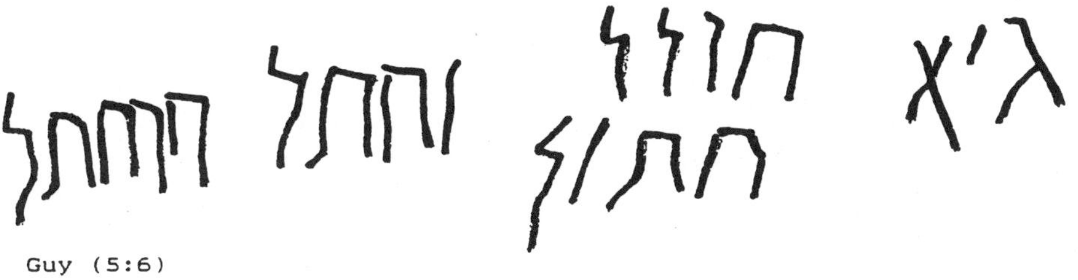

Guy (5:6)

interpreted relatively free of situational context while icons stand for things, events, or ideas. The whole history of writing is usually interpreted as a move from figurative-context-bound to linguistic-context-free ways of representation (Kaestle, 1985; Ong, 1982). A developmental analysis of children's writing may indicate a similar move. The question is whether and how children grasp that these graphic forms become meaningful as an act of social attribution of meaning, because they belong to a system of conventionally organized meanings rather than through their direct figurative resemblance. Or, in Vygotsky's terms, to what extent do children realize that writing stands for words rather than for things?

Vygotsky reported pioneer research by Luria (Vygotsky, 1978) in which 3- to 7-year-olds were asked to write a list of phrases "in a way they could remember." The productions of the youngest did not have any graphic cues hinting at the phrases the children had to remember. In some of the productions of the 5-year-olds, however, some graphic elements appeared suggesting the meaning of the phrases by direct figurative means; for example, the color of a mentioned object was utilized by the child for writing it. Vygotsky interpreted these findings as proof that children relate to writing as representing things directly rather than through language. Our first experiment, the one reported above, provided some support for Luria's findings. We also found 5-year-olds who utilized graphic elements that suggest the referents of the phrases they were asked to write in their shape or color. They wrote, for instance, "a red flower" with red (Tolchinsky Landsmann & Levin, 1985). According to Ferreiro's description of early writing (1982c), the use of shape is very rare and very primitive. Moreover, Sinclair (1982), when referring to Ferreiro's findings, pointed out that "it is noteworthy that iconic symbols are almost never found. When a child attempts to write 'a house' or 'a flower' the shapes he uses do not resemble a pointed roof or the petals of a flower" (translated from Spanish). Nevertheless, there are extensive indications, both in Ferreiro and other studies, that preschoolers may look for "semantic congruence" (Lundberg & Torneus, 1978; Lundberg, 1978)—that is, for a correspondence between the graphic features of the written display and the semantic features of the noted word. For instance, children may look for correspondences between the size of the written word and the size of the word's referent. Accordingly, the word "daddy" may be written with many letters, because "he is very tall." This phenomenon is not one of iconic representation, because in this case children are looking for an analogical correspondence between an intrinsic graphic resource of writing, that is, the number of marks and a quantifiable feature of the referent. That is why the correspondences would be restricted to those characteristics of the referent that can be expressed quantitatively, such as size, age, or amount, and not to qualitative characteristics such as shape or color. The fact that children resort to the "semantic congruence" hypothesis is usually interpreted as an outcome of their lack of metalinguistic awareness (Perfetti, 1984). The capacity to conceive writing as related to the phonetic parameter of an utterance rather than to its referent seems to require a certain degree of differentiation between form and meaning. Previous studies on metalinguistic development have shown that preschoolers have certain difficulties with this differentiation. They "confound" the formal features of words with their referential features. (Markman, 1976; Papandropoulu & Sinclair, 1974). When asked to say long words, for instance, they name long things. Hence, it is reasonable to expect that preschoolers' attempts to write and identify written words will be characterized by a tendency to referentialization, that is, a tendency to reflect in their writing some feature of the referent. To test this expectation, we asked 5- and 6-year-old preschoolers to write pairs of nouns which represent objects that are differentiated by a particular salient feature, such as shape, color, size, or quantity (Levin & Tolchinsky Landsmann, 1990). In addition, we presented them with two cards having the same nouns and asked them to identify which card carried which word. Since older children may tend to write more marks for longer-sounding words, we wished to distinguish this tendency from the tendency to write more marks for words representing bigger or numerous referents. To allow for this distinction, within the pair of words representing size or inclusion relation, the shorter-sounding Hebrew word stood for the bigger or included referent (*pil/nemala*—elephant/ant and *lool/tarnegolet*—coop/chicken in Hebrew). The two other pairs of words, representing shape and color differences, were each composed of two words of about the same length (rope/ball—*hevel/kadur* and tomato/cucumber—*agvania/melafefon*). Almost half of the children introduced one or more referential elements in their writing or utilized at least one referential explanation to justify their identification of written words.

In Figure 5.3 we can see examples of written productions including referential elements. The left-most column shows four writings illustrating the use of shape. The first two appear as a schematic representation of a ball and a rope by a single sign, while the second two are composed of round and straight "letters" for noting each object. Notice that the children do not produce figurative replicas of the object as in drawing. They rather select conventional letters or nonletters resembling letters which shape resembles or can be adapted to the shape of the referent. In this

Figure 5.3. The Utilization of Referential Elements.

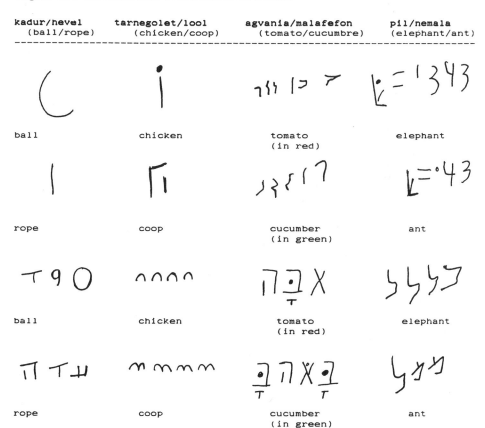

sense, the figurative elements appear as a sort of compromise between the shape of a letter and that of the referent.

The second column presents two pairs of writing suggesting a notation of the inclusion relation by the use of a referential strategy. In the first, chicken is written with one letter which is then "included" in another letter to represent coop. In the second the same string of "letters" is duplicated so that the first writing resulted in inclusion in the second one.

The third column shows examples of the use of color. The first two on pseudoletters, the second two on conventional Hebrew letters. The last column presents two pairs of examples of the utilization of number of signs to note the difference in referent's size. In the first pair, the Hebrew word *pil* (elephant) is written with more pseudoletters than the Hebrew word *nemala* (ant). In the second pair, although the letters are conventional Hebrew letters phonetically related to the words, still *pil* is written with more letters than *nemala*. This last example suggests very strongly that referentialization and phonetization appear as alternative principles regulating the written representation. This claim becomes especially clear when observing the writing process. In this example, the child wrote sounding out the word and searching for letter-sound correspondences. Once he finished writing he looked at the resulting written display and decided to reiterate the last letter, thus obtaining a longer string for *pil* (elephant). Therefore, succeeding in conciliating between referentialization and phonetization.

The use of referential elements presented different tendencies with age. The referential use of shape tended to decrease, as children grew older. The referential use of letter size was almost nonexistent; as presented in the example, the size differences of the referents were translated by using different numbers of marks. The referential use of numbers of marks tended to increase with age, while the use of color was very popular in both age groups.

Children's preferences for a particular graphic element (e.g., shape, color) as referential seem to be motivated by the extent to which it is regarded as intrinsic of writing and the extent to which its use is conceived as producing a significant transformation in the written display.

The referential use of shape implied a sort of direct replica of the referent and figurative replication is indeed foreign to the written system. This would explain why shape is abandoned very early. The referential use of different numbers of marks, the use of color or letters of different sizes, are all legitimate resources of writing, although they differ in their representational nature. A word can be written in another color or the size of its letters can be relatively modified without losing its identity. In contrast, a change in the number of letters would necessarily imply producing another word. If preschoolers become aware of the distinction between transformations which do and do not change the word's identity they will choose changes in the number of letters rather than in their color or shape whenever they want to note something different. This may explain why the number of written marks becomes the major representational resource of a child's writing system as he gets older. This may also explain why color is used throughout the full age range. Children seem to know that they can use it as an adornment, without producing any change of meaning. It is important to note that children are assimilating legitimate writing devices within their particular representational hypothesis: They are translating features of the referent into features of writing while at the same time utilizing the graphic resources of writing to sustain a referential difference.

A similar move from referential to phonetic strategies appeared when children were asked to explain why they thought a particular word was written on a particular card. As the reader will recall, children were orally presented with a pair of words and were asked to decide which card carried which word. Let us examine four different explanations as to why the Hebrew word *pil* (elephant) is written on one card and the Hebrew word *nemala* (ant) is written on the other:

Lior explained that he decided *nemala* was written on a particular card and on another *pil* because "you put this card first and this second." The experimenter asked him to look for another explanation; to explain his answer based on what he was seeing then. To this intervention Lior responded "I don't understand."

Meirav explained her selection thus: "It is because of this letter - pointing to the second letter of the word *nemala*-the *mem*, and here is written *pil*" (The Hebrew letter *mem* is neither related to the shape nor the phonetic value of any letter in the Hebrew word *pil*).

Roi explained that "It is written *pil* (elephant) here—pointing at the written word for *nemala* (ant)—because elephants are big."

Maia explained that "*nemala* (ant) has to be written with many words—meaning letters—and *pil* (elephant) is heard short."

Each explanation successively reflects, in our view, a gradual approximation to a more formal parameter as a possible frame of reference to explain the differences observed between the two written cards. Lior provided what we call a *contextual explanation,* utilizing clues related to the experimental setting. Neither the graphic features of the written word nor the phonetic or referential features of the oral one were utilized to justify a selection of a particular card. Meirav provided what we call a *textual explanation,* centrating on one element of the text itself, but without establishing any relationship between this element and the whole word. Meirav, like other children, seems to understand that "you have to look at the letters in order to know what is written," but she doesn't know what the letters relate to. Roi provided a *referential justification,* centrating on the word's referent to justify his preference.

Finally, Maia used a *phonetic justification,* resorting to the acoustic length of the spoken utterance as her frame of reference to justify the graphic characteristics of the text.

Each type of justification presented a different developmental path. The tendency to phonetic justifications increased with age while the tendency to utilize contextual explanations decreased with age. Referential and textual justifications remained almost stable in both age groups.

Age was not the only relevant factor in the type of justification children preferred; rather they tended to vary their justification for the different pairs of words.

The two pairs of words that elicited more referential reasonings were *pil/nemala* (elephant/ant) and *lool/tarnegolet* (coop/chicken). Perhaps this is because the referential feature which differentiates both pairs, that is, size, is congruent with the graphic feature that differentiates the written words, that is, number of letters. It is congruent from the child's point of view because, in conventional Hebrew writing, the difference in the number of letters is actually *inverse* to the size of the referents. The child, however, interpreted it as *directly* related to the size of the referent).

The pair of words that elicited less referential explanations was *agvania/melafefon* (tomato/cucumber). We think this is because there is no difference in the number of letters so the difference between the referents cannot be easily translated into feature of the written text. Hence, children had to resort to contextual explanations more. The few children who tried to use referential reasoning and referred to the different sizes of cucumber and tomato looked somehow disillusioned when they were shown by the experimenter that both words have the same number of letters (as though they had not seen it by themselves!).

The pair, *kadur/hevel* (ball/rope), represents an intermediate case: *Kadur* has four letters and *hevel* only three. Because of this small difference, and the fact that shape is the salient referential difference between rope and ball, the children could not resort to number of letters as a justification.

Resorting to the characteristics of the referent as a criterion for deciding between written words seems to be one of the possible hypotheses through which the graphic features are assimilated. This hypothesis is obviously supported by those cases in which a congruence can be established between the referential difference and the graphic difference. In cases where there is a lack of congruence the children look for other kinds of justifications.

To conclude, in their first attribution of meaning to a written string children seem to assume that it must reflect the content of the words. This assumption takes into account the graphic features of writing and of the words children are asked to write.

Although the use of referential strategies may sound like a primitive mean when thinking about the conventional rules of the written system, it constitutes a crucial step in the process of conceptualization of writing. It may be the first clear indicator that children relate to writing as a cultural fact. Unlike physical and biological facts, cultural facts are always dual: They refer to something else (Barthes, 1964). Maybe referentialization is the first step toward understanding the duality of writing. This supposed frame of reference, however, is both fragile and unreliable. Referential differences cannot be proposed for every pair of words.

The limitation of this frame of reference may explain why, as children grow older, they resort to other, more stable criterion to differentiate between words: the phonetic criterion—the criterion by which the number and type of letters in a written string is related to the acoustic differences between words.

Representing Sounds

Resorting to the phonetic factor as a guideline for producing and interpreting written materials constitutes a real turning point in the ontogenesis of writing—as it was in its sociogenesis. It is the discovery of a stable frame of reference. Referential similarities or differences can be found only between certain words; phonetic similarities and differences can be found between any pair of words. The problem children still have to solve is on which unit the phonetic written correspondence is to be established. Writing represents language, but in the history of writing we can find written systems based on different linguistic units. Logographic systems are based on graphema-morphema correspondences; alphabetic systems are based on graphema-phonema correspondences, and so on.

According to Ferreiro (Ferreiro & Teberosky, 1979), once children realize that writing relates to the phonetic factor, the unit on which their written system is based is the syllable. Children's first attempts at letter-syllable correspondence appear when they interpret their own writing; they break the word into its syllabic components and try to make a correspondence between a syllable and a written sign. Later on, children learn to break the word into syllables before writing it, deciding on the number of written signs according to the number of syllables. Ferreiro called this "the syllabic period" because children assume a letter-to-syllable correspondence (Ferreiro & Teberosky, 1979; Ferreiro, 1982a, 1982b).

It is very understandable that when children try to attribute meaning to the graphic components of a written string they tend to do so in terms of syllables. There is a tradition in research which demonstrates that when preschoolers are required to segment words explicitly, they tend to do it into syllables rather than into phonemes (cf. Content, 1984; Stanovich, Cunningham, & Cramer, 1984). Phonemes are linguistic constructs whereas syllables are natural units of spoken segmentation. The question is, are syllables absolute, stable units on which the child's written system is based or is the selected unit relative to the unit level of the utterance they are asked to write? If syllables are absolute units, any utterance children are asked to write will be written "syllabically." If, by contrast, they are relative units, words could be written syllabically whereas sentences could not. The experiment reported above focused on children's ways of noting and judging differences between isolated words. Hence, the possibilities for differentiating between them are restricted to syllables or phonemes. Children seem to choose the smallest pronounceable segment between the two levels of units, the one possessing the more concrete phonetic support. But what would they do to represent differences between sentences?

Previous research on adult perception of speech has shown that the feasibility of detecting a particular segment depends on the distance, in terms of unit level, between the target unit and the initial unit (McNeill & Lindig, 1973). In the case of children, a study by Fox and Routh (1975) shows that when asked to segment units larger than one word, children tended to segment them into the immediate inferior unit level. Based on these studies it is not unreasonable to claim that the first attempts at differentiating written material in phonetic terms will be influenced by the unit level of the utterance children are required to note.

There is still another reason to compare the way children write words with the way they write sentences. Given the attachment to content we found in the study on word notation, the following question is imposed: Are children going to resort to phonological primes like syllables when the presented utterances are grammatical sentences, or rather to meaning-based units such as words? The notion of word is one of the most discussed in linguistic theory. Nevertheless, the word, or some basic notion thereof as a minimal kind of sound-meaning association, is critical in all linguistic theory and in language acquisition. What we are suggesting here is that, based on the same developmental description according to which referential differences are represented earlier than phonetic differences, children may begin to base their differentiation on words rather than on syllables.

We undertook our third study to determine the effect of different linguistic units (syllables vs. words) on children's writing. We asked 120 children in nursery school, kindergarten, and first grade (the last in their first week of classes) to write and to read back four pairs of words and two series of sentences. Table 5.1 presents the list of utterances the children were asked to write. By analyzing them, it will be easier to understand the rationale of the experiment.

The right half of Table 5.1 includes a series of phrases which increase in length inclusively from the first word. These will be referred to as sentences. There are two series here which differ: One of them has sentences composed predominantly of verbs and adverbs, while the other has sentences composed predominantly of nouns. Consequently, in the first series we have an increment of words but not of objects; a single girl is the actor of the four sentences. In the second series we have an increment of words and of referents.

The other half of Table 5.1 shows four pairs of words wherein we also see an interplay of similarities and differences. Each pair of words comprises a monosyllable and a bisyllable. The bisyllabic word repeats the monosyllabic one and adds another syllable. In the first three pairs of words we only have a phonological increment without a referential increment, because the added syllable turns one singular noun into another singular noun; in the fourth pair of nouns we have both a phonological and a referential increment because the added syllable is the morpheme bound of pluralization.

All the written productions elicited by these series of words and sentences were compared in terms of number and type of marks. We did not compare the child's writing to conventional writing but rather compared each child's productions to themselves in terms of number and type of marks. These analyses allowed us to assess children's ways of representing the differences and similarities existing between the utterances: We could see if children use more marks to write longer-

Table 5.1. Presentation of Tasks

Word-Task			Sentence-Task	
Hebrew Words	**English Translation**		**Hebrew Words**	**English Translation**
			yalda	a girl
gal	wave			
galgal	wheel		yalda rokedet	a girl is dancing
		Verb		
		Loaded	yalda rokedet	a girl is dancing
ta	drawer	Series	ve'shara	and singing
mita	bed			
			yalda rokedet	a girl is dancing
pe	mouth		ve'shara yafe	and singing very
perach	flower		meod	well
kad	jar			
kadim	jars		tali	Tali
		Noun	tali ve'eran	Tali and Eran
		Loaded		are building a tower
		Series	tali ve'eran	
			bonim migdal	
			tali ve'eran	Tali and Eran
		·	bonim migdal	are building a
			ve'rakevet	tower and a train

sounding words and sentences, and if they use the same marks to write the same syllables or words. We could also assess the effect of syntactic categories of linguistic elements on the order of their appearance, that is, if the morpheme bound of pluralization is represented earlier than any other syllable, and if nouns in sentences are represented earlier than verbs or adverbs.

Let us consider a few examples of children's ways of noting similarities and differences between words and sentences before turning to the general picture.

Figure 5.4 shows writing samples from three children for two pairs of words and two consecutive sentences. Roi (4:1) uses the same type and number of marks for everything. In spite of using a single type of character—perhaps the first letter of his name (ר)—he manages to produce variations inside the written production (intra variations) and also between written productions (inter variations) by manipulating the size and the position of the single character. Roi does not yet represent either the phonological differences or the referential differences existing between the pairs of words and the series of sentences.

Yafit (5:6) already works with a larger repertoire of Hebrew letters and numbers, which she changes for every utterance. Notice, however, that she only adds letters when the difference between the pairs of words or sentences is a referential one. After writing *pe, perach,* and *kad* with one letter—as well as every other singular

Figure 5.4. The Representation of Similarities and Differences Between Words and Sentences.

```
pe /        kad /              yalda rokedet /            tali ve'eran /
perach      kadim              yalda rokedet ve'shara  tali ve'eran bonim migdal
(mouth/     (jar/                  (a girl is dancing/  (Tali and Eran /
flower)      jars)            a girl is dancing and singing)(Tali and Eran are
                                                                    building a tower)
```

Roi (4:1)

Yafit (5:7)

Adi (6:8)

word—she writes *kadim* with three letters. After writing the whole series of verb-loaded sentences with a single letter—since they represent a single girl!—she writes two and three letters respectively, for noun-loaded sentences since they refer to two and three objects.

Adi's (6:8) written productions already represent the inclusion relationship between utterances. She writes the longer word in each pair and the longest sentence in each series with more letters and she reiterates the same letters for representing the repetition of syllables in words and of words in sentences. Note that Adi, like other children, produces a different segmentation for each type of sentence. She produces spaces between group of letters when writing the noun-loaded sentences while she writes the verb-loaded sentence in an unsegmented way. This is probably because she conceives the first as a composite of distinct units and the latter as a meaningful whole.

We found a gradual progression in children's use of type and number of marks for representational purposes. In more than half their written productions, 5-year-old children either used the same marks to indicate identical linguistic elements or increased the number of marks as the lengths of the utterances increased, but not both. Only in 6-year-olds was it possible to detect the simultaneous use of both repeated marks and longer strings to represent the inclusion relationship between pairs of words and series of sentences.

Nevertheless, identical words embedded in different sentences were reflected in the use of identical marks at a younger age than were identical syllables embedded in different words. Similarly, the addition of words was reflected in the addition of marks earlier than the addition of syllables. The addition of the morpheme bound of pluralization was represented at a younger age than the addition of any other syllables. Sentences containing mainly nouns were represented earlier than sentences containing mainly verbs or adverbs.

We think that the congruence between the phonetic and the semantic levels of an utterance and the form characteristics of writing facilitates the representation of certain differences more than others. In our experiment, the phonetic lengthening of the utterance coincided with the referential increment involved in both the plural form and in longer sentences referring to more objects, and both corresponded to the way the written system represented the modification, that is, the orthographic lengthening. Hence, it is not surprising that those cases were represented more accurately by more children and at a younger age.

Since we were dealing with the written representation of sentences, we looked for any graphic segmentation between words. As we shall see, the way children segment their written strings constitutes a new instance of interaction between children's hypotheses and the conventional characteristics of writing.

Modern Hebrew orthography includes different clues to indicate a word's segmentation: blanks between groups of letters, the final letters, and the orthographic representation of the morphosyntactic marks. Spacing between groups of letters is, as in English, the main clue for the separation of words. Every word, independent of its syntactic category, appears separated by blanks. Although Hebrew is a much more synthetic language than English, the intuitive definition of a word that any literate English speaker possesses is enough to grasp the Hebrew orthographic segmentation, except in the case of some prepositions and articles. In English, prepositions and articles are written as separate words, while in Hebrew most of the prepositions and the only existing article are written juxtaposed to the modified words. Another clue is the one provided by the so-called final letters. In English, every letter can be capitalized to indicate the beginning of a sentence, proper names, or titles. In Hebrew, however, the capitalization resource does not exist. However, five letters have graphically different alternatives that appear only at the end of a word. In addition, the orthographic representation of some morphosyntactic marks, like the marks for gender or number, can also act as clues for the end of words because their spelling is absolutely regular.

Children's written production for the two series of sentences were analyzed for any clue indicating a separation between words or any other unit.

Figure 5.5 presents an example of graphic segmentation.

Figure 5.5. Graphic Segmentation.

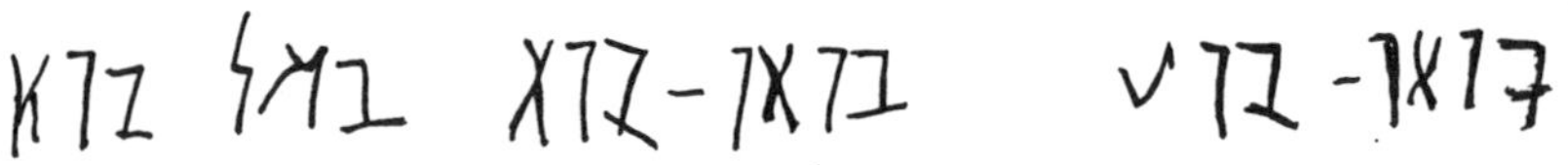

```
  migdal      bonim    ve'eran     tali              ve'eran      tali

(Tali and Eran are building a tower)              (Tali and Eran)
```

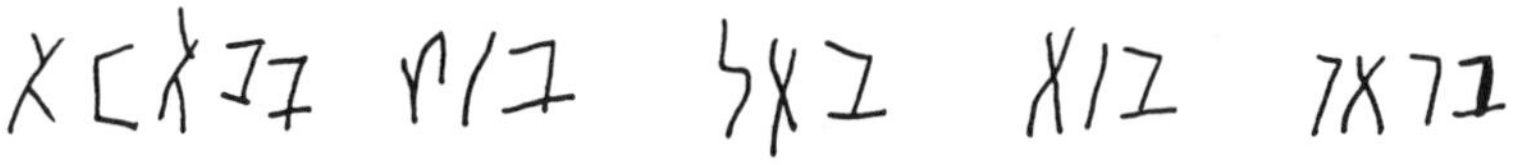

```
  ve'rakevet      migdal       bonim      ve'eran       tali

      (Tali and Eran are buiding a tower and a train)
```

```
meod yafe ve'shara rokedet yalda   ve'shara rokedet yalda   rokedet yalda

(A girl is dancing and singing      (A girl is dancing       (A girl is dancing
very well)                          and singing)
```

The example of Eldad (6:2) is very interesting because he uses three "conventions" to indicate the end of words: spacing, dashes, and also specific letters. The letter *beit* (ℶ) appears in the majority of the words as the first letter while the letter *nun* (ℸ)—in the graphic alternative for final letters—or *aleph* appears at the end of the words. Eldad uses these thee conventions for noun-loaded sentences. In writing verb-loaded sentences he does not separate groups of letters but rather indicates the end of each written string by the letter *aleph*.

In general, very few children produced any separation between groups of letters, especially in verb-loaded sentences. Most of the children that did so did not utilize the conventional segmentation, for example, they used dashes or wrote each group of signs on a different line. More interesting, they did not segment between words but rather between subject-object. Perhaps children find it unnecessary to create blanks in those sentences that are conceived by them as meaningful wholes. In any case, we again see an adaptation of writing conventions according to the child's own representational hypothesis.

Interactive Models of Psychological Development and the Conceptualization of Writing

Throughout this chapter we have tried to provide different examples of the interplay between children's language-processing and reflection, their hypotheses regarding the representational meaning of writing and the actual conventional features of the written system. Children's hypotheses appear as a sort of filter through which the graphic features of writing are understood. But, reciprocally, the conventional features of writing act like raw material on which children work out their own hypotheses.

Statements like the above, though unrelated to written language acquisition are very common in Piagetian descriptions. They simply express another instance of what Piaget defines as assimilation: a functional invariant of psychological development. Statements like this are not foreign in Vygotskian descriptions, either: "The mastering of nature and the mastering of behavior are mutually linked, just as man's alteration of nature alters man's own nature" (Vygotsky, 1978, p. 55). Sign systems transform the human mind in the same measure that the human mind transforms sign systems in the process of responding to it. Moreover, Vygotsky's pupil, Luria, used the assimilation metaphor—even differentiating between biological and psychological assimilation, as Piaget usually does—to explain Vygotsky's proposal regarding the origin of the higher forms of human consciousness (Luria, 1982). Nevertheless, although Piaget and Vygotsky may coincide in the role they assign to assimilation, they strongly differ in what constitutes the origin of higher forms of thought, a point we will dwell on later.

Besides agreeing on the interactive assimilatory processes, Piaget and Vygotsky also agree on the role they attribute to inter- and intrapsychological interaction and to activity in development, on the relevance they attribute to the study of ontogenesis and phylogenesis for understanding psychologal development, and on their experimental techniques. They probably agree on other points (and disagree on many more) but we would like to focus on the above. To be clear, we are not going to compare Piaget with Vygotsky; it is far beyond the goals of this chapter. Our intention is to mention some of the convergent points that were highlighted by the study of written language acquisition and which can orient further research in the field.

The internalization of interpsychological interaction is the main mechanism that accounts for psychological development in Vygotsky's terms. Higher functions originate in interpsychological functions and are later internalized, but, internalization is far from direct incorporation. The process of internalization consists of a series of transformations: (a) An operation that initially represents an external activity is *reconstructed* and begins to occur internally, (b) an interpersonal process is *transformed* into an intrapersonal one, and (c) The *transformation* of an interpersonal process into an intrapersonal one is the result of a long series of developmental events.

Most readers of Vygotsky, however, tend to overlook the transformations and reconstructions that must occur as the functions are internalized. Most readers of

Vygotsky prefer to recognize what Glick (1983) defined as Vygotsky II, a Vygotsky whose conceptual object is the ''identification of the manner in which sign systems transform organism environment relations and the means by which mind becomes socialized,'' rather than recognizing ''the developing antagonistic strains that serve to pit internal thoughts with external means of expression. The latter is the main concern of Vygotsky I, a Vygotsky who does not fully use a socialization model of mind.'' We think, however, that this is the most Piagetian Vygotsky.

In Piaget's theory, thinking is conceptualized in terms of interiorized and reversible coordination of actions (i.e., operations). These coordinations are both individually and socially organized: ''The general coordination of actions to which we have continually referred being an interindividual as well as an intraindividual coordination'' (Piaget, 1971). Within the Piagetian framework the mechanisms of development are: intrapersonal conflicts between existing but different assimilatory schemas; interpersonal conflicts between different ideas regarding the same problem, intra- and interconfrontation between one's own conceptions and socially established conventions. But, also and most important, reflection-on-one's-own action. What we are suggesting here is that although, both for Vygotsky and Piaget, the intrapsychological work is as essential as the interpsychological, a crucial difference appears when each author defines the ultimate impetus to higher forms of thought. The reflection on one's own action, ''abstraction reflechissante,'' is the main factor in Piaget's view (Piaget, 1979, p. 56) while internalization of social interaction, ''the external conditions of life'' (Luria, 1982) is the determinant in Vygotsky's perspective. In the simplest terms, while the Vygotskian direction of development is from *outside in* the Piagetian one is from *inside out*.

Most of the psychogenetic research work on literacy has focused on the child-written text interaction within the frame of a clinical interview. According to this work the development of writing appears as an outcome of intrapsychological as well as interpsychological interaction. A continual exchange of different internal principles, for example, referentialization vs. phonetization; the objective properties of written samples, for example, number and type of letters; and adult reading and writing practices help children understand the nature of the system of language representation that society has forged for them. Much more empirical work is needed to find out the relative weight of all these aspects in the acquisition process, especially regarding the role of peer-interaction of which only seminal research has been done (Teberosky, 1982).

Another point of agreement between the two interactive models of development regards the role Piaget and Vygotsky attributed to activity in psychological development. We would like to redefine here the ''activity'' construct and to discuss its educational implications for the teaching of reading and writing.

In almost every presentation of his theory, Piaget emphasized that the origin of thought lies not in perception or language but in action. However, it is very difficult to find psychologists today who will defend a nonactive view of perception or language. Hence, even from a Piagetian perspective it is difficult to rule out the construction of knowledge by means of perception or language or any other means that entails human functioning (Beilin, 1985). In any case, to see the functioning organism as active rather than passive in the acquisition of knowledge is absolutely central to Piaget's theorization. Similarly, the concept of activity is central for Vygotsky and for the whole of Soviet psychology. In the Vygotskian approach, human beings are viewed as essentially active participants in both their world and their learning. They are seen as the creators of their world and their history rather than simply products of that world and history.

Defining the sense of the activity construct may seem totally unnecessary for most of our readers. Nevertheless, we feel it is worthwhile to do it for the sake of the educational implications of this construct. Activity, according to both Vygotsky and Piaget, implies not only manipulation but also *mental action that transforms for understanding*.

The role of activity as manipulation has always been emphasized in the teaching of reading and writing. Children are encouraged to build words with block letters, to write with clay or on sand, and so on. The role of activity as mental action that transforms in order to understand is less recognized and far from being accepted. Children have to transform conventional systems in order to understand them. These transformations, however, are often viewed as lack of knowledge or mere mistakes that have to be fought. Our outlook emphasizes precisely that role of mental action. We have seen children transforming the semiotic function of writing, the rules of correspondence between graphic and linguistic units, the rules of graphic segmentation between words. These deviations from the conventions of writing could have been interpreted as mere novice behavior. In our view they represent real transformations for better understanding. Children's mistakes—even older children's mistakes—should not be viewed as something to be corrected but rather as something to be understood. Further research should be carried out to differentiate between mistakes that are necessary steps in the process of acquisition and those that are an outcome of learning disabilities.

An additional point of agreement is found in the importance both authors attributed to the need for studying behavior historically, both in the individual and in society. The work of the psychologist should be, in their view, very similar to that of the anthropologist who tries to reconstruct vital processes through fragmentary evidence and resorts to ontogenesis to trace those vital processes experimentally (see Wertsch's introduction to Luria, 1982). This stance proved very fruitful in the study of written language development. Studying the history of writing provided us with valuable insights into children's written systems as well as suggesting possible research questions. Reciprocally, the ontogenesis of writing may illustrate some of the problems humanity has to solve in the creation of a system of language representation.

When acquiring written language children are not acquiring a code but rather a system of representation. A code is a means of translating the units of one modality to another. Once the system of representation called writing was socially created, it could be translated into diverse modalities. The historical process of the creation of writing, however, did not involve a mere translation from speech to graphics but rather a long process of selection of the aspects to be represented and the creation of the units of representation. A system of representation as compared to a code preserves certain features of one modality while ignoring others. By the same token, adults who know how to read and write can translate this knowledge to other modalities. In contrast, children who are learning how to read and write are not receiving a mode of translation, they are in the process of recreating a system of representation. This means that they have to discover its semiotic function and find out which units the system is based on.

Many researchers and educators see the process of learning to read as a process of acquiring a code, that is, a process of the creation of associative habits linking letters to sounds (Perfetti, 1984). The development of writing analyzed here appears rather as a complex process of the creation of a system of representation.

Piaget's and Vygotsky's interactive models of development defined not only the mechanism and the results of development but also the best experimental approaches to tap development. The technique was defined by Vygotsky as dynamic testing and by Piaget (see Inhelder, Sinclair, & Bovet, 1974, for a description of the evolution of the use of the clinical method in Piagetian studies) and Luria (1976) as clinical method. The clinical method, in Piaget's view, helps the experimenter to understand better, to confront his own hypotheses and those of the child; consequently a tester who does not know the experiment's theoretical suppositions is inconceivable in Piagetian research. The goal of the clinical method is to reach the child's maximal capacity and at the same time to demonstrate the child's limitations. The famous "countersuggestions" (which are exactly like the hypothetical opponent Luria brings to his own questionnaires) are used in a Piagetian clinical interview not only to explore the reasoning processes that the subject uses to solve the problem the task poses, but also to prove the strength of the cognitive structure, resistant to any suggestion of the experimenter. Vygotsky's attraction to dynamic testing, in contrast, was fundamentally oriented to prove to what extent children's notions can be changed and their performance improved. In our work the clinical interview enabled us to understand the children's manner of approaching writing. In this sense, the experimental situation worked very well for us. In line with Vygotsky, the experimental situation also worked very well for the child. Although it is very hard to prove, we strongly believe that, to a preschooler who is basically convinced he knows nothing about writing, the sole request to write provokes a kind of "mindstorm." We saw many children gaze at their written productions and say, "Did I know how to write?" This inquiry about their own knowledge, in addition to the feeling we transmitted that it is permitted to try, opened a new world of possibilities. The discussions between the children after the experiments, the anxiety they demonstrated in participating, and the reactions of teachers and parents to the newly discovered ability may indicate that a fundamental change has occurred. Nevertheless, and in line with Piaget's arguments, the strength of children's internal constraints was also evident. The following extract from an interview illustrates this claim very well.

Experimenter	Child
Write *gal* (wave)	ga - gal - ga - ll it is with a ga? what letter is a ga? I know it is gimel. (she writes correctly the letter gimel. Karen knows the conventional value of some letters) ga - lll, ga - lll, I know it is a lamed (she writes a lamed).
(With the written word *gal* still in front of her),	
Write the word *galgal* (wheel)	gal- gal- , ga-l,ga-l,gal-gal, It is with gimel! (she writes) galll-gall, ga-lll-ga-lll,galgal, gal-gal it is with gimel! (she writes another gimel) Yes, *gal, galgal*
You know you can look at the word you wrote before; listen, you wrote *gal,* now you are writing *galgal*	I don't need to look. I remember I wrote *gal*. Now I am writing *galgal*. (and she starts again) gal-gal ,gall-gall (Pointing to the two gimels she wrote.) It is done.

Can anything be simpler than repeating the same letters for the same syllables? Or looking at what she had already done with such difficulty and using it for the new production? All these reflections are valid from an adult point of view. For Karen *gal* and *galgal* are two different totalities whose rules of composition are still not comparable.

Most people working in developmental research have surely felt at one time or another what we felt at this moment: a sort of impenetrability of the child's mind, a sort of other-world-other-rules, yet a clear sense that we had to wait, that something would eventually happen intrapsychologically *without our intervention.*

This reflection leads us to two profound differences between Piaget and

Vygotsky, in spite of the mentioned convergences. One is the notion of structure that is at the core of Piaget's view. The notion of structure imposes serious restrictions on what can change and on the direction of change. This is perhaps the reason for Piaget's relative pessimism regarding the power of language, in particular, and of instruction, in general, to cause structural changes in the human mind. Vygotsky did not speak about limitations; Vygotsky was what Zebroski calls a realistic optimist (Zebroski, 1982) with almost unlimited faith in the power of instruction and of language to change people internally. Reading and writing are not mere instruments or motor skills; sign systems change people ''internally'' as differentiated from tools that change objects and people ''externally'' (Vygotsky, 1978, p. 55). Vygotsky's ideas have a psychological as well as a very strong sociopolitical motivation. If people can be changed internally by sign systems, and sign systems can be manipulated by active social and political forces, there is great hope that people could be changed—quickly—a hope rather imperious in a revolutionary process. Beyond cognitive or general psychological changes, we think Vygotsky aimed at profound attitudinal and ideological changes. Our opinion is that these kinds of changes are less likely to be produced by the system of signs per se. On this point we agree with Tolstoi's (Tolstoi, 1862/1972) view that it is not the written code but rather the way in which it is acquired that is crucial for changing people. Like Freire's view (Freire, 1970), written language can be used for increasing consciousness or for developing submission, depending on the way it is transmitted, on the content of the texts, and on the role of the pupil in the process of learning.

The study of written language acquisition has put into relief another crucial difference between Piaget and Vygotsky: the distinction between scientific and spontaneous knowledge. Although this distinction seems important to Vygotsky, we could not find a precise definition of what he meant by scientific concepts. His definition seems to overlap with content taught in school (Vygotsky, 1962). Although Piaget sometimes refers to spontaneous vs. nonspontaneous notions, this distinction is not relevant in Piaget's conception because his inquiry focused on the search for the building process of the categories of knowledge. The content taught at school may be different from that which children acquire outside school but the same categories would organize both. Scientific knowledge is spontaneous knowledge shaped by the principles of objectivity and reversibility. Piaget would not even label concepts as ''concrete'' or ''abstract'' per se but rather as regarding the operative system of which the concept can be the content (Sinclair, 1972).

For a long time, written language was considered something that could only be taught: a scientific knowledge, in Vygotsky's terms. According to this perspective, the child even needs to fulfill certain requisites and to be especially prepared to enter the ''world of print'' which is usually conceived as totally strange to his interests. Moreover, based on the supposition that reading has to be carefully taught in order to be acquired, titanic efforts were invested in developing teaching methods. The main assumption here is that the written code has to be gradually supplied in order to make it easy enough for the child to grasp. In this respect, we ascribe to one of

Venezky's statements: "Legions of reading specialists and misled graduate students, egged on by reputable educators, have compared Method A to Method B ad infinitum and ad nauseum. Although publishers will continue to extol the virtues of phonics or whatever method, there is every reason to believe that only a small part of the variance in reading acquisition is attributable to the real effects of such ill-defined practices" (Venezky, 1978, p. 4).

We believe there are no prerequisites for a child to enter the world of print. We think that the encounter with print is almost unavoidable. Hence, the encounter itself constituted our focus, not from the perspective of a teaching method but from the perspective of a reconstruction-of-knowledge-situation. We analyzed the interactions between the child and the written language and we saw how these interactions changed with age even before the child is taught to read or write. In so doing, we fulfill what Vygotsky considered the fundamental task of a scientific psychology. The study of written language acquisition only entered the psychological arena in the last decade. Vygotsky was one of the very few that considered the acquisition of written language as a psychological theme before then. Reading and writing are, in Vygotsky's view, higher psychological functions, that is, aspects of human behavior with a long social history. Thousands of years were necessary for the invention of the first rudimentary forms of writing. It took almost 9000 years from these first rudiments to our present orthographies. In Vygotsky's view the first task of a scientific psychology is to study the ontogenesis of these functions, because he believed that the internalization of culturally produced sign systems brings about behavior transformation and forms the bridge between early and later forms of individual development (Vygotsky, 1978, p. 7).

Essentially, however, by exploring the child's point of view toward literacy, we recognize the child as an epistemic agent, a producer of knowledge. This is the main message of the Piagetian model of psychological development.

References

Barthes, R. (1964). *Essais Critiques*. Paris: Seuil.

Beilin, H. (1985). Dispensable and core elements in Piaget's research program. *The Genetic Epistemologists, 13*, 1–16.

Bissex, G. (1980). *GNYS AT WRK. A child learns to write and read*. Cambridge, MA: Harvard University Press.

Clay, M. (1982). *What did I write? Beginning writing behaviour*. Auckland, New Zealand: Heinemann Educational Books.

Content, A. (1984). L'analyse phonetique explicite de la parole et l'acquisition de la lecture. *L'Anne Psychologique, 84*, 555–572.

Ferreiro, E. (1982a). The relationship between oral and written language: The children's viewpoints. In Y. Goodman, M. Hausler, & D. Strickland (Eds.), *Oral and written language development research: The impact on the schools* (pp. 47–57). Urbana, IL: National Council of Teachers of English.

Ferreiro, E. (1982b). *Literacy Development: The construction of a new object of knowledge*. Paper presented to the 27th convention of the International Reading Association, Chicago, IL.

Ferreiro, E. (1982c). El desarrollo de la escritura. In E. Ferreiro & M. Gomez Palacio (Eds.), *Nuevas perspectivas en el desarrollo de la lectura y escritura* (pp. 128–154). Mexico: Siglo XXI.

Ferreiro, E., & Teberosky, A. (1979). *Los sistemas de escritura en el desarrollo del nino.* Mexico: Siglo XXI.
Freire, P. (1970). *Cultural action for freedom* (Monograph No. 1). Cambridge, MA: Harvard Educational Review.
Fox, B., & Routh, D. K. (1975). Analyzing spoken language into words, syllables and phonemes: A developmental study. *Journal of Psycholinguistic Research, 4,* 331–342.
Glick, J. (1983). Piaget, Vygotsky and Werner. In S. Wapner & B. Kaplan (Eds.), *Toward a holistic developmental psychology.* New York: Lawrence Erlbaum.
Goodman, Y. (1982). El desarrollo de la escritura en ninos muy pequenos. In E. Ferreiro & M. Gomez Palacio (Eds.), *Nuevas perspectivas sobre los procesos de lectura y escritura.* Mexico: Siglo XXI.
Harste, J., Woodward, & Burke, C. (1984). *Language stories and literacy lessons.* Auckland, New Zealand: Heinemann Educational Books.
Kaestle, C. (1985). The history of literacy and the history of readers. *Review of Research in Education, 12,* 11–53.
Levin, I., & Tolchinsky Landsmann, L. (1990). Becoming literate: Referential and phonetic strategies in early reading and writing. *International Journal of Behavioral Development, 12,* 369–384.
Lundberg, I. (1978). Metalinguistic awareness and reading. In A. Sinclair, R. J. Jarvella, & W. J. M. Levelt (Eds.), *The child's conception of language* (pp. 83–96). Berlin: Springer-Verlag.
Lundberg, I., & Torneus, M. (1978). Nonreaders' awareness of the basic relationship between spoken and written words. *Journal of Experimental Child Psychology, 25,* 404–412.
Luria, A. (1976). *Cognitive development: Its cultural and social foundations.* Cambridge, MA: Harvard University Press.
Luria, A. (1982). *Language and cognition.* New York: John Wiley & Sons.
McNeill, D., & Lindig, K. (1973). The perceptual reality of phonemes, syllables, words and sentences. *Journal of Verbal Learning and Verbal Behavior, 12,* 419–430.
Ong, W. (1982) *Orality and literacy: The technologizing of the word.* New York: Methucen.
Papandropoulo, I., & Sinclair, H. (1974). What is a word? Experimental study of children's ideas on grammar. *Human Development, 17,* 241–258.
Perfetti, C. (1984). Reading acquisition and beyond: Decoding includes cognition. *American Journal of Education, 93,* 40–60.
Piaget, J. (1971). *Biology and knowledge: An essay on the relations between organic regulations and cognitive processes.* Chicago: University of Chicago Press.
Piaget, J. (1979). La psychogenese des connaissances et sa signification epistemologique. In M. Piattelli-Palmarini (Ed.), *Theories du langage, Theories de l'apprentissage.* Paris: Seuil.
Sinclair, H. (1972). Some comments on Fodor's "Reflections on L. S. Vygotsky's Thought and Language." *Cognition, 1,* 317–318.
Sinclair, H. (1982). El desarrollo de la escritura: Avances, problemas y perspectivas. In E. Ferreiro & M. Gomez Palacio (Eds.), *Nuevas Perspectivas en el Desarrollo de la Lectura y Escritura.* Mexico: Siglo XXI.
Stanovich, K., Cunningham, A., & Cramer, B. (1984). Assessing phonological awareness in kindergartner children: Issues of task comparability. *Journal of Experimental Child Psychology, 38,* 171–199.
Teberosky, A. (1982). Construccion de las escrituras a traves de la interaccion grupal. In E. Ferreiro & M. Gomez Palacio (Eds.), *Nuevas perspectivas sobre los procesos de lectura y escritura* (pp. 155–178). Mexico: Siglo XXI.
Tolchinsky Landsmann, L. (1986a). *The development of written language among preschoolers and first grade beginners.* Unpublished doctoral dissertation, Tel Aviv University, Tel Aviv: (in Hebrew).
Tolchinsky Landsmann, L. (1986b). *Literacy development and pedagogical implications: Evidences from the Hebrew written system.* Paper presented to the World Congress of the International Reading Association, London, England.
Tolchinsky Landsmann, L., & Levin, I. (1985). Writing in preschoolers: An age related analysis. *Journal of Applied Psycholinguistics, 6,* 319–339.

Tolchinsky Landsmann, L., & Levin, I. (1987). Writing in four to six years old: Representation of semantic and phonetic similarities and differences. *Journal of Child Language, 14,* 127–144.

Tolstoi, L. (1862/1972). *Tolstoi in education.* Chicago: University of Chicago Press.

Venezky, R. L. (1978). Reading acquisition: The occult and the obscure. In F. Murray & J. Pikulski (Eds.), *The acquisition of reading: Cognitive, linguistic and perceptual prerequisites.* Baltimore: University Park Press.

Vygotsky, L. (1978). *Mind in society.* Cambridge, MA: Harvard University Press.

Zebroski, J. (1982). Soviet Psycholinguistics: Implications for the teaching of writing. In W. Frawley (Ed.), *Linguistics and literacy* (pp. 51–63). New York: Plenum.

6
Towards A Developmental Model Of Instruction*

Of Instruction*

Sidney Strauss

Tel Aviv University

In this chapter I sketch out a developmental model of instruction that includes implications of learning and developmental psychology research for curriculum development. In order to do this, I present my view of (a) what a curriculum is, and (b) the level at which educational research and practice should be done (a middle level). I then present (c) a case study on the arithmetic average to demonstrate ideas that arise from my analyses about how developmental psychology and education can inform each other. And finally, I (d) summarize the chapter.

Definitions of Curriculum

I see the curriculum as having both a literal and an intentional meaning. The literal curriculum that is often understood as *the* curriculum is the content of the book and booklets or computer programs children learn from in the school. I do not buy into this as its sole definition because it leaves us at the essential but vacuous level of examining the accuracy of the textbook's or program's content relative to the subject matter, as understood by experts in the field.

In my view, a more interesting description of the curriculum is that of a system of intentions and meanings of the authors of the literal curriculum, even if the authors did not have these intentions and meanings in mind when writing it. It's the stuff between the lines that counts here. A novel or short story serves as a metaphor: Events and individuals, moods, ascending lines of force, clashes, conflicts, descending lines of force, and so on—these are not in the words and they cannot be located in the book in the literal sense. Authors choose specific words to create what they have in mind, of course. But the moods, lines of force, and so on are in interpretations and inferences created by the author when he or she writes the piece.

Curriculum authors also have something in mind when they write the curriculum as they do: They have implicit models of how children learn and develop. These are

---

* This is Working Paper Number 70 of the Tel Aviv University Unit of Human Development and Education. A section of it was presented at the Symposium of the SIG: Conceptual Structure and Conceptual change, at the annual meeting of the American Educational Research Association, Washington, DC, April 1987. I wish to thank Rochel Gelman, Tamar Globerson, and Liliana Tolchinsky Landsmann for their thoughtful comments on an earlier draft of this chapter.

not written in the literal curriculum as such, but they can be unearthed in a hermeneutic way. A very simple example of such a model is that children learn through example and repeated practice. We can know that a particular curriculum author thought that that's how children learn because he or she wrote, say, a mathematics curriculum unit that includes several examples of how to solve a particular problem and then provided a number of problems where the children are expected to solve them in a manner similar to that given in the examples.

My experience in these matters is that curriculum developers' implicit models of how it is that children learn subject matter content are generally not based on research or grounded in learning and developmental psychology theory; instead, they are based on common-sense notions about learning and development (in the rare cases when the curriculum developer sees them as being different).

One purpose of this chapter is to take these implicit models out of the closet, and I will attempt to make explicit how learning and developmental psychology theory and research can inform curriculum development and vice versa. To do so, I further describe the curriculum as the outward expression of an underlying conceptual system that includes (a) the structure of knowledge of a culturally-valued discipline, (b) a psychological model that has epistemological underpinnings, and (c) a model of how development and learning take place. I now turn to each of these points, touching on each only briefly, given space limitations.

Structure of Knowledge

Here I begin with the basics by noting three cutting points for decisions about what content should appear in curricula. The first pertains to the discipline itself. The discipline to be taught in schools is considered important for children to understand so that they can fit into and move along the general sociopolitico-economic structure of the society. This cut is often implicit in curriculum planning.

The second cut has to do with the content of the discipline. It should fulfill at least one of two requirements: It should be of central importance for the discipline (as in the case of, say, thermal phenomena for physics) and/or it should have generality across domains (as in the case of, say, the arithmetic average which is not central to any one discipline but is used across many). This cut is usually explicit in curriculum planning.

I have suggested elsewhere (Strauss, 1987) that the first two cuts alone are necessary but not sufficient for curriculum planning and development. The third cut has to do with psychological aspects of the curriculum content. Here I argue that what we want to teach in schools is that content that requires instruction to be learned at all (as in, say, the case of reading) or understood correctly (as in, say, the case of concepts of motion in Newtonian mechanics). There is little point in teaching a topic that will be understood correctly by a large majority of children without any clear school instruction. In order to determine if this psychological aspect is met, we must conduct normative developmental research. Whereas the first two cuts are generally taken in contemporary curriculum planning and development, the third cut, the psychological one, occurs rarely, if at all.

Psychology and Epistemology

A curriculum unit should also take into account the increasing psychological evidence that children have multiple representations of their knowledge about the world. These different ways of mentally representing that knowledge must be understood by curriculum developers so that they can engage and even take advantage of them.

Vygotsky (1966, 1978) has made epistemological distinctions about multiple representations that can be helpful for curriculum developers and teachers. He distinguished between spontaneous (common sense, intuitive) knowledge and school-learned knowledge. An elaboration of this distinction is found in di Sessa (1983) and Feldman (1980).

Spontaneous knowledge is described as being unconscious, nonreflective, originating in children's direct personal experiences with the world, nonsystematic, and not in need of formal instruction to be constructed mentally. School-learned knowledge is thought to be conscious, reflective, originating in the classroom (or informal school settings), systematic, and in need of formal instruction to be constructed mentally.

These different kinds of knowledge are clothed in different symbolic systems, each of which has its own developmental trajectory (Strauss, 1987). For example, spontaneous knowledge may be described in a qualitative symbol system, whereas school-learned knowledge can be numerical. I am using the term ''symbol system'' or language in Carnap's (1966) sense of the term.

For illustrative purposes, consider the case where cold water at the same temperature in two cups is poured into a third, empty cup, and children are asked if the mixed water is the same temperature as the water in the original cups. The same task can be given to children, but we now tell them that the water is ten degrees Celsius in the two cups, and we ask them about the temperature of the mixed water. The tasks are identical from the point of view of the physics of the problem, but we have found different developmental courses in children's understanding of these two tasks. The qualitative tasks showed a U-shaped behavioral growth curve (Strauss, 1981, 1982; Strauss & Stavy, 1982), whereas the numerical task showed a monotonically ascending curve. These findings suggest that there may be psychological reality to the epistemological distinction between spontaneous knowledge coded in a qualitative language, and school-learned, numerically coded knowledge.

Development, Learning and Instruction

My view here is that a developmental model of instruction must inform and be informed by work in normative development of how children spontaneously construct knowledge about content taught in schools. Common-sense knowledge has developmental courses, and without a clear understanding of their developmental landmarks, we will not be in a position to insightfully determine the sequence and timing of instruction for these concepts. The case study I present in this chapter illustrates this point. Similarly, school-learned knowledge has its own developmental course.

The developmental trajectories of the two kinds of knowledge have great importance because much of what we attempt to do when instructing children is to build links or bridges between them. I have found that children construct the links differently depending upon where they are in the developmental course of each kind of knowledge, the spontaneous and school-learned (Strauss, 1981). How to create these links in children's minds is a critical issue in schooling.

The developmental model of instruction also takes a position about developmental transitions. Without a model of how development takes place, we will be hard-pressed to decide how to foster progressive developmental transitions, one of the goals of instruction. The question of how novel knowledge comes into existence is, of course, the question of questions for cognitive developmental psychology, and I do not pretend to have a solution for it. However, there are two models of conceptual change that have been exploited in training children to come to more accurate and correct understandings of the concepts of interest: cognitive conflict and analogy. Both can be seen as ways to construct links between the two kinds of knowledge as presented in the last paragraph. What underlies both models of conceptual change is the idea that one uses knowledge children have already constructed to help them reorganize inadequate knowledge in the same or other domains. In the case study I present here, analogy training was used to induce progressive cognitive change.

Choosing A Middle Level of Educational Research

The choice of the level of psychological reality one chooses to investigate and teach to is, in part, determined by where one's professional identity lies (Strauss, 1986). A developmental psychologist often chooses to investigate the development of concepts located at a deep level of mental organization. Here the content investigated has biological, evolutionary constraints; they are so general, deep, and utterly tied to phylogenetic selection that occured scores of millions of years ago that they are understood to be unchangeable except, possibly, through genetic engineering. Development is seen as occuring naturally and spontaneously in the world of natural objects. Schooling cannot budge this level of mental organization.

In contrast, educational psychologists of the persuasion I am writing about (i.e., those adhering to some of the loose tenets of a developmental model of instruction) are dedicated to changing children's mental organizations, which means that they have to work at a level other than the deep mental organization. They do developmental work, but at the middle level. I have termed this the middle level because it occupies a space between the deep, biologically constrained level of organization and the more surface level that is very close to a description of children's behavior. This surface level is tapped by, say, Siegler's (1981) rule assessment procedure where there are asemantic rules tied to specific task situations without generality beyond those tasks.

The middle level contains intuitive models of the world. It is somewhat general and yields to intervention with difficulty. An example comes from work on thermal phenomena (Strauss, Wiser, & Carey, 1988). Children's (and adults') intuitive thermal models seem to be fairly general and coherent, including thermal equilibrium, heat as an intensive quantity, and a model of expansion due to heating. For psychologists working within the developmental model of instruction, this mild generality and coherence are both its hope and difficulty. By being general and coherent, its change should lead to moderately general cognitive restructuring; however, that same generality and coherence makes that change very difficult to bring off.

A Case Study: The Arithmetic Average

I now bring a case study about the arithmetic average to demonstrate some of the ideas sketchily presented about the developmental model of instruction.

The arithmetic average meets the criteria for what content should appear in curricula. First, it is part of a valued discipline, mathematics (actually, statistics), and it is likely to appear in school curricula. Second, it has great generality across domains. It is ubiquitous in that practically every domain that is quantified uses the average. And third, from the psychological point of view, Strauss and Bichler (1988) found that many aspects of the simple arithmetic average are not understood correctly even through age 14. In fact, Mevarech (1983) and Pollatsek, Lima, and Well (1981) found that even university students in education and psychology departments had inordinate difficulty solving weighted average problems. Often they solved them as if they were simple average problems. The bottom line from these studies is that the simple and weighted average are difficult concepts to grasp, and they are unlikely to be understood correctly in the normal course of development without formal instruction.

The developmental model of instruction suggests several phases to curriculum development. In particular, they are: (a) research assessing normative development of spontaneous concepts, (b) training research to help children learn to overcome conceptual difficulties found in the normative research, (c) curriculum development, (d) curriculum implementation and evaluation, and (e) teacher training.

Normative Spontaneous Development

Normative developmental research about children's developing understanding of the content chosen to be taught in schools is critical for curriculum development. Its data tells us quite a bit. It tells us how children understand (and misunderstand) that content. It also tells us how those understandings change over the years. It tells us which aspects of that content are understood correctly at which ages, which gives us important information about instructional timing; that is, when instruction for those aspects is appropriate. And it tells us which aspects of the subject matter content is particularly difficult for children to grasp. This is important for instructional purposes because those data suggest where it is that we ought to intervene.

With the exception of Strauss and Bichler's (1988) work, no developmental research has been conducted on children's changing understanding of the simple arithmetic average. We investigated how children understand seven properties of the average rather than investigate how children compute the average. Among the properties were: the average is located between the extreme values; the sum of the deviations from the mean is zero; the average does not necessarily equal one of the values that was summed; the average is influenced by values other than the average. A total of 80 children ages 8, 10, 12, and 14 were asked a number of questions tapping each of the seven properties we had determined to be central to the concept of the average.

The results were that: (a) most of the properties were difficult for the 8-year-olds, (b) four of the seven properties were solved by many of the 10-year-olds and virtually all of the 12- and 14-year-olds, and (c) few of the children at all ages had a correct understanding of three of the properties. In addition to these levels of difficulty we found that there were developmental trends in that there were characteristic ways children solved tasks measuring different properties, and these ways changed similarly across ages.

I now elaborate on the property that the sum of the deviations from the mean is zero because it best serves the purposes of this chapter, namely, to show how developmental research at the middle level of psychological reality can inform curriculum development. I present our experimental data only for this property.

Let us begin with a simple example of the property. The average of the numbers 1 and 3 is 2. Now, we must calculate the deviations from the average, and we do this by subtracting each number from the average. The first number was 1 and the average was 2, so $(1 - 2 = -1)$. We make the same calculation for the second number we averaged, 3, and find that its deviation from the average is $+1$ $(3 - 2 = 1)$. The property we are exemplifying here is that the sum of the deviations around the average is zero, which means that were we to add these deviations, they should sum to zero. In our example, we add -1 and $+1$ and arrive at zero.

This property is easy enough to demonstrate via examples such as the one just provided, but it is my experience that it is not an easy property to grasp when we go beyond demonstration. Once children (and adults) are provided with an example such as the one above, they have few difficulties computing other examples to demonstrate the property; however, there is a distance between being able to demonstrate such a property and understanding just why it is that the sum of the deviations around the average equals zero.

I now report an aspect of Strauss and Bichler's (1988) research. In our study to assess the development of children's reasoning about the properties of the average, we asked five questions about qualitative aspects of the property in question. One of them, which I call the cards task, was: "The children in a class brought picture playing cards to school. They put all of their cards into a pile and then passed them out to every child so that each one got the same number of cards. When they did that it turned out that each child got four cards. Afterwards, each child got back all of the original cards he brought to school. The teacher then divided the class into two groups: those who had more than four cards and those who had less than four cards. The children who had more than four cards gave their extras to the teacher. The teacher then passed out the extras to the children in the other group, and she passed them out so that each child in the group would have four cards. When she did this, did she have any cards left? Did she have too few to hand out to the children? Why do you think so?'' The basic idea here is that the number of cards that were extras (above the average) equaled the number of cards missing in the group that had less than four cards (below the average) and the teacher had none left (zero) when she finished passing them out.

This task may seem especially wordy and complex, thus requiring considerable mental space to "keep the problem in mind," making it a task that even older children could not solve correctly. But we gave other, less complex tasks that tapped this property, and found similar results (to be described). An example of such a task was: "Children brought cookies to a party they were having. Some children brought many and some brought few. The children who brought many gave some to those who brought few until everyone had the same number of cookies. Was the number of cookies given by those who brought many the same as the number of cookies received by those who brought few? Was it more? Less? Why do you think so"?

The findings were that 10%, 10%, 10%, and 30% of the 8-, 10-, 12-, and 14-year-olds, respectively, produced correct judgments for the five tasks. The dominant justification offered for *correct* judgments was that since we passed out the cards the first time and everyone received equal numbers, the same should happen when we pass them out the second time. This is a rather practical solution and is perfectly adequate, although it does not indicate whether the children understood the property. A second justification was that when passing out the cards, the surplus should equal the deficit and several children even stated the principle behind the property. The last justification did not occur with regularity until age 14. For *incorrect* judgments, the dominant justification was, "It depends." When this justification was probed further we learned that children meant something like: "I do not have enough data. Were I to know how many children and/or cards there were, I could tell you if the teacher was left with any extras, but since I don't know the exact numbers, I can't tell you." Children also erred when they attempted to work out one-to-one exchanges. This reasoning will be described in the section on training, so I won't elaborate on it here.

These findings indicate that even by age 14 there is a rather significant percentage of children who do not solve correctly the questions tapping their spontaneous, qualitative understanding of this property. If children had such difficulties when the questions were asked qualitatively, it seems reasonable to assume that they would not have a good understanding of this property were it to be presented in school-learned numerical form. I reiterate here: The children could solve the procedural side but they would not understand its significance.

One of the purposes of normative developmental research in the middle level developmental model of instruction is to determine the nature of the normative development for the content of interest. That's what the above developmental research was intended to do. A second purpose is to find areas where children have difficulties grasping the content. The above research did that, as well. In the next phase of the model, attempts are made to help children overcome these natural difficulties via training.

Analogy Training

An analogy is a partial correspondence between mental representations of elements of two domains, these elements being objects, properties, and relations (Gentner & Gentner, 1983). Analogical thinking involves mapping these elements from one domain to another and, thus, finding the partial correspondences that exist between domains.

The main purpose of the training study (Strauss & Salinger, 1988) was to determine the effects of using analogical thinking as a tool for teaching material to 9- and 12-year-old children who built analogies from a base domain of spontaneous knowledge clothed in a qualitative symbol system to a target domain of school-learned knowledge clothed in the numerical symbol system. If our training is successful, then its principles could be incorporated into a curriculum unit.

In the present study we take as given that analogical thinking is a powerful tool of learning with potential to be a source of generating an understanding of domains yet unknown or partially understood. Here we used analogical thinking to help children overcome conceptual difficulties. The teaching involved mapping knowledge representations from a base domain which was well-understood by some children and not by others, to an intermediate domain, and then to a target domain that was poorly understood by all of the children.

As mentioned, an argument of the developmental model of instruction is that the epistemological distinction between spontaneous, common-sense, qualitative and school-learned knowledge is a useful way to categorize knowledge. In this study, we attempted to have children construct analogies between these two kinds of knowledge about the same principle: The property of the arithmetic average that the sum of the deviations from the mean is zero.

I now exemplify these notions with three tasks, found in Figure 6.1, presented to children in our study.

The analogies of these tasks' objects, properties, and relations can be found in Figure 6.2. In the analogy training we asked children to build up these analogies. Some had a good understanding of the qualitative base domain about sand, and others did not. This allowed us to see how the analogy was built from their different understandings of the qualitative *base domain sand task* to the qualitative cards task to the *target numerical domain*.

Our study involved a pretest-training-posttest format. All children chosen for our study gave incorrect pretest judgments for the target domain numerical task.

In order to test the effectiveness of the analogy training we compared its effects to that of two other groups. The first group, the numerical demonstration training group, was given a series of demonstrations of the property, much like the one found in Figure 6.1 for the numerical task. I won't elaborate on this treatment because of space limitations. The second group, a control group, received a pretest

Figure 6.1. Three Analogous Tasks Tapping a Property of the Arithmetic Average.

Sand Task

"Suppose we want to build a sand castle in a sand box which has hills and valleys of sand. We can start by making the sand flat. What happens when we do that"? Through questioning the children answer that the hills fill in the valleys and that eventually leads to the leveled sand. They were then told the following: "Let's say that we decide to mark the height of the leveled sand and do that with a rope. We then put the sand back where it was before so that we have the same hill and valleys. We then take all of the sand that's above the rope and put it into a wheelbarrow. It we were to put the sand in the wheelbarrow into the valleys, would the sand come to the level of the rope, would there by any left in the wheelbarrow, or would there be too little sand in the wheelbarrow to fill in all the valleys. Why do you think so?"

Cards Task

"The children in a class brought picture playing cards to school. They put all of their cards into a pile and then passed them out to every child so that each one got the same number of cards. When they did that it turned out that each child got four cards. Afterwards, each child got back all of the original cards he brought to school. The teacher then divided the class into two groups: those who had more than four cards and those who had less than four cards. The children who had more than four cards gave their extras to the teacher. The teacher then passed out the extras to the children in the other group and passed them out so that each child in the group would have four cards. When she did this, did she have any cards left? Did she have too few to pass out? Why do you think so?"

Numerical Task

Here we wrote the following numbers on a piece of paper in front of the children: 1,1,2,3,5,5,5,7,7. We asked the children to add up the numbers (they sum to 36) and divide that number by the number of numbers (9) yielding the average ($36/9 = 4$). We then asked them to draw a line separating those numbers above four from those below four. They were then asked to calculate how much extra each of the numbers had in the group that was above four ($+9$) and how much each number was missing in order to reach four in the group that had less than four (-9). It was then pointed out to the children that the number of extras above four was the same as the number of those missing to get to the number four, and that were we to add the extras to the missing, they would sum to zero. The children were then asked if the same thing would happen were we to take another set of numbers and perform the same operations on them and to explain why.

and a posttest without any intervention. Our first hypothesis was that significantly more children in the analogy training group would solve correctly the posttest numerical tasks than children from the two other groups.

We also tested children from different ages: 9- and 12-year-olds. On one hand, we might expect that more older than younger children would solve the posttest numerical tasks correctly after training; however, there is nothing of developmental interest in such an expectation. Age, per se, does not tell us much about developmental considerations. On the other hand, it does tell us a great deal for instructional decisions. In particular, it can give us information about instructional timing. Were we to find, for instance, that the training was not successful for the 9-year-olds and

Figure 6.2. Analogies Between Sand, Cards, and Numbers Tasks.

	Sand	Cards	Numbers
Relations	above, below	more, less	above, below
Operations	more into less	extras to missing	add differences from mean
Product	no sand above below rope	no leftover cards	sum of deviations is zero

was successful for the 12-year-olds, we would be in a position to decide that the curriculum activities, based on the training research, should be aimed towards 12-year-olds. Recent research has shown, however, that age differences in an analogy training study were not a significant factor in grasping the analogy and in arriving at a correct understanding of the target domain (Crisafi & Brown, 1986). As a consequence, we leave our second hypothesis open about whether or not there would be age effects for solving the qualitative and numerical posttest tasks.

In the Vygotskian tradition, attention has been paid to how knowledge is built up during learning sessions in discussions between those who are more expert and those who are less so (Rogoff & Wertsch, 1984). Indicators used to determine ease of knowledge construction have been the number and organizational level of cues given during training. Those who are given fewer cues at general levels of knowledge organization are more likely to construct the target domain knowledge than those who are given more cues at levels of increasingly higher specificity (i.e., at more specific levels of knowledge organization). Our third hypothesis was that more children who immediately build the analogies than those who need the analogies to be built up through discussion will give correct judgments on the posttest numerical tasks. This hypothesis also gets at a diagnostic issue; that is, that the ease with which one constructs analogies via training can be a good guide for predicting posttest scores.

Each child was tested individually in a semiclinical interview. All children were given the same initial questions and the experimenter then followed up the children's answers according to their answers.

The research had three phases. All children were first given a pretest to determine their initial level on the qualitative sand and cards tasks and the numerical task. Those who answered incorrectly on the numerical task were then assigned to either one of the two training groups (analogy or numerical demonstration) or the control group (that received no training). Immediately following the pretest, training was given to the children in the two training groups. A posttest was given one month after the pretest. For the children in the training groups the pretest and training were given in one session which lasted between 20 and 60 minutes. The pretest for the control group and the posttest for all the children lasted approximately 30 minutes.

There were three tasks on the pretest: the sand, cards, and numerical tasks. These tasks are described in Figure 6.1.

There were two training conditions: the analogy and numerical demonstration conditions. In the analogy training condition, the experimenter presented the sand task. The first part of the task, which involved leveling sand, was understood correctly by all children. This constituted a correct understanding of an aspect of the qualitative representation of the problem. The experimenter then presented the second part of the sand task. A rope indicated the level of the sand, and the sand that was above that level was placed in a wheelbarrow and was then put into the valleys of the sand box. The children's answers to the questions about this part of the task were recorded, and it was noted if their answers were spontaneously correct, or whether probing questions on the part of the experimenter were required.

The experimenter then turned to the cards question which, it will be remembered, had already been presented in the pretest. The experimenter asked, "Do you see any resemblance between the sand task and the cards task"? Here, too, the experimenter noted the children's answers, as well as whether or not the answers were spontaneous or evoked through discussion. In the event that a child did not spontaneously produce an analogy between aspects of the two tasks, the experimenter asked, for example, "Is there a resemblance between the sand above the rope and the extra cards some of the children had"? Only when children seemed incapable of making the analogy did the experimenter supply them the information. This task is intended to bridge the base and target domain knowledge in a manner similar to that done by Clement and his coworkers (Brown & Clement, 1987; Clement, 1987).

The experimenter then reminded the children of the numerical task and asked them, "Do you see any resemblance between it and the sand and cards tasks"? Once again the experimenter noted if the child's answers were spontaneous or evoked.

The posttest consisted of four tasks: two qualitative and two numerical tasks—an even and odd number task.

A total of 84 middle-class children were tested. There were six groups (two age groups and three treatment groups) and 14 children per group. The number of boys and girls per group were approximately equal. The mean ages and standard deviation in months for the two age groups were: (a) $M = 103$; $SD = 2.6$, and (b) $M = 138$; $SD = 2.7$. For reading ease, we refer to these groups as 9- and 12-year-olds, respectively.

The experimental results were as follows: On the pretest, the children were given the cards and numerical tasks. All children failed the pretest numerical task, and we were interested to test whether or not the age and treatment groups affected posttest numerical task scores.

Our first hypothesis was that more children from the analogy training group than from the numerical demonstration and control groups would correctly solve the posttest numerical tasks. As will be remembered, we gave two posttest numerical tasks: the even and odd number tasks. We combined the two tasks and set the criterion for a correct judgment to be correct judgments on both the even and odd number tasks. We ran an ANOVA test and found significant differences between treatment groups: $F(2,79) = 7.07$, $p < .01$. A Tukey test indicated that among the younger children, more from the analogy group than from the other groups solved correctly both tasks. For the older children, more from the numerical demonstration group than from the control group correctly solved both posttest numerical tasks, whereas the analogy group was not significantly different than the other two groups.

The second hypothesis, that there would be age effects for the posttest numerical tasks, was not confirmed. Also, there was no interaction between age and treatment. The findings for posttest numerical tasks were that for the analogy training group, seven younger and seven older children judged the posttest numerical tasks correctly; for the numerical demonstration group, one younger and seven older children judged them correctly; and for the control group, one child judged them correctly from both the younger and older children.

We now present detailed data (see Tables 6.1 and 6.2) about what happened at each stage of the procedure for those children in the analogy training group. These data detail the findings from the first hypothesis and will be useful in understanding the results from the second and third hypotheses.

In Tables 6.1 and 6.2 we present data for the younger and older children who were in the analogy training group. For the younger children, 3 out of 14 children judged correctly on the pretest cards task. Six children spontaneously produced the analogies in the training session, yet at the end of that session, only two children solved the numerical task correctly. On the posttest, 7 out of 14 children solved both the even and odd numerical tasks correctly, and few solved the qualitative cards task correctly.

For the older children, 10 of the 14 children solved the pretest cards task correctly. Twelve children spontaneously produced the analogies during the training, and at the end of that session, six children solved the numerical task correctly. On the posttest, 7 out of the 14 children solved correctly both numerical tasks.

Table 6.1. Correct (+) and Incorrect (−) Judgments Among 9-Year-Olds in the Analogy Training Condition.

Pretest		Training		Posttest	
Subject	Cards	Spontaneous	Numerical	Numerical	Cards
1	+	+	+	+	−
2	+	−	−	−	−
3	+	−	−	+	−
4	−	+	+	+	−
5	−	+	−	+	+
6	−	+	−	−	+
7	−	+	−	+	+
8	−	+	−	+	−
9	−	−	−	+	−
10	−	−	−	−	−
11	−	−	−	−	−
12	−	−	−	−	−
13	−	−	−	−	−
14	−	−	−	−	−

Table 6.2. Correct (+) and Incorrect (−) Judgments Among 12-Year-Olds in the Analogy Training Condition.

	Pretest	Training		Posttest	
Subject	Cards	Spontaneous	Numerical	Numerical	Cards
1	+	+	+	+	+
2	+	+	+	+	+
3	+	+	+	+	+
4	+	+	+	−	+
5	+	+	+	−	+
6	+	+	+	−	+
7	+	+	−	+	+
8	+	+	−	+	+
9	+	+	−	−	+
10	+	+	−	−	+
11	−	+	−	−	−
12	−	+	−	+	+
13	−	−	−	+	−
14	−	−	−	−	+

The third hypothesis, that the number of correct judgments on the posttest numerical tasks would be greater among those who immediately constructed the analogy (i.e., needed no further questions) than among those who did not do so immediately was confirmed. Among the 17 younger and older children who judged correctly on the even number posttest task, 15 constructed the analogy immediately and 2 did not (Binomial $N = 17$, $x = 2$, $p < .001$), and among the 14 children who judged correctly on the odd number posttest task, 13 children constructed the analogy immediately and 1 did not (Binomial $N = 14$, $x = 1$, $p < .001$).

We found characteristic misconceptions among those children who had solved incorrectly the sand, cards, and numerical tasks. These misconceptions led to incorrect analogies between the tasks' properties. I begin by describing the misconceptions on the individual tasks. The misconceptions for the numerical tasks were already described. For the sand task, we found the following: (a) an inability to understand that the amount of sand remained the same (a version of nonconservation of quantity), (b) the slope of the hill defines both the amount of sand in the hill and the amount of emptiness of the valley, (c) the amount of sand above the rope that signified the level sand was understood as being from the bottom of the sandbox, as if one was supposed to take all the sand and put it into the valleys and not just the amount of sand above the rope.

For the *cards* task, we found that some children thought in terms of one-to-one exchanges without considering an essential feature of the average: the overall number of children; for example, "If one child has 6 cards and another has 2, then it's alright because in the end they'll both have 4. But if one has 6 and the other has 3, then there will be one left over, so the teacher will have some left." The numerical task was solved incorrectly when children thought that the lawfulness of the property depended on the numbers in the sample.

There were also characteristic errors in constructing the analogies which stemmed from misconceptions of the tasks themselves. For example, if a child understood for the cards task that the teacher would have some left over because of one-to-one exchanges, she or he would have difficulties making the analogy between the cards task and the numerical task.

There was another category of difficulties we found that had to do with the tasks' contents. Children who did not immediately construct analogies attended to the differences in task content rather than in their structural similarities. For example, children argued that there were no similarities between the cards task and the numerical task because the former was "real" while the latter was not "real," it was about numbers. Cards exist out there in reality whereas numbers do not.

In the most general terms, these data indicate that analogy training has potential to help children overcome conceptual difficulties and learn a different way to think about the content at hand. It is not a foolproof method, though, as seen by the number of children in the analogy training group who did not solve correctly the posttest tasks.

To remind the reader, one of the central ideas of the middle-level developmental model of instruction is that it is at a level of psychological reality that yields somewhat to intervention and is fairly general. Analogy plays into the issue of generality because it involves an understanding of a principle that is common across different content.

In our study, there were two ways to address the issue of generality. The first involved the reasoning that those who had a correct pretest understanding of either the sand or cards tasks or both would be more likely to benefit from the analogy training than those who had an incorrect pretest understanding of those tasks: It may be that the structure of the principle was already understood by those who solved correctly the pretest sand and cards tasks. This also gets at a diagnostic issue, namely, that static pretest scores can be a good guide for predicting the effectiveness of training via posttest scores. The data do not bear out this way of testing generality. Prior knowledge of the principle under test, when tested statistically, was not a good predictor of posttest results.

The second way to test generality was to see how pretest to posttest change in numerical knowledge affected children's pretest to posttest understanding of the cards task. The argument is that if the numerical and qualitative knowledge tapped in our tasks are linked psychologically by a common principle in our youngster's minds, change in understanding the numerical tasks should lead to change in understanding the cards task. I had reported that those who had spontaneously constructed analogies were more likely to change their incorrect pretest understanding of the numerical task to a correct posttest understanding. Hence, we looked at what, if any, changes occured on the cards task from the pretest to the posttest among those who constructed the analogy immediately and who also changed their pretest incorrect judgments on the number task to correct ones.

The data for the younger children, found in Table 6.1, were that six children produced spontaneously analogies during the training and eight did not. Among the former group, four of the six children (66%) changed their posttest judgments on the cards task relative to their pretest judgments. Three of the four changed from an incorrect pretest to a correct posttest cards judgment, whereas one changed from a correct to an incorrect judgment. Among the eight children who did not immediately produce analogies during the training, two (25%) changed their pretest to posttest judgments on the cards task. For the 14 older children, 12 had immediately constructed the analogy during training, so a comparison of these children to the remaining two would not have been informative.

These data, culled from a dynamic assessment, bear out one of the tenets of middle-levelness; that is, it is fairly general. Change in one of the expressions of a principle is accompanied by change in another expression of that same principle.

The above findings suggest that analogies can be constructed by both 9- and 12-year-olds, and ways can be devised to help children overcome difficulties they may have in constructing them. This was done for a property of the concept found to be difficult for children when we conducted our normative research. This leads to the next phase of curriculum development based on developmental and learning research.

Curriculum Development

Here I am brief in my comments. After the normative development and training research have been completed, the curriculum developer may be in a position to write curriculum activities. In our case study, we wrote several activities whose intention was to teach the property of the arithmetic average that the sum of the deviations from the average is zero. The activity pages were designed to build on the analogies between children's spontaneous understanding of the qualitative sand and cards problems and the numerical, school-based knowledge of the same principle. The pages, found in Figure 6.3, were constructed such that the children were asked to work together to discuss the problems posed, allowing children at different levels to interact.

There were three stories in the activities: the sand, cards, and number stories. I only briefly present an aspect of the sand story and the analogies. Notice that on the first page of the sand story, the children are asked if the amount of sand in the

Figure 6.3. Curriculum Activities.

Sand Story

In front of you is a sandbox. The sand is not level and it
looks like hills and valleys.

Figure 6.3. (*continued*)

You level the sand with your hand until it is completely
straight, and you then mark where the leveled sand is
with a rope.

Now that you have leveled the sand, is the amount of sand in the sandbox the same, more, or less than the
amount of sand when it was hills and valleys? Why do you think so?

Now you return the sand so that it will be the exact hills and valleys we began with.

Now you take the sand that is above the rope and put it in a wheelbarrow.

Will the sand in the wheelbarrow be just enough to fill the valleys to the rope? Will there be some sand
left over? Perhaps there will be too little? What do you think? Why?

Cards Story

The children in a class brought picture playing cards to school.
They collected the cards into a big pile, and saw that if
they pass out the cards equally, each child would get exactly four cards.
Afterwards, they returned the original cards each child brought.
Those who brought more than four cards were in one group.
And those who brought less than four cards were a second group.
The children who brought more than four cards gave their extras to the teacher.
The teacher passed out the extra cards to those who had less than four cards
until each child had four. Did the teacher have any left? Why?

Figure 6.3. (*continued*)

Do you find a connection between the stories?
Are there similarities between them?

If yes, what are the similarities?

Why do you think they are similar?

Complete the table so that in each row there will be items that are similar to each other. If you find other similarities, put them in the empty rows.

Sand Story	Cards Story
Sand	
Hills	
Valleys	
Rope	
Wheelbarrow	

Number Story

Now we are going to learn how to calculate the average.

In front of you is a group of numbers. 1, 1, 2, 2, 3, 5, 7, 7, 8

Add ?
(All) all the numbers in the group.

The number you should have arrived at is 36.
1 + 1 + 2 + 2 + 3 + 5 + 7 + 7 + 8 = 36

Figure 6.3. (*continued*)

Now, count the number of numbers in the group and write it down.
The number of numbers is 9.

Now divide the sum of the numbers in the group by   9   36
the number of numbers. The result you should have come to is 4, and
that is the average of the group of numbers.

We see that the average is not one of the numbers that is in the group.
It is also larger than the smallest number in the group and smaller than the largest number in the group.

Now we will see another property, a third one, that characterizes the average.
To show it to you, we will have to perform a number of calculations.
Place a line between the numbers in the group that are larger than the average (4) and those that are
smaller than the average (4).

1, 1, 2, 2, 3, 5, 7, 7, 8

Above each number that is smaller than the average write the number that is missing for it to be equal to
the average (4).
Above each number that is larger than the average write the number that were we to subtract it, we would
get the average (4).

Add all the missing numbers.
The missing numbers are equal to _____.
Add all of the extra numbers.
The extras are equal to _____.
Now, subtract the sum of the missing numbers from the sum of the extra numbers.
What number did you get?

Here is another group of numbers.   1, 2, 6, 7, 9
If we were to perform the same operations that we did on the last group, would the missing equal the
extras?
Why?

Do you find a connection between the sand story, cards story, and the numbers story? Do you think there
are similarities?

Figure 6.3. (*continued*)

If yes, what are the similarities?

Why do you think they are similar?

Complete the table so that in each row there will be similar items. If you find other similarities, put them in the empty rows.

Sand Story	Cards Story	Number Story
Sand		
Hills		
Valleys		
Rope		
Wheelbarrow		

sandbox remains the same or changes when it is leveled, and to explain their judgment. This was put in because of our research findings that some children thought that the amount of sand changed. I reasoned that were there discussion about this aspect of the task among children at different levels of reasoning, the problem may be cued for those who had difficulty conceptualizing it correctly.

Also notice that the children were asked to construct analogies between the three stories by being asked questions such as: "Do you find a connection between the stories? Are there similarities between them? If yes, what are the similarities? Why do you think they are similar"? These questions were put in the activities to get the children to construct their own analogies by themselves and in discussion with their classmates. I also allowed room for children to construct analogies between various aspects of the tasks other than those I deemed critical by providing empty rows for them to fill in if they so desired. This was put in to enable the children to think further about the analogies between problems.

Curriculum Implementation and Evaluation
In this phase, I put the curriculum into two classrooms to evaluate its effectiveness to bring about the planned-for conceptual change on the part of those who learn from the curriculum unit.

Rather than attempt to evaluate the effects of curriculum implementation in many classrooms, I first looked at its in-depth effects in these two classrooms. Here the reasoning was that were we to find that the unit was successful, we could then implement it in classrooms on a larger-scale basis, working less in-depth at this juncture. If, on the other hand, we found the unit's success to be inadequate, we would have both a theoretical and research basis for attempting to revise it.

I discussed the activities' goals for approximately 45 minutes with the fifth-grade mathematics teacher. In Israel, there is some specialization in the fifth-grade so that mathematics is taught by a special math teacher rather than the teacher who teaches almost all the other subjects.

The activities were introduced as part of a curriculum unit on the arithmetic average, and they were given to two regular Israeli classes in a middle-class neighborhood in Ramat Hasharon, a city neighboring on Tel Aviv. One of the classes was somewhat stronger than the other. One class had 37 and the other had 38 children in it, but some were absent during the pretest and/or posttest sections of our work, so only the 31 children from each class who received both the pretest and posttest were included in the study.

The instructional conditions were not unusual, and included events such as children coming to class late, leaving the classroom to go to the bathroom in the middle of the lesson, the class being interrupted by announcements from the administration, and so on. The activities were presented to each class in two mathematics lessons, separated by two days, each lesson lasting approximately 45 minutes.

The evaluation of children's development and learning was done via a pretest-training-posttest design, where the tasks used to measure their conceptual levels were the very ones we built when testing children's normative development in the first phase of curriculum development. The posttest was administered a week after the children finished the classroom activities. Much emphasis is normally placed on the children's responses during the learning sessions and the answers they give in their booklets, that is, during the training part of the evaluation. However, due to space considerations, I present only the pretest-posttest data for the two classes on the tasks measuring the property under test. I feel compelled to mention that children's understanding of other properties was also measured to determine the extent of the generality of such change that took place.

Children were given qualitative and numerical questions on both the pre- and posttests. There were two qualitative tasks: the cards task and a structurally similar task about a baker and the amount of dough he had in his baking tins. There were also two numerical tasks: an even number and an odd number task. For the two numerical tasks, we present data about two aspects of the questions asked: if the extras are equal to the missing, and if they sum to zero.

The pretest-posttest data are found in Tables 6.3 and 6.4. The data for both class A, the stronger of the two classes, and class B indicate that the children improved significantly on the qualitative and numerical tasks from the pretest to the posttest.

The pretest data for all the tasks show that the children in class A were at a higher

Table 6.3. Percentage Correct for and Significant Differences Between Pretest and Posttest Judgments for Class A (N = 31).

Presentation	Pretest	Posttest	Significance (T-test)
Qualitative			
Cards	55	90	.001
Baker	52	87	.006
Numerical (Even number)			
Extra Equals Missing	23	74	.0001
Sum is Zero	23	65	.001
Numerical (Odd Number)			
Extra Equals Missing	23	55	.005
Sum is Zero	23	52	.02

level on the pretest than those in class B, and their posttest scores on all tasks were also higher. Also, for the numerical tasks, we found that the odd-number task was more difficult for children to solve correctly than the even-number task, a finding that confirms data from Strauss and Salinger (1988). However, despite the significant improvement in both classes from their pretest to posttest understanding of the numerical presentation of the property, the percentage of children solving these tasks correctly remains moderate. And finally, although not presented in the tables, there was change in children's understanding of other properties of the arithmetic average, properties that were not trained for. In other words, there was some generality in the effects of instruction.

In short, the data point to moderate gains made by children in understanding the qualitative and numerical aspects of the property when taught under normal Israeli classroom conditions. There was also some generality in this improved understanding.

Teacher Training
The training I have done with teachers is to work with them on the development and learning aspects of the problems they will be teaching in the classroom. My experience has been that although teachers find working with general developmen-

Table 6.4. Percentage Correct for and Significant Differences Between Pretest and Posttest Judgments for Class B (N = 31).

Presentation	Pretest	Posttest	Significance (T-test)
Qualitative			
Cards	39	77	.001
Baker	42	81	.001
Numerical (Even number)			
Extra Equals Missing	17	63	.0001
Sum is Zero	17	43	.02
Numerical (Odd Number)			
Extra Equals Missing	17	47	.01
Sum is Zero	17	37	.06

tal theories (such as Piaget's) an interesting intellectual experience, the day-to-day problems of how to teach the subject matter of the curriculum is of greater urgency and demands priority. Rather than teach teachers general developmental principles and ask them to apply them to classroom content, I work with teachers on the development of content taught in the classroom, what they will be teaching tomorrow, and from that we get to more general educational and developmental considerations.

The goal of the teacher training part is to assist teachers to be more astute observers of children's cognitive activities about the subject matter at hand. By virtue of my having done considerable developmental and learning spade work, I am in a position to guide the teachers to meet that goal. The training technique I have used has several phases that mirror the phases outlined above when constructing the curriculum materials. First, we analyze together the subject matter via problems about the content at hand. Often, teachers have misconceptions of the subject matter that resemble those of the children they will be teaching. In the next phase, we construct tasks that measure aspects of the concept the teachers have deemed important. The teachers then test children at different ages, getting impressions about how children mentally organize the concepts. After analyzing the data we plan learning interventions to change children's understandings of the concepts. Afterwards the teachers attempt to change children's conceptual frameworks. Among the ways we work to bring about this change are those that will appear in the curriculum. Together the teachers analyze the data they got from the training research, attempting to understand what difficulties the children had in solving the problems and learning about additional methods other teachers used to help the children overcome these difficulties.

After all of this, the teachers are quite well-prepared to teach the curriculum materials and, no less important, their view of themselves as teachers changes from the traditional role of imparter-of-knowledge to that of also being a detective whose job is to discover children's reasoning and conceptual products and, when necessary, to intervene to bring about progressive conceptual change.

Summary

What I attempted to outline in this chapter is how a developmental model of instruction looks. The model includes curriculum development with a middle level of psychological reality in mind. It also includes curriculum implementation and evaluation, and teacher training.

The claim was made that the intentional (as opposed to the literal) part of a curriculum must be informed by explicit models about the structure of knowledge of a culturally valued domain, epistemological categories of psychological reality, and children's learning and development.

The case study was about an important aspect of a culturally valued discipline, mathematics (more properly, statistics), and the content has generality across a number of domains. In addition, normative developmental research has shown that it is not understood correctly by the age of 14. All of this suggests that it is a candidate for curriculum development and developmental research that informs education.

The epistemological categories of children's multiple representations I presented were spontaneous, intuitive knowledge and school-learned knowledge that are clothed in different symbolic systems: qualitative and numerical. The first phase of curriculum development is to assess the normative development of children's intuitive knowledge. Our first study (Strauss & Bichler, 1988) did that for the case study we presented. This allowed us to gain insights into the development of children's understanding of the properties of the arithmetic average, and it also indicated places where children had difficulties conceptualizing the properties. These places then become candidates for learning and development research.

Here I suggested that two ways to put together these two kinds of knowledge at different points in each one's developmental trajectory are conflict and analogy. In the case study presented here, we helped children build analogies between their correct qualitative, intuitive knowledge about a property of the simple arithmetic average and their incorrect knowledge about the same property in the school-learned, numerical language. What we found was that children ages 9 and 12 can effectively draw analogies that help them understand the numerical, school-learned knowledge that the sum of the deviations from the mean equals zero.

These data were then translated into activities for a curriculum unit, these activities based on the above epistemological, psychological, developmental, and instructional considerations. By so doing, we are then in a position to explicitly state why the unit appears as it does, and we can have a basis for revising the curriculum if it runs into problems. If the basis for deciding what should appear in the curriculum is principled and backed up by the empirical studies, the problems encountered in children's learning can be understood and principled revisions can be made.

Of course, further theoretical, conceptual, and empirical work is needed to develop the ideas presented here in sketchy form. Nevertheless, I believe I have pointed to the beginning of a way to combine developmental psychology and education into a developmental model of instruction that has shown some promise and suggests that further work is justified.

References

Brown, D. E., & Clement, J. (1987). *Overcoming misconceptions in mechanics: A comparison of two example-based teaching strategies.* Unpublished manuscript, University of Massachusetts, Scientific Reasoning Research Institute, Amherst.

Carnap, R. (1966). *Philosophical foundations of physics.* New York: Basic Books.

Clement, J. (1987). *Overcoming children's misconceptions in physics: The role of anchoring intuitions and analogical validity.* Unpublished manuscript, University of Massachusetts, Scientific Reasoning Research Institute, Amherst.

Crisafi, M. A., & Brown, A. L. (1986). Analogical transfer in very young children: Combining two separately learned solutions to reach a goal. *Child Development, 57,* 953–968.

di Sessa, A. (1983). Phenomenology and the evolution of intutions. In D. Gentner & A. L. Stevens (Eds.), *Mental models* (pp. 15–30). Hillsdale, NJ: Lawrence Erlbaum Associates.

Feldman D. (1980). *Beyond universals in cognitive development*. Norwood, NJ: Ablex.

Gentner, D., & Gentner, D. (1983). Flowing waters or teeming crowds: Mental models of electricity. In D. Gentner & A. L. Stevens (Eds.), *Mental models*. Hillsdale, NJ: Lawrence Erlbaum Associates.

Mevarech, Z. R. (1983). A deep structure model of students' statistical misconceptions. *Educational Studies in Mathematics, 14*, 415–429.

Pollatsek, A., Lima, S., & Well, A. D. (1981). Concept or computation: Students' understanding of the mean. *Educational Studies in Mathematics, 12*, 191–204.

Rogoff, B., & Wertsch, J. (Eds). (1984). *Children's learning in the "zone of proximal development."* San Francisco: Jossey-Bass.

Siegler, R. S. (1981). Developmental sequences within and between concepts. *Monographs of the Society for Research in Child Development, 46*, 75–80.

Strauss, S. (1981). Cognitive development in school and out. *Cognition, 10*, 295–300.

Strauss, S. (Ed.). (1982). *U-shaped behavioral growth*. New York: Academic Press.

Strauss, S. (1986). Three sources of differences between educational and developmental psychology: Resolution through educational-developmental psychology. *Instructional Science, 15*, 275–286.

Strauss, S. (1987). Educational-developmental psychology and school learning. In L. Liben (Ed.), *Development and learning: Convergence or conflict?* (pp. 133–157). Hillsdale, NJ: Lawrence Erlbaum Associates.

Strauss, S., & Bichler, E. (1988). The development of children's concepts of the arithmetic average. *Journal for Research in Mathematics Education, 19*, 64–80.

Strauss, S., & Salinger, A. (1988). *Instructing via analogies for the understanding of a property of the arithmetic average: A case study from a developmental model of instruction* (Working Paper No. 64). Tel Aviv: Tel Aviv University, Unit of Human Development and Education.

Strauss, S., & Stavy, R. (1982). U-shaped behavioral growth: Implications for developmental theories. In W. W. Hartup (Ed.), *Review of developmental research* (pp. 547–599). Chicago: University of Chicago Press.

Strauss, S., Wiser, M., & Carey, S. (1988). *Final report for the Binational Science Foundation: The development of children's thermal concepts*. Unpublished manuscript.

Vygotsky, L. S. (1966). *Thought and language*. Cambridge, MA: MIT Press.

Vygotsky, L. S. (1978). *Mind in society: The development of higher psychological functions*. Cambridge, MA: Harvard University Press.

7

Interactive Learning and Individual Understanding:* The Case of Reading and Mathematics

Ann L. Brown
Joseph C. Campione
University of California
at Berkeley

Roberta A. Ferrara
University of Kentucky

Robert A. Reeve
University of Illinois at Chicago

Annemarie Sullivan Palincsar
University of Michigan at Ann Arbor

Introduction: Self-Directed vs. Other-Directed Learning

A well-respected tradition in the developmental psychology of learning accords a minor role to social agents. Short of acting as models for imitation, it is argued that social agents play little part in inducing conceptual change. In the extreme case, this position holds that all ''meaningful'' conceptual change is self-directed. There can be little doubt that human beings are intrinsically motivated to understand the world around them. Some argue that learning is guided by systems of internal structures or principles that seek support in the environment for their growth and development (Gelman, 1986). But, in addition, children come equipped with a propensity to extend knowledge by systematically monitoring naturally occurring variations and the results of their own active experimentation (Gelman & Brown, 1985). Herein lies the foundation of such metaphors as the child as scientist (Piaget, 1950) or tireless explorer (Chukovsky, 1968) central to many conceptions of cognitive development. Children are seen as essentially self-directed learners seeking data to test and modify their current theories and hypotheses about how things work (Carey, 1985; Gelman & Brown, 1985; Inhelder, Sinclair, & Bovet, 1974; Karmiloff-Smith & Inhelder, 1974–75).

At the opposite extreme from theories of self-directed learning are theories of cognitive development that emphasize other-direction almost exclusively. According to such theories, conceptual development has an essentially social genesis.

* The preparation of this manuscript was supported by grants HD 05951 and HD 06864 from NICHHD and from funds from the McDonnell Foundation. Portions of the Introduction and the section on Reciprocal Teaching are abstracted from Brown and Palincsar, 1989, and Brown & Campione, 1990. The reflection board discussed in this chapter is being developed in a collaboration between Ann Brown, Joe Campione, and Allan Collins. A simpler planning board for use with arithmetic problems is being developed by Lauren Resnick and her colleagues (Resnick, 1989).

Conceptual change in children is a process of the gradual internalization of cognitive activities originally experienced in the company of others (Vygotsky, 1978).

We have argued elsewhere that a coordination of the two positions comes somewhat nearer the truth (Brown & Reeve, 1987; Brown & Palincsar, 1989). In fact, both Vygotsky and Piaget acknowledged social and individual influences on learning. Piaget certainly considered the role of social experience in cognitive development, noting "the fact that human intelligence develops in the individual as a function of social interaction is too often disregarded" (Piaget, 1967, pp. 224–225). In particular, Piaget regarded peer interactions as an ideal forum for helping children take the leap to a higher level of understanding. A group of peers holding opposing opinions must cause reflection in a reasonable child. Interactive experiences help children "decenter" their thinking, shifting them away from an egocentric perspective, thus enabling them to consider multiple perspectives. Piaget argued that "social interaction is a necessary condition for the development of logic" (Piaget, 1976, p. 80). The process (the group interactions) as well as the product (the solution to the problem) are internalized as part of the child's emergent thinking repertoire. Piaget certainly did not believe in feral children, raised in cognition isolation.

A central tenet of Vygotsky's developmental theory is an essentially social concept: the notion of a *zone of proximal development* (Vygotsky, 1978). Vygotsky argued that one cannot understand the child's developmental level unless one considers two aspects of it: the *actual* developmental level and the *potential* developmental level. "The zone of proximal development is the distance between the actual developmental level as determined by independent problem solving and the level of potential development as determined through problem solving under adult guidance, or in collaboration with more capable peers" (Vygotsky, 1978, p. 86). What children can do with the assistance of others is "even more indicative of their mental development than what they can do alone" (Vygotsky, 1978, p. 85).

By observing learners operating within a zone of proximal development, we are able to mark bandwidths of competence within which a particular child can navigate. At the lower boundaries are the "fruits of learning" or "developmental cycles already completed," a conservative estimate of the child's status. At the upper bound are just emerging competences that *are created by* the interactions in a supportive context. Gradually, however, the "newly awakened processes . . . are internalized, they become part of the child's independent developmental achievement" (Vygotsky, 1978, p. 90). The upper bound of today's competence becomes the springboard of tomorrow's achievements.

It is important to note that social settings can provide learning zones for children even in the absence of an explicit instructional goal. Cooperative learning groups provide a learning forum for their members, although the goal is successful problem solution, regardless of individual contributions or the potential for personal development. And many of the situations examined by those interested in the zone of proximal development involve informal apprenticeships, where the teaching function is a minor part of the total activity. Typical of learning in informal settings is a reliance on *proleptic teaching* (Rogoff & Gardner, 1984; Wertsch & Stone, 1979). Proleptic means ''in anticipation of competence'' and refers to situations where children or novices are encouraged to participate in a group activity before they are able to perform unaided. Novices may be held responsible for some simple aspect of the task while at the same time they are permitted to observe experts, who serve as models for higher-level participation. In such settings, novices learn about the task at their own rate, in the presence of experts, participating only at a level they are capable of fulfilling at any point in time. ''Collaborative learning environments, through a nexus of social support, shared goals, modeling and incidental instruction, awaken new levels of competence in the young'' (Brown & Palincsar, 1989).

Plan of Chapter
In this chapter we describe three aspects of our work that have been directly influenced by these ideas about collaborative cognition and the zone of proximal development. The bulk of the chapter is in the next section, where we concentrate on reciprocal teaching in which children interact with each other under the guidance of an adult teacher, that is, *teacher-child* interactions. The following section contains a discussion of our work on *tester-child* interactions designed to assess a child's readiness to learn. Finally, in the last section, we consider *mother-child* interactions as a form of guided learning.

Reciprocal Teaching: Teacher-Child Interaction

The Procedure
In this section we focus on cooperative learning groups as embodied in a procedure known as reciprocal teaching (Brown & Palincsar, 1982, 1989; Palincsar & Brown, 1984, 1986). Reciprocal teaching was designed to provide a simple introduction to group discussion techniques aimed at understanding and remembering text content. To illustrate, consider the discussion below that took place between a group of first graders, at high risk for academic failure, and their regular classroom teacher. The children have just been read a section of a story about aquanauts. Student 1 begins the discussion with the question:

Student 1: (*Question*) My question is, what does the aquanaut need when he goes under water?
Student 2: A watch.
Student 3: Flippers.
Student 4: A belt.
Student 1: Those are all good answers.
Teacher: (*Question*) Nice job! I have a question too. Why does the aquanaut wear a belt? What is so special about it?
Student 3: It's a heavy belt and keeps him from floating up to the top again.
Teacher: Good for you.

Student 1: (*Summary*) For my summary now: This paragraph was about what aquanauts need to take when they go under the water.

Student 5: (*Summary*) And also about why they need those things.

Student 3: (*Clarify*) I think we need to clarify gear.

Student 6: That's the special things they need.

Teacher: Another word for gear in this story might be equipment, the equipment that makes it easier for the aquanauts to do their job.

Student 1: I don't think I have a prediction to make.

Teacher: (*Prediction*) Well, in the story they tell us that there are "many strange and wonderful creatures" that the aquanauts see as they do their work. My prediction is that they'll describe some of these creatures. What are some of the strange creatures you already know about that live in the ocean?

Student 6: Octopuses.

Student 3: Whales?

Student 5: Sharks!

(Palincsar & Brown, 1986, pp. 771–772)

These students and their teacher are engaged in reciprocal teaching, a procedure that features guided practice in applying simple concrete strategies to the task of text comprehension. An adult teacher and a group of students take turns leading a discussion on a test section that they have either read silently, or listened to the adult teacher reading aloud (depending on their reading skill). The learning leader (adult or child) begins the discussion by asking a question on the main content and ends by summarizing the gist. If there is disagreement, the group rereads and discusses possible question and summary statements until they reach consensus. Questioning provides the impetus to get the discussion going. Summarizing at the end of a period of discussion helps students establish where they are in preparation for tackling a new segment of text. Attempts to clarify any comprehension problems that might arise occur opportunistically when someone misunderstands, or does not know the meaning of a word (gear) or phrase. And, finally, the leader asks for predictions about future content.

Note the cooperative nature of the procedure. The group is jointly responsible for understanding and evaluating the text. All members of the group, in turn, serve as learning leaders, the ones responsible for guiding the dialogue, and as learning listeners (Yager, Johnson, & Johnson, 1985), those whose job it is to encourage the discussion leader to explain the content and help resolve misunderstandings. The goal is joint construction of meaning: The strategies provide concrete heuristics for getting the procedure going; The reciprocal nature of the procedure forces student engagement; and Teacher modeling provides examples of expert performance (Brown & Palincsar, 1989).

Theoretical Rationale

The reciprocal teaching procedure is based on several theoretical principles concerning the strategies taught, the environment in which they are taught, and the role of the instructor in guiding learning.

Strategies. Questioning, clarifying, summarizing, and predicting were chosen because they are excellent self-testing mechanisms: Incidentally, they afford the learner an opportunity to monitor current understanding. For example, if one cannot summarize what one is reading, this is a sign that comprehension is not proceeding smoothly and, therefore, some remedial action is required.

Another theoretically important aspect of these particular strategic activities is that they serve to structure individual as well as social dialogues. Reviewing content (summarizing), attempting to resolve misunderstandings (clarifying), anticipating possible future text development (predicting), and assessing the state of one's gradually accumulating knowledge (questioning) are all activities that an experienced learner engages in while studying independently, by means of an internal dialogue. The reciprocal teaching procedure was intended to make such internal attempts at understanding external and, hence, observable to all. Reciprocal teaching provides social support during the inchoate stages of the development of internal dialogues. In the course of repeated practice such meaning-extending activities are gradually adopted as part of the learner's personal repertoire of learning strategies.

The learning environment. Reciprocal teaching was designed to provoke a zone of proximal development within which novices could gradually take on greater responsibility for learning. The group cooperation ensures that a reasonable level of understanding is reached, even if individual members could not achieve this unaided. It embodies a form of proleptic teaching (Wertsch & Stone, 1979) that can best be understood by comparison to what it is not. The more traditional method of teaching, for example, reading skills, is to introduce a skill by starting out on a decontextualized easy version of it. Upon success, a more difficult version is presented and this step is repeated through gradually incrementing levels of difficulty until the learner is confronted with the "mature" version of the target task. Thus, one way of making the task easier is to divide it into manageable subcomponents and to provide practice on these, in isolation, until they are perfected. But it is usually the case in educational settings that the role of recombining the subcomponents (vertical transfer) or using them flexibly on an array of tasks of which they are elements (lateral transfer) is left up to the student, with disastrous results (Gagne, 1965), that is, the thorny problem of transfer (Brown & Campione, 1981, 1984).

In proleptic teaching, by contrast, the integrity of the target task is maintained; components are handled in the context of the entire task; skills are practiced in context. For example, in reciprocal teaching, the aim of understanding the texts remains as undisturbed as possible, but the novice's role is made *easier* by the provision of a supportive social context that does a great deal of the cognitive work until the novice can take over a greater degree of responsibility. But the task remains the same, the goal the same, the desired outcome the same. There is little room for confusion about the point of the activity: understanding the text (Brown, 1978; Brown & Campione, 1984).

The cooperative feature of the learning group in reciprocal teaching, where everyone is seeking consensus concerning meaning, relevance, and importance, is an ideal setting for novices to practice their emergent comprehension skills. All of the responsibility for comprehending does not rest with one person and even if a learning leader fails, the other members of the group including the adult teacher, are there to keep the discussion going. Because the group's efforts are externalized in the form of a discussion, novices can learn from the contributions of those more expert than they on any particular point. It is in this sense that reciprocal teaching dialogues create a zone of proximal development (Vygotsky, 1978) for their participants, each one of whom may share in the co-construction of meaning to the extent that she or he is able. Collaboratively, the group, with its variety of expertise, engagement, and goals, gets the job done; the text gets understood. What changes over time is who has the major responsibility for the learning activities.

The role of the instructor. The idea that reciprocal teaching provides a zone of proximal development for its members in which they can exercise cognitive activities that are just emerging, should not be equated with the notion of expert scaffolding, which it closely resembles (Griffen & Cole, 1984). For the participating children are not explicitly intending to tutor each other. Just by being privy to the group activities allows the novices to witness comprehension strategies that they might not have understood before, thereby opening up wider and wider potential zones for development. But within reciprocal teaching, one member of the group, the adult teacher, does have an explicit instructional goal, and it is part of her responsibility to engage in deliberate *scaffolding* activities when she works with the current discussion leaders in an attempt to improve their level of participation. Thus, reciprocal teaching is *both* a cooperative learning group jointly negotiating the understanding task *and* a direct instruction forum wherein the teacher attempts to provide temporary scaffolding to bolster the learning leader's inchoate strategies.

In addition, the adult teacher closely monitors the learning leaders, giving them feedback that is tailored to their existing levels. Because the students must participate when it is their turn to be the leader, the teacher can engage in online diagnosis of their competence. On the basis of this diagnosis, responsibility for the comprehension activities is transferred to the students as soon as they can take charge of their own learning. The idea is for the teacher to take control only when needed and to hand over the responsibility to the students whenever they are ready. Through interactions with the supportive teacher, the students are guided to perform at an increasingly challenging level. In response, the teacher gradually fades into the background and acts as a sympathetic coach, leaving the students to handle their own learning. The teacher is always monitoring the discussions, however, and is ready to take control again when understanding fails.

Finally, the adult teacher acts as a model of expert behavior. She models mature comprehension-promoting strategies, thus making overt, explicit, and concrete thinking activities that are usually not open to inspection. Instead of being told to ''monitor your comprehension,'' the students see how the teacher does this: by retelling content in her own words, by asking what something means, and by posing questions about main points.

Over the past seven years, we have conducted many studies of reciprocal teaching, including a concentration on reading comprehension in sixth to eighth graders and a minilongitudinal study of first- to third-graders' reading and listening comprehension. Common to all our studies are that (a) the interventions are fairly extensive by experimental standards (between 20 days to 60 days), (b) the older students are at least two years behind on standardized tests of reading comprehension and the younger students have been diagnosed as "at risk" for academic delay, (c) progress is measured not only by observable changes in the students' participation in the discussions, but also by repeated independent tests of their understanding of novel passages (i.e., itself a form of transfer), (d) long-term maintenance, transfer, and generalization are all measured along with improvements in standardized test scores.

Main Findings

Success of experimental program. The reciprocal teaching procedure has been used successfully as a reading and listening comprehension intervention by average classroom teachers with academically at-risk grade and middle school children. Since 1981, when the program began, 287 junior high school students and 366 first- to third-grade children have taken part in reading and listening comprehension experiments, respectively. These interventions were conducted by regular classroom teachers working with small groups (the ideal group size is six, but the teachers have handled much larger groups). Students enter the study scoring approximately 30% correct on independent tests of text comprehension and continue in the program for at least 20 instructional days. We count as successful any student who achieves an independent score of 75–80% correct on five successive days. With this as the criterion, approximately 80% of the students at both ages are judged to be successful. Furthermore, students maintain their independent mastery for up to six months to a year after instruction ceases (Brown & Palincsar, 1982); they generalize to other classroom activities, notably science and social studies; and they improve approximately two years on standardized tests of reading comprehension (Palincsar & Brown, 1984). In terms of research into practice, currently, in one school district alone 50 teachers and 700 students are using the procedure as their regular reading comprehension instruction.

Reciprocal teaching is more than the sum of its parts. Such improvements in comprehension scores are not an automatic outcome of strategy training. For example, to test the effectiveness of the reciprocal teaching procedure, we have conducted a series of comparison studies where the method is pitted against a variety of alternative instructional practices. We will give just one example here. Groups of closely matched junior high school students, all with reading comprehension problems, were assigned to one of three training conditions or to a control group. The three instructional groups were reciprocal teaching (RT), modeling (M), and explicit instruction (EI). In the modeling group, the teacher modeled how to use the four strategies on each segment of the passages and the students' role was to observe and answer the teacher-posed questions. In the explicit instruction group, the teacher demonstrated and discussed each strategy for the first half of the session, and in the second half, the students completed pencil and paper exercises in applying the strategies to the remaining text segments. Thus, modeling consisted of an expert talk-aloud procedure in which the teacher herself used the strategies for the students to see (Bereiter & Bird, 1985). Explicit instruction was based on normal classroom demonstration and practice routines. In both cases, however, the explicit teaching in the modeling and demonstration procedures was focused on the strategies themselves, not a common classroom practice (Durkin, 1984).

All groups improved except the untreated control as can be seen in Figure 7.1. But the reciprocal teaching students' performance was significantly better than that of the other two instructional groups. Reciprocal teaching, where the students receive instruction, modeling, and practice, gradually taking charge of their own learning, is by far the most effective form of intervention.

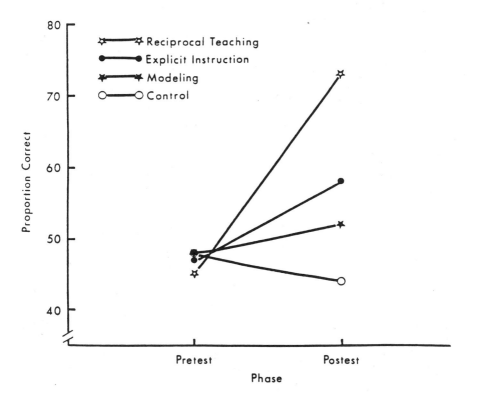

Figure 7.1. The independent comprehension scores of four seventh-grade groups: Reciprocal Teaching (RT), Modeling (M), Explicit Instruction (EI), and a Control group (C) (from Palincsar & Brown, 1984).

Maintenance and generalization. These improvements in individual learning scores are maintained over time, for up to six months to one year (Brown & Palincsar, 1982). Perhaps a more dramatic indication of the effects of reciprocal teaching is the extent to which the students improved in settings other than those we control. In our 7-year period of study, we have found three types of transfer: (a) generalizations to the classroom, (b) improved performance on posttests that tap the trained strategies, and (c) improvement in standardized test scores. Representative transfer data (taken from Palincsar & Brown, 1984) are shown in Figure 7.2. Entries 1 and 2 present data taken from classroom generalization probes where the students read science and social studies content passages in their regular classes and answered comprehension questions on them from memory. No mention was made of the fact that these tasks formed part of the study. All seventh graders in the school ($N = 130$) took the tests as part of their regular classroom activity. In the top part of Figure 7.2, the performance over time of the reciprocal teaching group is compared with that of matched control students. The reciprocal teaching group showed steady improvement; the control students did not. Perhaps of more interest are the data shown in the second part of Figure 7.2. Here the reciprocal teaching students' improvement in percentile rankings is compared with all of the seventh graders in the school (students drawn from the full range of ability). Whereas the control group showed only random fluctuations in their rankings, the reciprocal teaching students improved dramatically, bringing their level to *above* the average for their age.

The third set of statistics shown in Figure 7.2 are the reciprocal teaching students' improvements on standardized tests of reading comprehension. The improvement was dramatic; one-third of the students tested at or *above* grade level. Similar findings were found when nonselected teachers conducted the program with students in reading groups improving 11 months and those in the science classes 15 months after a few weeks of instruction.

Finally, reciprocal teaching students showed significant improvement on laboratory tests that differed in appearance from the training task, but could be said to tap the same underlying processes. They were better at (a) applying macrorules to the task of writing *summaries* (Brown & Day, 1983), (b) constructing appropriate comprehension *questions* to accompany a text, and (c) detecting (*clarifying*) anomalous sentences (Harris, Kruithof, Terwogt, & Visser, 1981).

Reciprocal Teaching and Coherent Content

In the majority of our work on reciprocal teaching of reading comprehension we have followed the typical pattern of "reading group," that is, each day the children read a text that is not related in any way to the previous texts. Passage follows passage with no coherent link between them (a story about volcanos follows one on dinosaurs, which follows one on aquanauts, etc.); there is little opportunity for cumulative reference. Such procedures positively encourage the child to acquire encapsulated "inert" knowledge (Whitehead, 1916).

We will give the details of just one study in which we bypassed this typical procedure; here "at-risk minority" third-grade children were trying to learn a coherent body of knowledge about animal defense mechanisms, such as camou-

Classroom Generalization Data

1) <u>Classroom Probes</u>

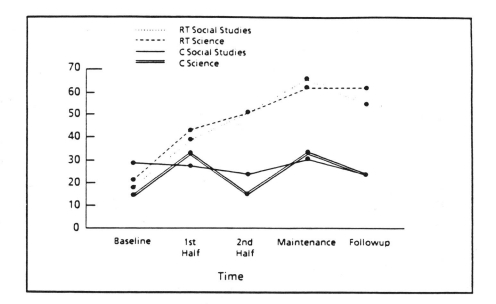

2) <u>Changes in Percentile Rankings</u>

		Pretest	Posttest
Reciprocal Teaching:	Social Studies	25	78
	Science	5	69
Control Groups:	Social Studies	13	11
	Science	20	18

3) <u>Standardized Tests</u> (<u>Gates-McGinitie</u>)

	Comprehension	Vocabulary
Reciprocal Teaching:	+ 20 month	+ 4 months
Control Groups:	+ 1 month	+ 3 months

4) <u>Laboratory Transfer</u>

Significant transfers to novel tests of summarizing, questioning, and clarification.

Figure 7.2. Generalization and transfer measures of seventh grade Reciprocal Teaching students vs. Control (from Palincsar & Brown, 1984).

145

flage, mimicry, protection from the elements, extinction, parasites, and natural pest control. These themes repeat during the discussions and are also taken up in the daily independent tests of comprehension.

In the discussions, the students are forced to explain and justify their understanding to others, and in so doing, come to understand the theme better themselves. An example of this explanatory process can be seen in the dialogue in Table 7.1. The learning leader (S_1) does not fully understand the meaning of the term camouflage

Table 7.1. The Meaning of Camouflage.

S_1:   (*Question*) What does camouflage mean?
S_2:   It means you invisible like G.I. Joe (*spontaneous analogy*).
S_1:   (*Question*) What color can it (the chameleon) be?
S_3:   Brown.
S_1:   No.
S_2:   Green?
S_1:   No.
All: What? (*confusion*)
S_1:   (*Question*) What color would it be if it was on a fire engine—red, right? And if it's on a car—black, right? And on a cab—yellow, right?
All: No! No!
S_4:   It can only be greenish or brownish, like in nature.
S_1:   (*Indignant*) It says (*reading text*), "A chameleon can take on the color of its background"—so it can be *any* color, right?
S_4:   No, no! It can only be colors like brown earth and green trees and yucky color like mud—like G.I. Joe.
S_6:   So he matches.
T: (*Scaffolding weaker student: repeating text line*) Yes he matches, he's almost invisible.
S_6:   He changes colors so his enemy won't get him.
T: Good. That's right.
S_1:   (*Question—confused*) But what if he's not in the grass, what if he's in a whitish kinda color?
S_6:   He would turn white?
All: No.
S_1:   (*Question—still confused*) But what if he doesn't have that color? What if he can't turn that color?
S_5:   He just moves on down to another spot that has his color.
S_4:   No, only green and brown and yucky.
S_1:   (*Question, persistent*) Can it be blue like water in the forest?
S_3:   Water in the forest isn't blue, it's yucky colored, so chameleons can be yucky colored too.
S_1:   (*Summary*) OK. OK. I summarize, it change color.
T: What does?
S_1:   (*Sigh*) Chameleon change color to hide from its enemies. It can be green—umh brown—yucky color (*pause*) so it has to stay in the forest 'cause those colors are there.
S_1:   (*Question*) I have another question. How does it change color?
T: Good question. Anyone know?
S_6:   It doesn't say.
T: Do we really know how it changes?
S_1:   No.
T: Any predictions? No?
T: (*Prediction*) I think it might be a chemical in its body, let's read to find out.

because she is unduly influenced by the inconsiderate text comment that ''a chameleon can take on the color of its background.'' This she takes to mean any color whatsoever. The ensuing discussion forces the learning leader to reevaluate her understanding and come to terms with the constraints placed on the mechanisms. Note Subject 1's confusion and persistence. She attempts to understand by asking about special cases. She really wants to know, and eventually, in her final summary, she appears satisfied. It is also Subject 1 who sets up the motivation to find out *how* the mechanism works. Several days later, when discussing another instance of camouflage, the walking stick insect that disguises itself by changing its shape, Subject 1 shows she has mastered this idea.

> OK, it goes invisible because it looks like a twig. It's frozen and twig-like on the tree and on the ground. Some things change color, to nature colors, green and brown; some things hold still, some things pretend to be twigs, I get it.

Twenty days of such discussions led to dramatic improvement in both comprehension processes and theme understanding. In Figure 7.3 are the daily independent assessment results of four groups. Students were assigned to reading or listening procedures depending on their decoding competence. RTE refers to reciprocal teaching groups where the teacher mentioned the theme explicitly and RTI refers to groups where the theme is implicit and the teacher did not intervene; however, as most of these groups concentrated on the repeated themes anyway, this turned out not to be an interesting variable. The two control groups are C (control), untreated except for taking the pre- and posttest and P (practice), a group that took all the daily assessments but had no instruction. As can be seen in Figure 7.3, the reciprocal teaching groups' improvement is large and reliable. Even *12 months* later the effect of instruction was apparent.

Each day the discussion and test passages were directly analogous. For example, under the natural pest control theme, the children might discuss the manatees, large sea mammals, that for their own protection (from sharks) were moved inland, where they took to eating the water hyacinths that had previously clogged Florida's inland waterways. The manatees were thus welcomed by the residents because they provided a biological (rather than chemical) solution to an environmental problem. Immediately after discussing this example of a biological deterrent, or natural pest controller, the students read and answered questions on a passage that contained the analogous problem of how to rid a garden of mosquitos, where they are told that (a) purple martins eat mosquitos, and (b) purple martins like to live in man-made bird houses. This crucial information is buried under other facts about the lifestyle of these birds. When asked, in the questioning, how the gardener might rid himself of mosquitos, an observant child would respond like Jeremy:

> ''the house-owner could build a home for purple martins at the bottom of the garden . . . but I think Raid is best—but it's just like the manatees we talked about . . . and the ladybugs eating the farmer's a- a-[Teacher—aphids] right aphids—we talked about that last week.''

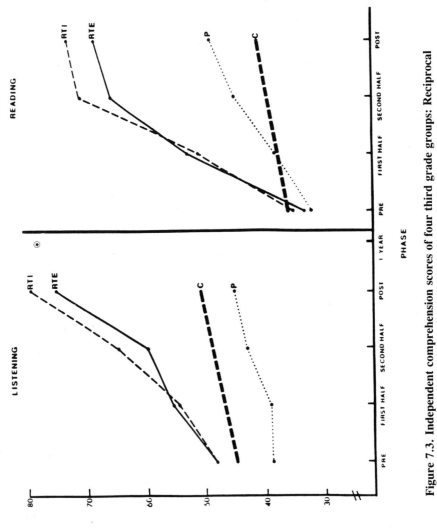

Figure 7.3. Independent comprehension scores of four third grade groups: Reciprocal Teaching Explicit (RTE), Reciprocal Teaching Implicit (RTI), Practice (P), and untreated Control (C). Students were assigned to reading or listening condition based on their decoding competence.

Regular practice greatly improves the ability to use analogous information to solve problems; that is, guided practice creates a mind set to reason by analogy (Brown & Kane, 1988). The children began by noting few of the analogies, but, after several days, they were able to solve 90% of the analogies by cross-reference to the discussion passages.

The students also made use of the analogous themes in their discussion. In Table 7.2, a group of six children are discussing the critical paragraphs in passages about natural pest controllers. Note that the children readily hone in on the usefulness of

Table 7.2. Repetitive Themes in Reciprocal Teaching Dialogues:
Natural Pest Control
Third Grade High Risk Children (N = 6).

Day 5 Ladybugs

Student 1: (*Question*) What do they eat?

Teacher: What do what eat?

Student 1: (*Question*) The ladybugs. What do ladybugs eat?

Student 2: Aphids, little white bugs.

Student 1: (*Question*) Right. Why do farmers like them?

Student 3: Because they eat the little bugs off the farmers' plants.

Student 1: That's the answer I want. (pause)

Student 1: (*Question*) I have another question, where do they live?

(overlapping discussion of potential places to live not accepted because they are not mentioned in the text)

Student 4: I know, they crawl on leaves and rosebuds as in the grass.

Student 1: (*Summary*) Okay it's about the ladybugs that crawl in the grass and help the farmer by eating bad little insects.

Teacher: Good summary.

Day 17 Manatees

Student 4: (*Question*) How does the manatee clean up the river?

Student 3: By eating water plants?

Student 4: No you missed one word.

Student 3: By eating water hedge-whatever.

Teacher: Hyacinth.

Student 4: Yea that's right.

Student 4: (*Question*) How many years ago people moved some of the manatees from the sea in the inland river? Amelia?

Student 6: A few years.

Teacher: (*Scaffolding*) Anne (S$_4$)—another way you could have asked that question would be— *when* did the people move the manatees.

Student 4: (*Question*) What did the people want the manatees to eat?

Student 2: The plants.

Student 4: I want the whole sentence.

Student 2: The people wanted the manatees to eat the water hyacinths that grow in the river.

Student 4: (*Summary*) Okay, that's it; it tells where the people moved them and what they wanted them to eat, and why.

Teacher: Good summary.

Student 1: (*Noting analogy*) The manatees went through and ate all the plants so that's helping like the ladybugs because they eat all the aphids, bad bugs.

Table 7.2. (*continued*)

Year Follow-up Day 1 Lacewings

Student 6:	(*Question*) Okay, what do lacewings eat?
Teacher:	Good question.
Student 5:	Bugs and insects.
Student 3:	Aphids and other bugs.
Student 2:	And, they, eat the farmers' crops.
Students:	No.
Student 6:	(*Clarification and question*) No the bad bugs eat the farmers' crops. Okay, let me see (pause). Are insects nice to crops?
Student 1:	Not always, some are.
Student 6:	(*Question, clarify*) What's the story about, any one need clarifying?
Student 2:	It's about how the lacewing is destroying the insects that are in the fields trying to eat crops.
Student 6:	Okay, people often think of insects as just good for nothing bugs.
Students:	You told the answer. That's not a question.
Student 6:	(*Question*) Okay, let me see (pause). Why does the farmer like the (pause), oh yea, we already know this. I'll ask it anyway. Why does the farmer like the lacewing?
Student 1:	(*Analogy*) Because they can stop other things from eating crops. I remember we read about farmers that don't want animals on their crops because they kill 'em.
Student 2:	They put spray on it?
Student 1:	No ladybugs.
Student 4:	The ladybugs ate them all up so they don't hurt no crops.
Student 6:	So they quit messing up crops.

ladybugs, remember ladybugs 12 days later when discussing the manatees, and finally, even a year later, they discuss the analogy between ladybugs and lacewings.

Not only did the children remember how to conduct the reciprocal teaching dialogues and score well on independent tests, they also remembered the content. Asked to sort pictures of animals into the six themes, they scored 85% correct immediately after being in the study, and 82% correct one year later. Scored as correct were responses where the child could name the theme and justify why the animal in question was an exemplar of that theme. Finally, on both the long- and short-term tests, the children were able to classify novel exemplars of the themes and place them in appropriate habitats. Reciprocal teaching experience enables the children both to learn a body of coherent, usable, knowledge and to develop a repertoire of strategies that will enable them to learn new content on their own.

Reciprocal Teaching and Mathematics Understanding

Reciprocal teaching of text comprehension strategies was originally designed in response to the overwhelming evidence that many children fail to develop such skills on their own. Similarly, there is considerable agreement that the way in which mathematics is taught in school leads to students' failure to understand what they are being taught. Many children master basic algorithms if provided with enough drill and practice, but they have considerable difficulty achieving a robust understanding of the conceptual basis of these algorithms (Gelman & Greeno, 1987;

Resnick, 1988). Students need practice connecting together their fragmentary knowledge into systems of "meaningful mathematics" (Davis, 1984; Noddings, 1985). When this opportunity is provided by an expert classroom teacher, the results are quite dramatic (Lampert, 1986). Lampert's students argue about the meaning of mathematical expressions and attempt to convince each other of the appropriateness of the algorithms they invent. They engage in lively discussions about the meaning of what they are doing, and it is these reflective processes that are largely absent from traditional mathematics classes (Schoenfeld, 1985; Stodolsky, 1988). The question is, can we develop a procedure that would ensure such discussions even when average teachers are engaged in teaching mathematics, that is, the equivalent of reciprocal teaching in reading?

The first problem was to select appropriate strategic activities to scaffold the discussion as, obviously, the reading strategies could not be transported to the new domain unchanged. We decided to use the same selection criteria we had used in the case of reading. Questioning, summarizing, clarifying, and predicting were not randomly selected activities. We settled on them only after *diagnosing* that they were comprehension-monitoring activities rarely engaged in by weak students. They were also selected because they could be readily taught—the student could produce some questions or summaries right from the start, thereby assuring that a discussion of sorts got going; the activities were readily engaged in by inexperienced learners when instructions to "monitor your understanding" or "be strategic" provoked blank stares; and, most important, they were selected because a byproduct of summarizing what one has just read, asking for clarification, and so on is to force comprehension monitoring. If you cannot summarize, you need to reread, seek help, and so forth. The four activities became rituals that ensured that a discussion took place and forced comprehension monitoring of oneself and others.

In order to determine which comprehension activities needed to be practiced in mathematics, we again observed groups of children engaged in the target task, in this case sixth to eighth graders solving algebraic word problems, and diagnosed six characteristic monitoring errors. The students had trouble (a) estimating an approximate answer, (b) extracting relevant facts from the story, for example, the goal, the givens, the unknowns, relations among givens, and so on, (c) keeping track of the quantities that the algebraic expressions stood for (X = the number of marbles that Linda had, etc.), (d) drawing visual representations when appropriate, (e) checking arithmetic facts, and (f) sense making.

Given this diagnosis, we asked what ritual activities comparable to questioning, summarizing, and so on could be used to (a) scaffold a discussion, and (b) force reflection. Note that the choice of the activities was determined not by what experts would do to attack the problems but by what students were failing to do on their own.

Our first step was to introduce a reflection board on which the group externalized their problem-solving activities. All other aspects of the interactive learning environment remained the same. The students worked together with an instructor in small cooperative groups. The students and adult teacher again took turns being learning leaders responsible for leading a discussion aimed at understanding algebra word problems while the others acted as supportive critics. The procedure embodied expert modeling, scaffolding, and coaching on the part of the teacher; the method forced externalization of strategies, monitoring of progress, and attempts to impose meaning. What differed is that the strategies selected to scaffold the discussion were tailored to the domain.

The reflection board is illustrated in Table 7.3. It was designed to be directly responsive to the six characteristic monitoring errors of the target students. The board was designed to support efforts at problem solving and meaning imposition (Resnick, 1988) rather than rote drill and practice. The solution path was made explicit, was in plain sight, and was the object of reflection. The repetitive use of the board both generated an external record of the group's problem-solving attempts, and forced communal monitoring and reflection.

In this implementation, the solution path is parsed into four general categories: goal setting, planning, problem solution, and sense making/checking. *Goal setting* involves stating clearly the exact problem that is to be solved, along with identifying any unknown quantities that are relevant to the problem.

The *planning phase* is the most elaborate and consists of two general sets of activities, one "required" and one "optional." The required component consists of having the student identify the quantities given in the problem, along with the relations between those quantities. It is emphasized that whenever a quantity is selected, a description of that quantity *must be appended* so that students do not lose touch with the semantics of the problem. If the students wish to do so, they can also draw a sketch representing the problem statement and use that to facilitate their planning. It is emphasized that a sketch may help identify the quantities needed to satisfy the goal. Estimation is another optional activity that is incorporated into the planning phase. If desired, students can try to predict what the answer might look like, for example, specify a range of possible solutions or constraints on the solution. And they can do this at any stage in the procedure.

When the group is satisfied that they have extracted all the necessary information, the students proceed to the *problem solution phase*, where they attempt to generate their specific answer. This can be accomplished either by going directly to some arithmetic activities (adding, multiplying, etc.) or by taking the intermediate step of generating a more abstract algebraic representation of the problem (an equation).

Once an answer has been generated, the *sense making/checking phase* begins. This phase involves several related activities, including checking the actual computation for arithmetic errors, checking the answer against the problem statement, or the estimation if there was one to see if the answer makes sense in the context of the actual problem.

Next, the group reflects on the overall problem-solving process to see if they want to make any changes. During this *reflection phase*, the students review the steps taken in solving the problem, discuss choice points that were encountered, talk about alternatives that were or might have been considered, and so on. Particular

Table 7.3. First Pass on Marble Problem.

Problem: John has 4 marbles more than Karen, who has twice as many marbles as Linda. The 3 together have 24. How many does John have?

GOAL: STATE GOAL(S) Number of marbles that John has = X

STATE UNKNOWN(S)   Y = number of marbles Karen has

Z = number of marbles Linda has

Planning	Problem Solution	Sense Making & Checking
State givens and relationships between them	Tutor: You want to find the one unknown. (prompt)	1) Answer make sense?
		2) Computations correct?
Z = 2Y (Karen has twice as many as Linda)	Tutee: I know more about Y so let's get rid of the Z, can I?	3) Review method(s) of solution.
X = Y + 4 (John has 4 more than Karen)		
X + Y + Z = 24 (all 3 together = 24)		
		Checking:
	Equation:	1) 5 + 9 + 10 = 24
	(Y + 4) + Y + Z = 24	
(Error not noticed)	Y + 4 + Y + 2Y = 24	2) John = 9
	4 Y + 4 = 24	Karen = 5, 9 − 5 = 4
	4Y = 20	
	Y = 5 = Karen	
	X = 9 = John	3) Error accepted . . .
Estimating, Sketching, Etc.	Z = 10 = Linda	
		Accept the answer without validating relation between Karen and Linda
	(Error still not noticed)	

153

attention is given to any fix-up strategies that might have been brought into play, that is, methods of identifying unproductive paths and ways of getting the process back on track.

The final component of reflection involves what we term *problem extension*. Here the idea is to pose a variety of related problems, either by modifying some of the quantities included in the original problem, or by exchanging some of the givens for unknowns. The goal is to make clear that the group has been working on not only a single problem, but also one of a family of related problems. To the extent that they understand the quantities involved in the original problem and the relations among those quantities, they should be able to "play" with their specific solution and solve related problems. Thus, extension serves to accentuate the need for understanding the problem, as well as providing a way of checking to see if the students do in fact understand the nature of the solution they have generated. This is also training for transfer which we strongly endorse (Brown & Campione, 1978, 1984).

An example of what a problem path might look like is given in Table 7.3. This represents the first unsuccessful attempt to solve the problem. This solution path was taken from pilot work with an expert tutor and a naive tutee working collaboratively. They begin by stating the goal, the number of marbles John has, which they label X because the tutee believes algebra has to have things like Xs and Ys. They then go on to map out the givens and the relations among them, connecting X, Y, and Z with the quantities. Unfortunately, they confuse Karen and Linda, writing $Z = 2Y$, whose meaning is that Linda has twice as many as Karen rather than the correct $Y = 2Z$, that Karen has twice as many as Linda. They do not detect the error but go on to the problem solution phase, lose track of the quantities, and come up with an answer that satisfies one of the constraints of the problem; $5 + 9 + 10$ does add up to 24 which they check and are duly satisfied, overlooking the fact that Karen has half as many as Linda rather than the reverse.

Although that ended the session, the tutee later reworked some of the problems independently to check on progress. With most of the problems, the correct answer was obtained, a satisfying outcome. However, for the problem shown in Table 7.3, something quite different occurred—the answer was not the same.

This second attempt is shown in Table 7.4. Here the tutee begins by extracting the goal *and estimating* an approximate answer, a step not engaged in on the first go round. The estimate of 12 is also (by chance) the correct answer. During the planning phase, the unknowns are labeled and the tutee is careful to always keep track of the actual quantities tied to the variables. The manipulation (problem solution) phase is successfully negotiated, with decimals converted to whole numbers in order to do the needed division (the tutee had forgotten the algorithm for dividing decimals). Having reached the goal, the arithmetic is checked, and the answer, 12, is checked against the constraints of the problem and the original estimate, with which it fits nicely. The answer, of course, is different from the one reached collaboratively in the teaching session. Noting the difference between the answers in Tables 7.3 and 7.4 prompts a subsequent discussion leading to the detection of the original error and the reason it was made.

Table 7.4. Second Pass on Marble Problem.

Problem: John has 4 marbles more than Karen, who has twice as many marbles as Linda. The 3 together have 24 marbles. How many does John have?

GOAL: STATE GOAL(S) Number of marbles that John has = X = Goal

STATE UNKNOWN(S)   Y = Karen's marbles

                         Z = Linda's marbles

Planning	Problem Solution	Sense Making & Checking
State givens and relationships between them	Equation:	1) Answer make sense?
	$(Y + 4) + Y + Z = 24$	2) Computations correct?
Unknowns:	$(Y + 4) + Y + (1/2)Y = 24$	3) Review method(s) of solution
	$(2\,1/2)Y = 20$	
X = number of marbles John has = Goal	$Y = 20 - (2\,1/2) = 8$	
Y = number of marbles Karen has		
Z = number of marbles Linda has	$\begin{array}{c} 2.5\,\overline{|20} = \\ 25\,\overline{|200} = 8 \end{array}$ $\quad\begin{array}{l} Z = 4 \\ X = 12 \end{array}$	Checking:
		1) $12 + 8 + 4 = 24$
	$X + Y + Z = 24$	
Relations:		2) John = Karen plus 4
$Y = 2Z$ $\quad$ Karen = Linda $\times$ 2 (2Z)	John has 12 marbles = Goal	$Y + 4 = 12$
$X = Y + 4$ $\quad$ John = Karen + 4 (Y + 4)		$Y = 8$
$X + Y + Z = 24$		$8 + 4 = 12$
Estimating, Sketching, Etc.		3) Karen = 8
		Linda = 4 $\quad$ $4 \times 2 = 8$
If all had the same, John would have 8. $(3 \times 8 = 24)$ but John has 4 more than Karen, and Karen twice as many as Linda, so Linda is small, Karen middle and John has the most. Estimate 12 approximately.		4) Answer fits with estimated number.

155

At present, we only had pilot data on the success of these procedures (see Brown & Campione, 1990; Campione, Brown & Connell, 1988), but the initial results are encouraging. Discussions do take place, students are engaged, the reflection board serves the intended purpose of provoking group discussion and argumentation. It remains to be seen if such experiences result in better independent learning than traditional practice as it did in the reciprocal teaching of reading.

Summary. In this section we have reviewed our research program on reciprocal teaching, a procedure intended to provide supportive contexts for learning in a variety of domains. Based on our previous work in the reciprocal teaching of reading comprehension, we have attempted to transfer the philosophy behind the reading work to the new domains. In describing the similarities and differences between reading, science, and math, we illustrate the domain-specific nature of the activities that promote discussion, argumentation, explanation, and reflection, as well as the domain-independent philosophy of the interactive learning environments. The development of these supportive environments has been greatly influenced by our interpretation of Vygotsky's (1978) theory.

Social Interaction and Assessment (Tester-Child Interactions)

Vygotskian notions about the role of social interaction in cognitive development have also influenced our approach to the assessment of individual differences. In defining the zone of proximal development, Vygotsky (1978) distinguished between the levels of performance a student could achieve working either independently or in collaboration with others. He argued that in evaluating this difference, we would be led to consider, not simply the learning *products* of past experience, but also the *processes* of learning as it actually takes place. That is, by observing learning in the zone of proximal development, we would glean information about the efficiency with which students could build up new resources.

This distinction between assessment of the products of prior experience and the learning processes themselves has been made frequently in the literature on testing (Brown & Campione, 1986; Mann, 1979). It is interesting to note that this idea has been particularly salient to those working with disadvantaged populations. For both Vygotsky (1978) and Feuerstein (1980), a major impetus for their attempts to develop alternative assessment methods was the need to evaluate individuals who had been exposed to suboptimal learning environments to say the least. Vygotsky, in his role as director of the Institute of Defectology in Moscow, had the task of dealing with students raised in the aftermath of the Russian Revolution. Feuerstein worked with children who were refugees from displaced persons camps in the wake of the Second World War. In both cases, it was safe to say that students' opportunities for learning had been severely restricted, and that performance on standard tests of aptitude, intelligence, or achievement would provide virtually no valid information. The point is an important one, as standard tests are used for the purposes of prediction and classification of students, with strong implications for the type of educational program they will receive. In the case of both Vygotsky and Feuerstein, their approach was to observe students as they were actually learning to deal with novel problems, and to use this performance as the basis for instructional intervention.

Our own particular approach (Campione & Brown, 1984, 1987) was influenced by (a) translations of Vygotsky's writings (notably *Mind in Society*, 1978), (b) observations of Soviet clinicians' interpretations and implementations of Vygotskian ideas (Brown & French, 1979), and (c) our own longstanding interest in learning and transfer processes as sources of differences between academically successful and less successful students (Brown, 1974, 1978; Brown & Campione, 1978, 1981, 1984; Brown & Ferrara, 1985; Campione & Brown, 1977, 1978, 1984; Campione, Brown, & Ferrara, 1982). Our idea was to assess the facility with which students learned from others and the flexibility with which they could use what they learned. Of interest was whether these indices of learning and transfer would provide important diagnostic information about individual students.

General procedures. Toward this end, we conducted a series of experiments in which we evaluated how much help students needed to come to deal with problems they could not solve individually. The student was set to work on a problem, and the tester/teacher provided a series of hints until the student could solve the problem. The hints provided a form of scaffolding to enable the student to progress. The tester estimated the level of hint required by a student, providing more or less help as needed, just as in "natural" scaffolding (see pp. 162-167). Early hints were quite general, later hints were much more specific, with the tester eventually providing a blueprint for solving a particular problem if the learner failed to catch on. This phase of the process continued until the student could solve an array of target problems with no help from the teacher. The amount of help each student needed was taken as the estimate of her learning efficiency *within that domain* and *at that particular point in time*.

After achieving independent learning, students were given a series of transfer problems, varying in terms of their similarity to the items learned originally. The idea was to evaluate the extent of lateral transfer (Gagne, 1965) that individuals could accomplish, based on a metric of "transfer distance." Transfer problems were classed as involving near, far, or very far transfer as a function of the number of transformations performed on the learning problems to generate the transfer probes. The amount of help needed to deal with each of the transfer problems was then used as an estimate of the student's "transfer propensity" (Campione & Brown, 1984). This transfer performance was taken as an index of the extent to which the students *understood* the procedures they had been taught, that is, having learned the procedures, could they access and modify them in flexible ways? We have applied these general procedures to the domain of inductive reasoning and early mathematics learning.

Inductive Reasoning Tasks

In a series of studies using tasks such as the Raven Progressive Matrices and series completion problems, we were able to establish that the learning and transfer scores possessed reasonable psychometric properties, including both concurrent and predictive validity. In terms of concurrent validity, we found that grade school children of higher academic ability, as compared with those of lower ability, required less help to learn sets of rules and principles, and more readily transferred use of those rules to novel problems (Campione, Brown, Ferrara, Jones, & Steinberg, 1985; Ferrara, Brown, & Campione, 1986). In addition, differences between ability groups were greater on transfer tests than on the initial learning problems, and group differences increased as transfer distance increased. Higher-ability students showed greater degrees of lateral transfer. It appears that academically weak children have particular difficulties applying what they have learned to novel but related situations.

To investigate predictive validity, we conducted a series of studies again involving inductive reasoning tasks. Preschool children were asked to solve either simple series completion items or matrix problems with a format similar to that of the Raven Progressive Matrices, but involving double classification problems. In these studies (Bryant, 1982; Bryant, Brown, & Campione, 1983), children were given a series of pretests assessing both general ability (IQ measures, including subscales of the WPPSI and the Raven Coloured Progressive Matrices) and task-specific competence (unaided performance on the kinds of problems they were later to learn to solve). They were then given sets of learning and transfer sessions as described above and a final posttest on the kinds of problems they had been asked to learn. The transfer sessions included maintenance, near transfer, and far transfer problems as defined above. In these studies, we were particularly interested in the change from pre- to posttest performance, or the extent to which individuals had profited from the instructional sessions; and the specific question was, what are the *best predictors* of this gain score: (a) static scores, that is, general ability, entering competence, or (b) dynamic scores, that is, learning and transfer measures?

The first point to note is that there were large gains from the pretest to the posttest. As Vygotsky and Feuerstein both emphasized, the initial unaided performance is a dramatic underestimate of the level of performance some children can achieve independently after receiving a little aid. There were also sizable differences in the gain scores, and regression analyses were undertaken to determine the factors associated with those differences. The estimated IQ score and the Raven score were related to the gain scores, accounting together for around 36% of their variance. Even after the effects of the ability scores were extracted, however, the learning and transfer scores still accounted for significant additional portions of the variance in gain scores, an additional 39% in the matrices tasks and 22% in the case of series completion. Thus, taking the learning and transfer scores into account did provide further diagnostic information about individual children. Also of note, if one considers the simple correlations, the dynamic learning and transfer scores are better predictors of gain score than either of the static ability measures. Finally, within the set of dynamic measures, the tendency is for the transfer scores to be more strongly associated with gain than the learning index. This latter result is consistent with the earlier studies, where ability group differences were larger on transfer than learning. Even though students had learned the initial problem to the same criterion they differed dramatically in how flexibly they could apply their newfound knowledge.

In short, dynamic assessment measures provide a different picture of individual competence than do traditional static procedures. Static measures tend to underestimate many children's ability to learn in a domain in which they initially perform poorly, and the estimates obtained under more favorable conditions provide greater insights into the current competence. These findings were dramatic when IQ test items were the domain in question. We turn now to the case of mathematics.

Early Mathematics

Having established that guided learning and transfer measures have reasonable psychometric properties, we were interested in extending the method to academically more salient, and conceptually richer, domains. Our choice was early mathematics. This step was taken for both theoretical and practical reasons. Theoretically, there is a dominant view that individual or developmental differences can be explained largely in terms of variations in amount and quality of domain knowledge. In contrast, we emphasize the importance of processing skills underlying the acquisition and use of that knowledge, for how did individuals come to have different amounts of knowledge in the first place (Brown, Bransford, Ferrara, & Campione, 1983)? The strong interpretation of the knowledge position is that students equated for amount and quality of knowledge are equally "ready" to proceed within a domain and should improve at comparable rates. Our contrasting, dynamic, view is that students may have taken different routes to acquire knowledge, and that predictions of future trajectories require an examination of individuals' learning efficiency as well. Although the results of our early studies were consistent with the dynamic view, they could not be said to provide a particularly strong comparative test, since inductive reasoning tasks are featured on standard ability tests in good part because they do not require specific background knowledge. Students are thus equated for knowledge by their lack of it. Mathematics understanding demands knowledge and skill and, therefore, we choose this domain for an extension of our assessment work.

The practical issues are straightforward. There are good reasons to believe that alternative methods of assessment in mathematics need to be developed. Although prediction and classification are still goals of assessment, a more important goal is to guide instruction. As we have noted elsewhere (Brown & Campione, 1986; Campione & Brown, 1987), standard tests do not contribute to this goal. While they may help identify students likely to experience difficulties (i.e., the student is two grade levels behind or in the lowest percentile ranking vís-a-vís her peers), they provide no information on the design of remedial instructional programs. So too, our dynamic measures are silent with respect to instruction. Knowing that a child is a fast learner or a broad transferrer on inductive reasoning rules does not have immediate implications for instruction. An assessment vehicle that is based on sound theoretical analyses of the skills and knowledge required for performance within a domain does, in contrast, have the potential to provide that kind of information. For example, if a child does not have rapid access to number facts, does not understand one-to-one correspondence, counts all rather than counts-on, and so on, we now know what to teach.

Understanding and Assessment in Mathematics

How do we currently measure what children know about mathematics? We do it mainly by teacher evaluation and standardized tests. In both cases, there is a tendency to assume that children who get the answer to a problem right know what they are doing, and those who fail to get it right don't know. In addition, it is assumed that what a child does *now* on a test is a reasonable reflection of his knowledge, and that knowledge *predicts* readiness to learn. Reasonable though they may sound, we quarrel with both assumptions.

Static tests. On standardized tests, children are given a problem, usually in some familiar form. It is assumed that children who get the answer correct know what they are doing, whereas those who get it wrong do not. However, Erlwanger (1973) has shown that getting an answer correct on a test does not mean that the child knows what he is doing. More recently, Peck, Jenks, and Connell (1989) interviewed fourth to sixth graders who had just taken a standardized math test used by their school district for placement in appropriate instructional groups. On the basis of the interviews, they found four types of students: (a) those that got it right and knew why, (b) those who got it wrong and didn't know much at all—the two categories that tests are meant to separate. But there were a large number of students, comprising 41% of the sample, who fell into the other two possible combinations: (c) those who got the wrong answer but understood what they were doing, and (d) those who got the right answer but really did not understand (i.e., they could not resist countersuggestions). Thus, in addition to the general problems with static tests emphasized by Vygotsky and Feuerstein, there are more specific problems encountered in the math domain. These tests do not adequately assess understanding of principles, but rather evaluate algorithm use.

Readiness. It is assumed that the scores obtained on a static test provide an index of the student's readiness to go on to more advanced portions of the curriculum. We also take issue with this position. We argue that readiness can best be assessed by evaluating as directly as possible the student's ability to benefit from instruction. Our work on dynamic assessment is designed to evaluate how rapidly students can acquire skills that are just beyond their current competence. Further, we attempt to assess student understanding of these new skills by evaluating their performance on transfer problems, where they are required to put those nascent skills to work in novel contexts.

Early Mathematics: A Case Study

In a dissertation undertaken by Ferrara (1987), the aim was to extend these analyses to the domain of early arithmetic. The goal was to compare the predictive utility of dynamic learning and transfer measures with measures of overall ability and with indices of students' initial mathematical competence. The research was conducted in two phases—the development of a *theoretically* based static test of number knowledge and the use of that test in a subsequent study comparing its predictive validity with that of standard ability tests, other standardized tests of mathematical skill, and domain-related learning and transfer measures.

Static Test. Although we cannot go into detail here, we can summarize some aspects of the static knowledge test. Eleven subscores were obtained. Three of the subscores measured the child's knowledge of the conventional number-word sequence. Four measured the child's knowledge of basic principles of counting which have been described by Gelman and Gallistel (1978). The final four tapped advanced counting skills. The knowledge test has been administered to several samples of preschoolers with consistent results. Factor analysis indicates the existence of three factors that account for approximately 60% of the variance in test performance. Details of this instrument are given in Ferrara (1987).

Dynamic assessment. The second phase of the research involved 5-year-old children learning to solve word arithmetic addition and subtraction problems. For each child, we had IQ scores, standardized math scores, and initial indices of each subject's ability to solve the targeted problems, along with the knowledge scores derived from the new instrument.

During the initial learning sessions, the student and tester worked collaboratively to solve problems that the student could not solve independently. The problems were simple two-digit addition problems, for example, $3 + 2 = ?$, $5 + 4 = ?$, and so on, presented as word problems, such as:

> Cookie Monster starts out with 3 cookies in his cookie jar, and I'm putting 2 more in the jar. Now how many cookies are there in the cookie jar?

When the student encountered difficulties, the tester provided a sequence of hints or suggestions about how he should proceed. Again, these hints were standardized and proceeded from general to specific. The interaction continued until the student could solve a series of such problems without help, and the amount of aid needed to achieve this degree of competence was recorded.

Following this, a variety of transfer problems were presented in the same interactive, assisted format. These problems required the student to apply the procedures learned originally to a variety of problems that differed in systematic ways from those worked on initially. Some were quite similar (near transfer: addition problems involving new combinations of familiar quantities and different toy and character contexts); others were less similar (far transfer: $4 + 2 + 3 = ?$);

and some were very different indeed (very far transfer: missing addend problems, 4 + ? = 6). What was scored was the amount of help students needed to come to solve these transfer problems on their own. The aim of the transfer sessions was to evaluate understanding of the learned procedures. That is, the goal was to both program transfer and use the flexible application of routines in novel contexts as the measure of understanding. Can students use only what they were taught originally, or can they go further and apply their routines flexibly?

After these learning and transfer sessions were completed, a posttest was given to determine how much the student had learned during the course of the assessment/ instruction, the gain from pre- to posttest. The question of interest concerns which variables or combination of variables best predict the gain scores. The major data are summarized in Table 7.5. The main features are that the dynamic scores are better predictors of gain (mean correlation $= -.57$) than are the static knowledge and ability scores (mean correlation $= .38$). Further, in a hierarchical regression analysis, although the static scores when extracted first did account for 22.2% of the variance in gain scores, the addition of the dynamic scores accounted for an additional 33.7% of the variance, with transfer performance doing the majority of the work; it accounted for 32% of the variance.

Summary. Although static measures of general ability and task-specific competence do predict the amount of gain individuals achieve, the dynamic measures—learning and transfer scores—are: (a) better individual predictors of gain, (b) account for significant additional variance in gain scores beyond ability and knowledge, with (c) transfer, or *understanding*, scores being significantly more diagnostic than learning scores. If the interest is in predicting the learning trajectory of different students, the best indicant is not their IQ or how much they know originally, nor even how readily they acquire new procedures, but how well they understand and make flexible use of those procedures in the service of solving novel problems. Again, the development of these supportive contexts for assessment, just as the supportive contexts for learning described earlier, was influenced by Vygotsky's theory.

Spontaneous Tutoring: Mothers and Children

Beyond formal tutoring, much of cognitive development, according to Vygotsky, is due to more informal interactions, including those between parents and children. Although not necessarily having an explicit instructional goal, parents model and

Table 7.5. Regression Analysis of Gain Scores (from Ferrara, 1987).

Step Variable	F to Enter	p	Mult. R	R^2	R^2 Change	Simple r	Overall F	p
1 Background Knowledge	8.00	.009	.47	.222	.222	.47	8.00	.009
2 IQ	0	.967	.47	.222	.000	.28	3.86	.034
3 Learning	0.58	.454	.49	.239	.017	−.41	2.72	.067
4 Maintenance	18.12	.000	.75	.559	.320	−.73	7.92	.000

$N = 30$

scaffold a number of their children's cognitive skills. It has become an increasingly frequent assumption in the literature that parents aid learning by providing a cognitive scaffold that enables children to solve problems that would be beyond their unassisted efforts (Brown & Reeve, 1987; Wertsch, Minick, & Arns, 1984; Wood & Middleton, 1975). From this perspective, effective learning-teaching involves two interrelated components: (a) the diagnosis by the parent of the child's current level of competence, and (b) the ability of the parent to provide problems that are just beyond the child's current ability level. Though the usefulness of this framework has been demonstrated in carefully controlled research studies with the researcher taking the role of the expert teacher (see pp. 156-162), there is some question regarding the extent to which parents naturally use scaffolding techniques in teaching their preschool children. And we do not really know whether there are any consequences of providing good, poor, or mediocre scaffolding, nor whether parents, like the experimenters in the assessment studies described earlier, can be taught to provide adequate scaffolding.

In this section of the chapter, we consider the functional significance of mothers' teaching strategies for their preschool child's immediate and relatively long-term math problem-solving skills (Reeve, 1987). Again the major reason for focusing on the math domain is that there exists a well-articulated knowledge base about the expected developmental sequence of skill acquisition (e.g., Gelman & Gallistel, 1978; Romberg & Carpenter, 1986). Moreover, although numeracy is highly valued in American culture, with the exception of work by Saxe and his colleagues (e.g., Saxe, Guberman, & Gearhart, 1987), little is known about the role parents play in fostering their child's number skills. Indeed, it is possible that parents have minimal impact on facilitating children's number and computation skills (Gelman & Massey, 1987).

We began by assessing the number and computation ability of a large number of middle-class 4-year-olds in order to select a sample with predetermined characteristics. The selected children (a) could count accurately to 20, (b) counted all presented items rather than counting on from one of the two presented sets of addends (Resnick & Ford, 1981), (c) had a good understanding of the cardinality and order irrelevance number principles (Gelman & Gallistel, 1978), and (d) exhibited poor addition inability when adding together two groups of objects.

Mother-child interactions. The laboratory testing phase was divided into five distinct phases: (a) pretest of child's addition ability, (b) mother-teaching child addition, (c) posttest of child's addition ability, (d) one week follow-up of mother-teaching child addition, and (e) follow-ups of children in their homes four times over a 6-month period.

The addition problems used in the pretest and mother's teaching sessions were all candy problems in which candies were available for counting and the sum of two addends was between 5 and 11. The posttest addition problems were either (a) *identical*, (b) *similar* (candy problems where the sum was greater than 10 but less than 16), or (c) *different*—no candies present.

Mother's teaching style. Of central interest is the mother's teaching style. The mothers were instructed to teach their child to solve candy problems. It was emphasized that the goal of their teaching was for the child to be able to solve similar sets of problems unaided in an immediately following posttest, and they were told to give only the amount of help necessary for the child to solve the immediate problem. What did they do? A coding scheme was developed to capture the mother's "degree of cognitive support." It is illustrated in Table 7.6. On the basis of this coding scheme, three interactive styles were readily and reliably identified (see Reeve, 1987, for further details): (1) *Scaffolding* mothers (n = 20); (2) *Directing* mothers (n = 16); and (3) *Inconsistent* mothers (n = 10). Scaffolding mothers were those who appeared very sensitive to their child's abilities, offering directions contingent upon their child's response to a previous directive. Characteristically, scaffolding mothers rarely took complete responsibility for their child's problem-solving (level 6 directive in Table 7.6). In contrast, directing mothers frequently gave level 5 and level 6 directions, taking charge cognitively of problem-solving activity. Scaffolding mothers appeared to be using what might be termed a "joint-referring style" (Clark & Wilkes-Gibbs, 1986). A mother would start to give information on how to solve part of the problem (e.g., how to line up candies so they can be counted), but the child would elaborate upon the mother's comment before she had finished speaking. In contrast, the children of directing mothers took a more passive role. Directing mothers tended to give clear and concise directions to their children who, in turn, waited until their mothers had finished speaking before responding to the directive. Inconsistent mothers appeared not to exhibit an identifiable teaching pattern, at least in the context of the coding scheme used in the current study.

These interactive styles were relatively consistent. When the mothers revisited the laboratory one week after the initial tutoring session, 17 of the 20 initial scaffolding mothers were classified similarly on the second occasion; 14 of the 16 directing mothers were similarly classified; and all 10 of the inconsistent mothers were classified the same way.

Table 7.6. Classification of Mother's Instructional Directives in Terms of "Degree of Cognitive Support."

Level	Allocation of Responsibility
1	Mother cedes all cognitive responsibility to child. Child is simply urged to solve problem.
2	Focuses child on problem, but urges child to solve problem by herself.
3	Mother breaks problem down into subgoals, urges child to solve problem, but does not inform child how to solve problem.
4	Mother decomposes problem into subgoals and identifies potential problem-solving strategies, but child left to apply the strategies.
5	Mother provides all problem-solving steps and leads child through the problem, but encourages child to provide the answer.
6	Mother assumes responsibility for entire problem-solving sequence and may even produce the answer for the child to repeat.

Table 7.7. Proportion of Problems Solved Correctly on Pretest and Posttest.

Mothers Group	Pretest	Type of Posttest Problem		
		Identical	Similar	Different
Scaffold	.31	.62	.27	.15
Direct.	.30	.27	.13	.15
Inconsist.	.36	.25	.13	.13

Effect of teaching style. The proportion of problems solved correctly is shown in Table 7.7. There were no differences in the pretest performance of children whose mothers would subsequently be classified as scaffolding or otherwise. This raises an interesting question: If scaffolding is a consistent style, and these mothers do engage in it spontaneously, why is it that their children do no better initially? It could be that the mothers have not concentrated on addition. Or it could be that spontaneous scaffolding is actually rare, appearing in laboratory studies because of the demand characteristics of such settings. But within this study scaffolding was effective. As can be seen in Table 7.7, the children of mothers in the scaffolding group outperformed the children in the other groups, and the effect was especially pronounced for identical problems.

Training mothers to scaffold. Given that scaffolding was related to improved performance, the next question was, could mothers be instructed in the method? After all, in the assessment studies described earlier in this chapter, an experimenter was trained in the method and used it with success. Therefore, in the long-term follow-up to the study, a subsample of children was evaluated four more times over a 6-month period (Scaffolding $n = 15$, Directing $n = 13$). All testing occurred in the home. Immediately prior to the beginning of the follow-up assessments, half of the mothers in both groups were taught the principles of scaffolding, and were encouraged to use that teaching technique. Mothers were shown a tape of a good scaffolder, and the experimenter discussed the philosophy of scaffolding cognitive activity with them. The remaining mothers were given no additional instructions.

The data from the follow-up study are shown in Table 7.8. First it is interesting to note that the advantage shown by children of scaffolding mothers on the laboratory posttest has dissipated by the first in-home test. Again this raises the question of the frequency or effectiveness of the scaffolding experiences outside laboratory settings. But within the study, the effects of scaffolding are apparent. The children of mothers who were initially identified as scaffolders outperformed the children of mothers who were initially classified as directors. In addition, the children of mothers who received training in scaffolding solved more problems correctly than the children of mothers who were given no additional instructions.

Although all children solved more problems correctly over time, the children of scaffolders improved at a faster rate than did the children of directors. Moreover, the children of the trained mothers improved more quickly than did the children of

Table 7.8. Mean Number of Problems Correct in the Home Follow-Up Evaluations (from Reeve, 1987).

GRP	Time 1			Time 2			Time 3			Time 4		
	Same	Sim.	Diff.	Same	Sim.	Diff.	Same	Sim.	Diff.	Same	Sim.	Diff.
ST	2.7	2.1	1.5	2.8	2.4	2.4	4.3	3.5	2.9	5.4	4.3	2.8
SNT	2.4	2.3	2.1	2.6	2.6	2.8	3.6	3.4	2.6	4.3	3.4	2.9
DT	2.6	2.4	1.0	2.6	2.3	1.0	3.1	2.6	1.7	4.4	2.9	1.7
DNT	2.8	1.7	1.5	2.2	1.5	1.3	2.5	1.8	1.8	2.7	1.3	1.5

(Time of Test and Problem Type)

1. Groups: ST = Scaffold Training (n = 8); SNT = Scaffold No Training (n = 7); DT = Directing Training (n = 7); DNT = Directing No Training (n = 6).
2. Problem types: Same = Candy problems, where the sum of the two addends is greater than 5 and less than 11; Similar = Candy problems, where the sum of the two addends is greater than 10 and less than 16; Different = Word problems, where the sum of the two addends is greater than 5 and less than 11.
3. Six problems of each of the three types were given to children on each test occasion.

the untrained mothers. Training had a greater impact on some problem types. This latter finding appears due to the relatively rapid improvement of ''same'' and ''similar'' problems over time for the training compared to the non-training groups; the ''different'' problems, in contrast, did not appear to be similarly affected by training.

Finally, some of the children of scaffolding mothers moved toward using more sophisticated problem-solving strategies during the course of the study. Children were selected for the study because they used some version of a count-all strategy (Resnick & Ford, 1981), typically pointing to all the to-be-counted items in sequence. At the conclusion of the study, 8 out of 15 of the scaffolded children, but only 1 out of 13 of the directed children, exhibited some form of counting-on strategy, typically counting-on from the first mentioned addend. The count-on strategy is thought to represent increased numeracy sophistication.

Summary. There are four major outcomes of our study of mother-child interactions. First, it is clear that we can identify differences in teaching style. Second, such differences are relatively stable at least over short periods of time, in the same cognitive domain, and under the demand characteristics of laboratory settings. Third, scaffolding does lead to more effective problem solving. And fourth, mothers can be trained to improve their scaffolding style.

What remains unclear is just how often mothers engage in these activities on their own volition. Note that the ''scaffolded'' children did not begin as better problem solvers. And the beneficial effects of scaffolded instructions had dissipated by the time of the first home visit. Is it the case that mothers rarely engage in such practices? Gelman and Massey's (1987) observation of parents and children at a numbers display in a museum suggest that only a very few children are subjected to such parental aid. The frequency and efficiency of such practices warrants investigation on both theoretical and practical grounds.

Conclusion

We have reviewed an extensive research program conducted in our laboratory over the last 10 years. The work was influenced by our interpretation of Vygotsky's theory, particularly as expounded in the translations in *Mind and Society* (1978). We have considered both assessment and instruction in innovative social settings. Interactive learning environments, where a mother, a peer, a teacher, or a tester provide graduated aid, both promote and reveal competence hitherto unsuspected on the basis of independent performance. Children perform activities in the social context that later become part of their individual repertoire of cognitive competence.

Common to our innovative learning and assessment environments is the key notion of supportive contexts for learning. Four main principles are involved: (a) Fostering conceptual *understanding* of procedures rather than just speed and accuracy should be the aim of assessment and instruction; (b) *expert guidance* is used to reveal as well as promote independent competence; (c) *proleptic teaching* aims at one stage beyond current performance, in anticipation of levels of competence not yet achieved individually but possible within supportive learning settings; and (d) *microgenetic analysis* permits estimates of learning as it actually occurs (Brown & Campione, 1986).

References

Bereiter, C., & Bird, M. (1985). Use of thinking aloud in identification and teaching of reading comprehension strategies. *Cognition and Instruction, 2*, 131–156.

Brown, A. L. (1974). The role of strategic behavior in retardate memory. In N. R. Ellis (Ed.), *International review of research in mental retardation* (Vol. 7, pp. 55–111). New York: Academic Press.

Brown, A. L. (1978). Knowing when, where, and how to remember: A problem of metacognition. In R. Glaser (Ed.), *Advances in instructional psychology* (Vol. 1, pp. 77–165). Hillsdale, NJ: Erlbaum.

Brown, A. L., Bransford, J.D., Ferrara, R. A., & Campione, J. C. (1983). Learning, remembering, and understanding. In J. H. Flavell & E. M. Markman (Eds.), *Handbook of child psychology* (Vol. 3, pp, 77-166). New York: Wiley.

Brown, A. L., & Campione, J. C. (1978).Permissible inferences from the outcome of training studies in cognitive development research. *Quarterly Newsletter of the Institute for Comparative Human Development, 2*, 46–53.

Brown, A. L., & Campione, J. C. (1981). Inducing flexible thinking: A problem of access. In M. Friedman, J. P. Das, & N. O'Connor (Eds.), *Intelligence and learning* (pp. 515–530). New York: Plenum Press.

Brown, A. L., & Campione, J. C. (1984). Three faces of transfer: Implications for early competence, individual differences, and instruction. In M. Lamb, A. Brown, & B. Rogoff (Eds.), *Advances in developmental psychology* (Vol. 3, pp. 143–192). Hillsdale, NJ: Erlbaum.

Brown, A. L., & Campione, J. C. (1986). Psychological theory and the study of learning disabilities. *American Psychologist, 41*(10), 1059–1068.

Brown, A. L., & Campione, J. C. (1990). Interactive learning environments and the teaching of science and mathematics. In M. H. Gardner, J. G. Greeno, F. Reif, A. H. Schoenfeld, A. DiSessa, & E. Stage (Eds.), *Towards a scientific practice of science education* (pp. 111–139). Hillsdale, NJ: Erlbaum.

Brown, A. L., & Day, J. D. (1983). Macrorules for summarizing texts: The development of expertise. *Journal of Verbal Learning and Verbal Behavior, 22*(1), 1–14.

Brown, A. L., & Ferrara, R. A. (1985). Diagnosing zones of proximal development: An alternative to standardized testing? In J. Wertsch (Ed.), *Culture, communication and cognition: Vygotskian perspectives* (pp. 273–305). New York: Cambridge University Press.

Brown, A. L., & French, L. A. (1979). The zone of potential development: Implications for intelligence testing in the year 2000. *Intelligence, 3*, 253–271.

Brown, A. L., & Kane, M. J. (1988). Preschool children can learn to transfer: Learning to learn and learning from example. *Cognitive Psychology, 20*(4), 493–523.

Brown, A. L., & Palincsar, A. S. (1982). Inducing strategic learning from texts by means of informed, self-control training. *Topics in Learning and Learning Disabilities, 2*(1), 1–17.

Brown, A. L., & Palincsar, A. S. (1989). Guided cooperative learning and individual knowledge acquisition. In L. B. Resnick (Ed.), *Knowing, learning and instruction: Essays in honor of Robert Glaser* (pp. 393–451). Hillsdale, NJ: Erlbaum.

Brown, A. L., & Reeve, R. A. (1987). Bandwidths of competence: The role of supportive contexts in learning and development. In L. S. Liben (Ed.), *Development and learning: Conflict or congruence?* (pp. 173–223). Hillsdale, NJ: Erlbaum.

Bryant, N. R. (1982). *Preschool children's learning and transfer of matrices problems: A study of proximal development.* Unpublished master's thesis, University of Illinois, Urbana-Champaign.

Bryant, N. R., Brown, A. L., & Campione, J. C. (1983, April). *Preschool children's learning and transfer of matrices problems: Potential for improvement.* Paper presented at the Society for Research in Child Development meetings, Detroit, MI.

Campione, J. C., & Brown, A. L. (1977). Memory and metamemory development in educable retarded children. In R. V. Kail, Jr. & J. W. Hagen (Eds.), *Perspectives on the development of memory and cognition* (pp. 367–406). Hillsdale, NJ: Erlbaum.

Campione, J. C., & Brown, A. L. (1978). Toward a theory of intelligence: Contributions from research with retarded children. *Intelligence, 2*, 279–304.

Campione, J. C., & Brown, A. L. (1984). Learning ability and transfer propensity as sources of individual differences in intelligence. In P. H. Brooks, R. Sperber, & C. McCauley (Eds.), *Learning and cognition in the mentally retarded*. Baltimore: University Park Press.

Campione, J. C., & Brown, A. L. (1987). Linking dynamic assessment with school achievement. In C. Lidz (Ed.), *Dynamic assessment* (pp. 82–115). New York: Guilford Publications.

Campione, J. C., Brown, A. L., & Connell, M. L. (1988). Metacognition: On the importance of understanding what you are doing. In R. I. Charles & E. A. Silver (Eds.), *Research agenda for mathematics education: The teaching and assessing of mathematical problem solving* (pp. 392–490). Hillsdale, NJ: Erlbaum.

Campione, J. C., Brown, A. L., & Ferrara, R. A. (1982). Mental retardation and intelligence. In R. J. Sternberg (Ed.), *Handbook of human intelligence*. New York: Cambridge University Press.

Campione, J. C., Brown, A. L., Ferrara, R. A., Jones, R. S., & Steinberg, E. (1985). Breakdown in flexible use of information: Intelligence-related differences in transfer following equivalent learning performance. *Intelligence, 9*, 297–315.

Carey, S. (1985). *Conceptual change in childhood*. Cambridge, MA: Bradford Press.

Chukovsky, K. (1968). *From 2 to 5*. Berkeley: University of California Press.

Clark, H. H., & Wilkes-Gibbs, D. (1986). Referring as a collaborative process. *Cognition, 22*, 1–39.

Davis, R. B. (1984). *Learning mathematics: The cognitive science approach to mathematics education.* Norwood, NJ: Ablex.

Durkin, D. (1984). Do basal manuals teach reading comprehension? In R. C. Anderson, J. Osborn, & R. J. Tierney (Eds.), *Learning to read in American schools: Basal readers and content texts* (pp. 29–38). Hillsdale, NJ: Erlbaum.

Erlwanger, S. H. (1973). Benny's conception of rules and answers in IPI Mathematics. *Journal of Children's Mathematical Behavior, 1*(2), 7–26.

Ferrara, R. A. (1987). *Learning mathematics in the zone of proximal development: The importance of flexible use of knowledge.* Ph.D. dissertation, Department of Psychology, University of Illinois at Urbana-Champaign.

Ferrara, R. A., Brown, A. L., & Campione, J. C. (1986). Children's learning and transfer of inductive reasoning rules: Studies in proximal development. *Child Development, 57*(5), 1087–1099.

Feuerstein, R. (1980). *Instrumental enrichment: An intervention program for cognitive modifiability.* Baltimore: University Park Press.

Gagne, R. M. (1965). *The conditions of learning.* New York: Holt, Rinehart & Winston.

Gelman, R. (1986, August). *First principles for structuring acquisition.* Presidential Address to Division 7 of the American Psychological Association, Washington, DC.

Gelman, R., & Brown, A. L. (1985). *Early foundations of cognitive development.* The 1985 Annual Report for the Center for Advanced Study in the Behavioral Sciences, Stanford, CA.

Gelman, R., & Gallistel, C. R. (1978). *The child's understanding of number.* Cambridge, MA: Harvard University Press.

Gelman, R., & Greeno, J. G. (1987). On the nature of competence: Principles for understanding in a domain. In L. B. Resnick (Ed.), *Knowing, learning and instruction: Essays in honor of Robert Glaser* (pp. 125–186). Hillsdale, NJ: Erlbaum.

Gelman, R., & Massey, C. M. (1987). The cultural unconscious as contributor to the supporting environments for cognitive development. In G. B. Saxe, S. R. Guberman, & M. Gearhart (Eds.) *Social processes in early number development* (pp. 138–152). *Monographs of the Society for Research in Child Development, S2* (2, Serial No. 216).

Griffen, P., & Cole, M. (1984). Current activity for the future: The Zo-ped. In B. Rogoff & J. V. Wertsch (Eds.), *Children's learning in the "zone of proximal development* (pp. 45–64)." San Francisco: Jossey-Bass.

Harris, P. L., Kruithof, A., Terwogt, M. M., & Visser, P. (1981). Children's detection and awareness of textual anomaly. *Journal of Experimental Child Psychology, 31*, 212–230.

Inhelder, B., Sinclair, H., & Bovet, M. (1974). *Learning and the development of cognition.* Cambridge, MA: Harvard University Press.

Karmiloff-Smith, A., & Inhelder, B. (1974–5). If you want to get ahead, get a theory. *Cognition, 3*(3), 195–212.

Lampert, M. (1986). Knowing, doing, and teaching multiplication. *Cognition and Instruction, 3*(4), 305–342.

Mann, L. (1979). *On the trail of process: A historical perspective on cognitive processes and their training.* New York: Grune & Stratton.

Noddings, N. (1985). Formal models of knowing. In E. Eisner (Ed.), *Learning and teaching the ways of knowing: Eighty-four yearbook of the National Society for the Study of Education* (Part II pp. 116–132). Chicago: Chicago University Press.

Palincsar, A. S., & Brown, A. L., (1984). Reciprocal teaching of comprehension-fostering and monitoring activities. *Cognition and Instruction, 1*(2), 117–175.

Palincsar, A. S., & Brown, A. L. (1986). Interactive teaching to promote independent learning from text. *The Reading Teacher, 39*(8), 771–777.

Peck, D. M., Jencks, S. M., & Connell, M. L. (1989). Improving instruction via brief interviews. *Arithmetic Teacher 37*(3), 15–17.

Piaget, J. (1950). *The psychology of intelligence.* London: Routledge & Kegan Paul.

Piaget, J. (1967). *Biologie et connaissance.* Paris: Gallimard.

Piaget, J. (1976). *The grasp of consciousness: Action and concept in the young child.* Cambridge, MA: Harvard University Press.

Reeve, R. A. (1987, April). *The functional significance of parental scaffolding as a moderator of social influences on children's cognition.* Paper presented at the biennial meeting of the Society for Research in Child Development, Baltimore, MD.

Resnick, L. B. (1988). Treating mathematics as an ill-structured discipline. In R. Charles & E. A. Silver (Eds.), *Research agenda for mathematics education: The teaching and assessing of mathematical problem solving* (pp. 32–60). Hillsdale, NJ: Erlbaum.

Resnick, L. B., & Ford, W. W. (1981). *The psychology of mathematics for instruction.* Hillsdale, NJ: Erlbaum.

Rogoff, B., & Gardner, W. (1984). Adult guidance of cognitive development. In B. Rogoff & J. Lave (Eds.), *Everyday cognition: Its development in social context* (pp. 95–116). Cambridge, MA: Harvard University Press.

Romberg, T. A., & Carpenter, T. P. (1986). Research on teaching mathematics: Two disciplines of scientific inquiry. In M. C. Wittrock (Ed.), *The handbook of research on teaching* (3rd ed., pp. 850–873). New York: Macmillan Publishing Co.

Saxe, G. B., Guberman, S. R., & Gearhart, M. (1987). *Social processes in early number development. Monographs of the Society for Research in Child Development, S2* (2, Serial No. 216).

Schoenfeld, A. H. (1985). *Mathematical problem solving.* New York: Academic Press.

Stodolsky, S. (1988). *The subject matter: Classroom activity in math and social studies.* Chicago: University of Chicago Press.

Vygotsky, L. S. (1978). *Mind in society: The development of higher psychological processes* (M. Cole, V. John-Steiner, S. Scribner, & E. Souberman, Eds. and Trans.). Cambridge, MA: Harvard University Press.

Wertsch, J. V., Minick, N., & Arns, F. J. (1984). The creation of context in joint problem solving. In B. Rogoff & J. Lave (Eds.), *Everyday cognition: Its development in a social context* (pp. 151–171). Cambridge, MA: Harvard University Press.

Wertsch, J. V., & Stone, C. A. (1979). *A social interactional analysis of learning disabilities remediation.* Paper presented at the International Conference of the Association for Children with Learning Disabilities, San Francisco, CA.

Whitehead, A. N. (1916). *The aims of education.* Address to the British Mathematical Society. Manchester, England.

Wood, D., & Middleton, D. (1975). A study of assisted problem-solving. *British Journal of Psychology, 66,* 181–191.

Yager, S., Johnson, D. W., & Johnson, R. T. (1985). Oral discussion, group to individual transfer, and achievement in cooperative learning groups. *Journal of Educational Psychology, 77,* 60–66.

8

Peer Collaboration as a Context for Cognitive Growth

Erin Phelps
Radcliffe College

William Damon
Brown University

Any theory of instruction recognizes that cognitive growth can be stimulated in a number of ways. The real question for instructional theory is not whether learning can be fostered in diverse ways, but whether variations in forms of stimulation make a difference for the quantity or quality of knowledge that is learned.

This is, of course, the same question that must be asked more generally by any "social interactional" theory of development. All theories tell us that social interaction plays an essential role, and that many different types of social interaction make a contribution. The interesting part is when a theory links a type of social interaction to a particular cognitive acquisition, as for example, when Piaget wrote that relations of unilateral respect foster heteronomous moral concepts whereas relations of mutual respect foster autonomous ones (Piaget, 1965; Youniss, 1980).

This kind of "relational analysis" is necessary if we are ever to understand adequately and improve the contexts for children's learning. Unfortunately, the state of the art has not progressed very far in this direction. In this paper we take one step towards such an endeavor. We analyze here the special features and outcomes of a type of social interaction as a learning context that we have studied closely— the peer collaboration engagement.

Our interest in peer collaboration springs from our belief that it provides a form of social discourse with properties that are unavailable in most instructional relations. We believe that these properties are especially conducive to conceptual insights that depart radically from a learner's previous ways of knowing. We do not believe, however, that peer collaboration provides the one answer to children's education. Our expectation is that many important learning achievements are best accomplished in other settings. Thus we reach out for a pluralistic social interactional approach to the question of how instruction facilitates cognitive growth.

Parameters of Adult/Child Instructional Interactions

In order to provide a framework for understanding the overarching research/ instructional question of what social forms are best suited for learning what kinds of material, and how our research addresses one part of it, we can use some of Wertsch's (1984) work in the area of adult/child interaction as a contrast. This form has been studied more often than peer/peer interactions (cf. Rogoff, Malkin, & Gilbride, 1984; Saxe, Gearhart, & Guberman, 1984) and shows clearly the steps involved in making the connections between developing a social interactional analysis of the instructional form, deriving a process model of how the instructional form yields particular cognitive benefits, and providing a set of empirical associations between the form and hypothesized cognitive benefits.

Wertsch (1984) has offered a Vygotskian analysis of the social interaction patterns that characterize instructional dialogues between adults and children. The particular dialogue that Wertsch depicts arises from an experimental paradigm in which an adult helps a child construct a copy of a model. Adult and child approach the task with different understandings. Whereas the adult defines the task as a replication procedure, the child focuses solely on its construction aspect. Wertsch contrasts the two differing understandings by analyzing the "strategic, goal-directed action patterns" that result from each:

Action pattern 1 (Adult)

Step 1:   Consult the model to determine the identity and location of the piece needed next.
Step 2:   Select the piece identified in Step 1 from the pieces pile.
Step 3:   Add the piece selected in Step 2 to the copy object in accordance with its location in the model.

Action pattern 2 (Child)

Step 1:   Select a piece from the pieces pile.
Step 2:   Add the piece selected in Step 1 to the copy.

According to this analysis, the major instructional problem in the adult/child transaction is the negotiation of goals and strategic steps towards those goals. The two parties start from different sets of assumptions about the purpose of the task and the strategies to be used. If they are to communicate at all in solving the task, they must find a common ground for their collaboration. For both parties, this will require a qualitative shift in the definition of task goals.

The adult/child instructional transaction is based on a fundamental asymmetry: It is the adult, not the child, who plays the leading role in forging the "common ground" redefinition of the task goals. Further, for the adult, task redefinition is only temporary, and subsumes the further goal of helping the child gain an improved understanding of the task. The child, on the other hand, profits permanently from the act of task redefinition, because this act brings with it new insights about problem-solving goals and strategies.

The adult assumes the leading role through a series of guiding questions and directives. Sometimes these are quite explicit, as in:

1.   Pick up that red one and put it next to the blue one.

Sometimes they are more probing and ambiguous, as in:

2.   Show me what you need next.

The second example, of course, represents the Socratic method of teaching, whereas the first example represents a direct transfer-of-information approach. Whether the Socratic method more effectively provokes learning than direct teaching is a matter that has been debated for generations, and we have nothing further to add to this debate at the present time. However, the efficacy of each can be empirically tested. The point for now is that these two approaches, though different in spirit from one another, still have some core similarity. This similarity tells us something about the essential quality of adult/child instructional interactions.

Both methods rely on the adult's leading role and both communicate to the child a common ground between the child's task goals and the differing ones held by the adult. In the case above, this common ground between adult and child is the subgoal of using a particular piece, rather than just any piece, for the construction task. Eventually the adult will link this subgoal to another subgoal—perhaps, for example, linking the particular piece selected back to a matching one in the model. If successful, the instruction ultimately will result in the child's adopting the overall task goal of replicating the model.

With the child's acceptance of new goals comes insights about how to plan for these goals and achieve them through means-ends strategies. The adult/child collaboration guides the child towards goal-related acts that the child at that time could not possibly have accomplished alone. In the process, the child has the opportunity to learn through, about, and as a consequence of such acts.

Thus, it is easy to see how the asymmetrical leadership patterns in adult/child relations creates a particular kind of communicative setting that fosters particular sorts of mental sets. As Wertsch and his colleagues have shown, from adult/child interactions we can expect cognitive products like planning, goal-directedness, and means-ends reasoning on the one hand. On the other hand, as Piaget and Youniss have shown (Piaget, 1965; Youniss, 1980), we also can expect heteronomy and a centering on the existing order of things. Within these broad parameters, there are many significant variations in adult/child instructional dialogues, as in the two alternatives presented in the model-building example above. It remains for future research to link empirically such alternatives to their respective cognitive outcomes.

Peer Collaboration

As noted earlier, we also know from Piaget, Youniss, and others that peer/peer relations may foster a different sort of mental set than does adult/child interaction. Piaget loosely characterized this as "autonomous thinking"—a construct whose application, however, he limited to the moral domain. We believe that autonomous thinking occurs in the cognitive domain as well. Below we discuss such cognitive outcomes in relation to one type of peer engagement, a group learning format that we call "peer collaboration."

We have chosen peer collaboration as our extended "case in point" because we believe it to be the quintessential form of genuinely *peer* learning. Unlike "peer tutoring," for example, peer collaboration establishes an equal relation between its participants (Damon, 1984; Damon & Phelps, 1988). This is because none of the learners in a peer collaboration format is granted "expert" or "tutor" status (at least by adults). For our purposes, such a setting, with its extreme encouragement of interactional equality, enables us to characterize the special qualities of peer learning by observing its purest form.

In peer collaboration, a pair of children work together to solve tasks that neither could do previously. Peer collaboration forces children to communicate about task-solving strategies and solutions. It simulates the challenges of discovery learning, but places these challenges in a context of peer assistance and support. Like discovery learning, its promise lies in provoking conceptual insights and basic developmental shifts on the part of its participants. This is because it encourages experimentation with new and untested ideas and demands a critical reexamination of one's old assumptions. But it is a group, rather than an individual, form of discovery learning. Unlike individual discovery learning, where the child may feel like an isolated incompetent, peer collaboration provides a sympathetic forum for this sort of creative risk taking. As the child works with a fellow novice, the insufficiencies in his or her own knowledge become less discouraging and the challenge of discovery becomes less forbidding.

Peer collaboration as a systematic learning strategy emerged from Piagetian intervention studies in this country and abroad. Peer collaboration has proven to be the most consistently effective means of helping children acquire conservation and the basic reasoning skills underlying it (Damon, 1984). The dominant explanation of the success of peer collaboration has been the Genevan construct of "socio-cognitive conflict" (Doise, Mugny, & Perret-Clermont, 1976).

The idea is that social interactions between peers will inevitably lead to disagreements that present the participants with both a social and a cognitive conflict. This unsettling experience in turn leads children to a number of important realizations. First, they become aware that there are points of view other than their own. This is the Piagetian process of "decentering." Second, they reexamine their own points of view and reassess their validity. Third, they learn that they must justify their own opinions and communicate them thoroughly if others are to accept them as valid.

In this way, children can benefit both cognitively and socially from peer collaboration. The social benefits are their improved communication skills and their sharper sense of other persons' perspectives. The cognitive benefits derive from their forced reexamination of their own conceptions because of a peer's feedback. Piaget believed that these social and cognitive benefits were directly related, in that improved social communication instigates progressive change. When people feel the need to explain and justify their beliefs to others, they realize that these beliefs must be rationalized as fully as possible. This sense of "social responsibility" in communication ultimately leads to improvements in the logical quality of one's reasoning.

Piagetian theory, therefore, suggests that peer collaborations lead to learning because it creates a conflict of ideas. This conflict forces children to reexamine and rework their understanding of the world, thus triggering conceptual growth. This triggering process, it should be noted, does not provide the substance or "stuff" of change. In Piagetian theory the perturbing, conflictual feedback provided by peer interaction initiates a process of intellectual reconstruction, but it does not do the main work of formulating new knowledge. This is done by the individual, in solitary reflection, through symbolic manipulations of the world and inferences based on these manipulations. The ideas themselves, in other words, remain the product of the child's internal reasoning processes.

An alternative explanation emphasizes more the constructive, or "co-constructive" aspects of peer collaboration. In this view, elaborated by Youniss, children learn through peer interaction because it introduces children to the possibilities of cooperative activity (Youniss, 1980). In a cooperative effort, children devise plans together, share ideas, and mutually validate one another's initiatives. Not only is this a powerful procedure for generating new insights, it also yields solutions that are superior to those arrived at by an individual in isolation. Thus it can provide the substance of new ideas as well as the incentive to reformulate old ones—an important contrast to the Genevan position outlined above.

Unfortunately, there have been very few studies that have attempted to identify the peer interaction processes leading to progressive change. This requires lengthy and complex videotape analyses of the sort not always available in experimental studies. But the few empirical hints that we do have from such research also places in question the sociocognitive conflict model of learning through peer collaboration.

For example, in a training study of distributive justice concepts, children who disagreed with one another the most were the least likely to progress, whereas children who accepted one another's views and worked positively with them were the most likely to change (Damon & Killen, 1982). Constructive rather than conflictual interaction was clearly the key facilitator. A study of spatial concepts found that large degrees of conflict in peer dyads was inversely related to change (Bearison, Magzamen, & Filardo, 1986). This study also reported that moderate conflict was associated with change, but assessed moderate conflict in a way that made it indistinguishable from co-constructive activity. Finally, a recent analysis of peer interaction processes during task engagement found such interactions to be heavily loaded with "transactive" activity (Kruger & Tomasello, 1986). Transactions constitute a constructively-compromising form of social discourse especially suited for joint exploration into unknown areas of thought.

Peer collaboration, then, is a promising method of spurring basic conceptual development in children, but we still have much to learn about its nature and its potential. In particular, we need to know the interactional conditions under which peer collaborative learning flourishes. As was the case with Wertsch's adult–child instructional form, there are two (and possibly other) processes that have been identified as potential causes of cognitive gains. We would like to know the extent to which sociocognitive conflict promotes learning and the extent to which other notions like "co-construction" or "transaction" provide a more fertile context. What are the limits of peer collaboration in relation to other forms of peer learning, and what are its special strengths? How may peer collaboration be integrated with the other peer learning paradigms, and with other instructional models in general?

A Study of Children's Learning through Peer Collaboration

Some of our current work will be used to illustrate the benefits of peer collaboration in the domain of logical physical reasoning. These data come from a larger, longitudinal study of social interaction between pairs of children working together on a series of mathematical or spatial reasoning task (described in greater detail in Damon & Phelps, 1988). In the first year, fourth graders were assigned either to a mathematics or spatial problems group; the following year, they worked on a set of balance scale problems. The design of the study was determined by the desire to address several questions about how and under what conditions peer collaboration might promote learning in these areas. Among these research questions were:

1. Can children of equal abilities, working together with minimal adult assistance, make significant strides in achieving an understanding of basic math and science concepts?
2. Are some areas of math and science more amenable to learning through peer collaboration than other areas?
3. Assuming that some children will show marked gains through peer collaboration while others may not, are there differences in children's social interaction patterns that may explain how the "gainers" are able to profit from peer engagement?

In general, it appears that peer collaboration is an effective learning environment for tasks that require logical reasoning, but not for rote learning or copying situations. Further, some of the social interaction patterns that differentiate "gainers" from "nongainers" are beginning to be identified.

The design and results of the pretest-posttest analyses are briefly described in order to show that peer collaboration is an effective context for learning. This information provides the background for the following discussion of what occurs during the interactions themselves that differentiates pairs who change from those who do not.

In the first year, 152 fourth graders were randomly assigned to one of four groups, two intervention groups and two control groups. The two intervention groups participated in six weekly sessions in which they worked with math or spatial reasoning materials, and sessions 1 and 6 were videotaped. In Year 2, children in the original two intervention groups and children in one of the control groups participated in a six-week intervention with a series of increasing difficult balance scale problems. As in Year 1, sessions 1 and 6 were videotaped.

Analyses of the pretests and posttests show that children in the intervention groups showed significantly greater learning gains than did the control group children. This applied to children in the Year 1 mathematics and spatial groups as well as to children in the Year 2 balance scale group.

At the same time, certain tasks within the math and spatial domains were more likely to induce change than others. In the math area, children changed significantly on ratio and proportion problems, but not on the arithmetic word or numeral problems. In the spatial area, there was significant change on perspective-taking problems, but not on model-copy problems.

This pattern of findings reveals a great deal about the educational potential of peer collaboration. As expected, the method facilitates the discovery learning of basic concepts that often resist direct instruction. Proportionality is a good example of this. It is a central concept for the child's mastery of fractions as well as many other mathematical and logical operations. Educators and experimental psychologists frequently have reported difficulty in teaching the concept of proportionality to elementary school children.

The tasks that proved less successful in instilling change during our experiment rely less on conceptualization and more on knowing and remembering formulas and procedures that can be imparted through direct teaching. These included missing addend multiplication problems presented in word and numeral formats, and model-copying tasks.

Thus it appears that peer collaboration is not the best medium for showing children how to "carry" numbers, for reminding them about their multiplication tables, or for increasing the accuracy of their copying skills. This is because such collaboration orients children towards discovery and reflection rather than practice and implementation. While both types of learning activity are essential for educational achievement, these results suggest that the learning contexts should be tailored to the kind of learning that is desired.

Because of our longitudinal design, we could determine the extent to which our Year 1 intervention effects persisted into Year 2. We had two indicators of this. First, our Year 2 pretest included a range of items representing all of the Year 1 intervention areas. Second, our Year 2 intervention problem, based on Siegler's (1976) balance scale tasks, relies on conceptual skills closely related to the proportion tasks that we used in our Year 1 math intervention. Thus we expected that the children who took part in the Year 1 math sessions (Experimental Group) would be best prepared for learning about the balance beam. The children who took part in the Year 1 spatial sessions, we believed, would do better than the Year 1 control group, because the spatial group had the benefits of prior peer communicative experience. On the other hand we did not expect them to do as well as the Year 1 math group, because they did not learn concepts of mathematical proportionality in Year 1.

Our longitudinal results by and large confirmed our expectations, although more clearly in some areas than others. In math, Year 1 training effects persisted to Year 2, but did taper off considerably. Spatial training effects persisted and even increased to a significant degree by Year 2. Such accelerating post-post-test effects generally indicate that important and permanent learning gains have been made (Resnick & Glaser, 1976).

On the balance beam problem, trends were in line with our hypotheses concerning differential carry-over effects from the respective Year 1 experiences of the math, spatial, and control groups. The math group made the most progress during balance beam training, followed by the spatial group, followed by the Year 1 control group. The Year 2 control group showed no progress whatsoever.

We take these data as confirmations of our belief that peer collaboration can have lasting effects on children's understanding of difficult conceptual material like proportionality. Further, such effects can transfer to other closely related problem areas in the following predictable manner: the closer the area, the greater the transfer.

Taken together, these pretest-posttest findings are compatible with previous educational research on the value of various forms of peer learning (Johnson, Maruyama, Johnson, Nelson, & Skon, 1981; Slavin, 1983). Although this previous research has not tested peer collaboration directly, it has compared cooperative types of peer learning with peer tutoring (where an "expert" child instructs a usually younger "novice" child). Generally the previous findings are that in equal and cooperative peer interactions, children's "higher-order" reasoning skills become engaged, leading to developmental shifts in conceptual insight. Unequal tutoring interactions, in contrast, are more suited to the practice and consolidation of insights already attained (Sharan, 1980).

We did not have a peer tutoring comparison group in our study, but our peer collaboration technique established a context of learning interactions that is more equal and cooperative than anything previously attempted in educational research. The pattern of our results with this technique confirms the notion that equal collaboration engages children's reasoning skills, leading to conceptual change. We believe that this is because peer collaboration provides an ideal atmosphere for discovery learning. In this atmosphere, children become motivated to attack challenging problems. They also feel secure enough to risk expressing the new and untested ideas needed to solve such problems.

Some of these ideas about why peer collaboration can be an effective context for learning become clearer when the actual interactions are considered.

Examples From the Interaction Data

In both years of this project, sessions 1 and 6 were videotaped, transcribed, and coded according to a system of about 30 categories which may be roughly grouped as requests, solutions, explanations, other information about the problem, information about the children, procedures, agreements, and disagreements (cf. Damon, Phelps et al., 1988). We are currently analyzing these data in terms of percentage use of categories and sequences of interactions and relating these measures to amount of pretest-posttest change, problem type, and gender, a process which will no doubt take several years.

In this discussion, we will describe the kinds of interactions that occurred during the final (sixth) balance scale task that are related to progress in reasoning. This task was chosen initially because it has been used so extensively. As a result, it is very well described, and we know how to analyze it. More than the other tasks, the kinds of reasoning strategies that are required had been delineated previously. In addition, others have used if for studying peer interaction, so there are results available for comparison (Martin, 1985; Tudge, 1985).

A brief description of the task will facilitate the following discussion. In this task, children must predict which arm of a balance will go down when various configurations of weights and distances are set up (Siegler, 1976). Our balance scale had five pegs on each side of the fulcrum upon which metal washers were placed. Depending upon the placement and number of weights used, the arm could tip left, right, or remain balanced. Blocks of wood or paper cups were placed under each side to keep it stationary while the children set up the problems as indicated in drawings of each problem in a binder. Once the weights were arranged the children had to predict which side, if any, would go down when the blocks or cups were removed.

Children were given a booklet of 20 problems. For each one, they set up the balance scale with the arms blocked from moving. Then they were asked to predict which arm, if any, would go down and to write down their answer when they agreed. At that point, they removed the blocks or cups from under the scale arms in order to see what, in fact, would happen. If they had answered correctly, they circled their answer on the paper. In this way, they were provided feedback about their performance directly from the materials.

The simplest types of problems were basic balance, weight, and distance problems. Equal weights on matching opposing pegs (balance), unequal weights on matching opposing pegs (more weight), and equal weights on nonmatching opposing pegs (greater distance) were all fairly easy for most of the children. When the weights and pegs were varied beyond these simple mixtures, however, performances were much more inconsistent. These more difficult conflict-weight, conflict-distance, and conflict-balance problems were mixed into the easier problems in ever increasing numbers, until the final sessions primarily consisted of more difficult problems.

The general category that was used by all children was information about the problem (46%). This category includes statements concerning how to set up the problem, information about how to do the problem, solutions, explanations for solutions, and problem-solving strategies. Proportion use of information overall was significantly and positively related to change from pretest to posttest on the balance scale task.

In order to qualitatively understand these findings, we have looked closely at pairs in which both children change a significant amount and compared them with those pairs in which neither child changes. Out of the 46 pairs that continued through both years, there are 10 "changer pairs" and 10 "nonchanger pairs" in which both children either changed or did not. Within both groups are pairs from all three intervention groups (math, spatial, and Year 1 control) and boy and girl pairs.

Four pairs will be used to illustrate the findings. The two changer pairs were chosen because they changed more than any other pairs; the two nonchanger pairs were chosen because they match on sex (all boys) and original group assignment (math tasks group).

Selected data for the eight sample children are presented in Table 8.1. As shown, the changers give more information and solutions than the nonchangers, but not a

Table 8.1. Descriptive Statistics for Four Pairs.

	Numerical[1]		Siegler's Rules[2]		
	Pre	Post	Pre	Post	Information
Nonchangers					
128	19	18	II	III	.451
127	21	21	II	II	
260	16	19	1–2	III	.462
261	17	19	II	II	
Changers					
133	19	29	II	IV	.564
134	18	27	II	IV	
146	12	22	0–1	III	.550
147	20	26	III	IV	

[1]Possible range is from 0 to 30.
[2]Possible levels according to Siegler (1976) are I, II, III, IV. Tudge (1985) described some additional intermediate levels, such as 0–1 (pre level I) and 1–2 (in between levels I and II).

great deal more—55% versus 45%. A much clearer difference between changers and nonchangers appears when the kinds of information being exchanged is considered. In order to do this, the information was subdivided into the following subcategories:

1. Describing the problem—stating the setup. For example, "Put 3 washers on peg #1 and 2 washers on peg #2."
2. Giving solutions with and without an explanation. For example, "The black arm will go down." or "The black arm will go down because it has more weight."
3. Whether or not an explanation was given and its rule level, described in Table 8.2 (according to Siegler, 1976).
    a. "You can tell by looking at it." or "We haven't had any problems where the white arm goes down yet."
    b. "This arm has 5 washers and yours has 2."
    c. "Mine has 5 and yours has 5, but mine are out further."
    d. "On white, there are 3 washers on peg 2 and 2 washers on peg 3 equals— 12. On black, there are 2 washers on peg 5—equals 10. So white will go down."

Table 8.2. Siegler's Rule System.

I.	Weight alone used.
II.	If weights are equal, distance is used.
III.	When there is more weight on one side and more distance on the other, "muddle through."
IV.	Prediction made on the basis of which side has the greater product of the # weights times distance from fulcrum.

All children did a good job of describing and setting up the problem. They checked each other constantly. There are no differences here between changers and nonchangers.

Most of the time solutions are given without an explanation, so there are not enough explanations for a quantitative comparison to be fruitful. Overall, the range for proportion of statements that were either explanations to solutions or inferences about how to do the problem was 0.0 to 0.25. For the two nonchangers and one changer, the proportion was less than .05. For one exceptional changer pair, the proportion was .25.

Instead, looking at the *kinds* of explanations given proves to be the most fruitful way to understand differences between changers and nonchangers. In order to do this, explanations were classified according to Siegler's rule system, briefly characterized in Table 8.1. Some examples will show this most clearly:

Pair 134, whose members changed from using Siegler rule I to rule IV according to pretest-posttest change measures, used fully developed proportional reasoning strategies. Each boy would set up "his" arm and compute its value. They would compare values and state the solution. When errors were made, they would backtrack to see why they got the wrong answer, which was always an arithmetic error. This pair, however, was alone in showing such proficiency.

The other changer pair (*Pair 146*), whose rule use changed from a pre-Rule I to rule III from rule III to rule IV present a less clear cut picture. They only used a total of 8 explanations or inferences. However, those were all of a rule III type. For example, "there are more [washers] here, but these are further out." One of their explanations was nearly a full proportional strategy, "this is 8 [4 × 2] . . ." but the child never finished the statement.

In contrast to this, the nonchangers' explanations and inferences were less complete. *Pair 260* used weight, distance, and what could be called a "doubling" explanation about equally. The doubling strategy consisted of explaining that the scale would *balance* because although there were twice as many washers on one side, those on the other arm were farther out. It is a kind of qualitative compensation argument. However, it seems to be an intermediate step toward full compensation between weight and distance, which will ultimately prevail.

Pair 128 used weight explanations (Rule II), except for one type of problem. If the problem was 4 washers on peg 1 versus 1 washer on peg 4, or 5 washers on peg 2 versus 2 washers on peg 5, they would explain that "there's 4 here and 4 there," classified as Rule III. They always got these kinds of problems right, which is, again, a limited move toward proportional reasoning.

These findings suggest the following hypotheses for these four pairs. Exchange of information is related to more change. However, the quantity alone does not predict which pairs will change. Instead, for these categories, it is the level or quality of exchange that seems important. Children who communicate with more adequate reasoning are those who show both the greatest *amount* of change, in a quantitative sense, and change to the higher *levels*, in a qualitative sense.

These results look promising. Most striking is the finding that children who changed were particularly likely to share information about the task with their partners. It seems that these children were engaged in both solving the problem and communicating about ideas related to the problem.

Clearly, then, peer interactions around stimulating materials that draw children in to the logic of the problem—that is, in this case, those that encourage them to discuss why the left arm or right arm goes down—facilitate intellectual progress. We will be verifying the generality of these findings with the remaining transcripts. In addition, we are beginning to look at the changes in reasoning strategies that occur from session 1 to 6.

The pattern of the interaction results confirms the idea mentioned above that equal collaboration engages children's reasoning skills, thus promoting conceptual change. Further, in order to work productively with their partners, subjects must publicly recapitulate their own emerging understanding of the task in terms of explaining their solutions. This, we believe, is a process that strongly facilitates intellectual growth, because it forces subjects to bring to consciousness the ideas that they are just beginning to grasp intuitively. However, rather than voicing and justifying conflicting ideas about how to do the problem and obtain the correct answer, the changers in this example would suggest and test answers in an exploratory fashion, discovering strategies as they went along. The responsibility that children feel for communicating well with their peer partners induces them to gain greater conceptual clarity for themselves. In this way, the social demands of the peer encounter combine with its other motivational and affective benefits to spur cognitive growth.

A Pluralistic View of Instructional Contexts

The examples of peer collaboration and adult/child dyads as contexts for learning show that each can make a specific and distinct contribution to cognitive growth. We believe that there are other contexts, other social configurations that may each be maximally effective in engendering particular kinds of learning. More of these contexts and their associated cognitive outcomes need to be identified and studied, and there remains a great deal of research to be done.

Educational research generally has been directed towards confirming or disconfirming the efficacy of specified instructional methods. The purpose is to determine which forms of social stimulation yield the greatest cognitive benefits (however defined) for the student, rather than to establish connections between various types of social discourse and the distinct forms of knowledge that they may engender. The assumption behind such work is that some instructional approaches (and the modes of social stimulation that they embrace) are simply more powerful as inducers of intellectual progress than are others. Research efforts are directed towards promoting those that are powerful stimulators and discarding those that are not.

Even among educational researchers who are looking at "alternative contexts," there is disagreement about which alternative is better. In the area of group learning, in which groups of four or five children work together, Slavin (1983) argues that more learning occurs when there is an external reward structure imposed on the group while Johnson, Maruyama, Johnson, Nelson, and Skon (1981) conclude from a meta-analysis of various forms of group learning that such reward structures are less beneficial than cooperative group situations. Perhaps it would be more fruitful to ask the question of which instructional form is more beneficial for what kinds of cognitive outcomes.

In the area of child development research, theoretical models pose hypothetical processes to account for why cognitive growth does or does not take place under certain social stimulation conditions, but rarely show how a particular condition affects the nature of the learning outcome. Both with the adult/child dyad and the peer collaboration examples, we have shown that even within theoretical models for particular contexts, different interaction processes may be identified (e.g., direct tutelage versus Socratic method and sociocognitive conflict versus co-construction). The processes themselves need to be studied, in turn, to determine whether some are to be preferred over others or each is a potential stimulant for particular kinds of learning.

Thus, we propose a pluralistic view of the learning contexts issue. The notion of instruction legitimately can encompass a wide variety of social discourse forms without internal contradiction or incoherence. The agenda is not to decide which of these forms should be removed for maximum efficiency, but rather to identify the specific potential contribution of each. (Of course we still entertain the possibility that some types of instruction will be found to be entirely without merit, or even counterproductive, by any standard.) This entails: (a) developing a social interactional analysis of each instructional form, (b) specifying a process model providing a plausible account of how the instructional form yields particular cognitive benefits, and (c) obtaining a set of empirical associations between the instructional form and the predicated cognitive benefits. This is an ambitious research program, but a necessary one if an integrated view of learning contexts is to be achieved.

References

Bearison, D. J., Magzamen, S., & Filardo, E. K. (1986). Socio-cognitive conflict and cognitive growth in young children. *Merrill-Palmer Quarterly, 32*, 236–245.

Damon, W. (1984). Peer education. The untapped potential. *Journal of Applied Developmental Psychology, 5*, 331–343.

Damon, W., & Killen, M. (1982). Peer interaction and the process of change in children's moral reasoning. *Merrill-Palmer Quarterly, 8*, 347–367.

Damon, W. & Phelps, E. (1988). Strategic uses of peer learning in children's education. In T. J. Berndt & G. W. Ladd (Eds.), *Peer relationships in child development*.

Damon, W., Phelps, E., Yang, W., Clement, C., Hopfenbeck, J., Mitchell, R., & Staven, K. (1988). *Coding Manual: Observation codes for peer collaboration*. Unpublished manuscript, Brown University, Providence, R.I.

Doise, W., Mugny, G., & Perret-Clermont, A. (1976). Social interaction and cognitive development. *European Journal of Social Psychology, 6*, 245–247.

Johnson, D. W., Maruyama, G., Johnson, R., Nelson, D., & Skon, L. (1981). Effects of cooperative, competitive, and individualistic goal structures on achievement: A Meta-analysis. *Psychological Bulletin, 89*, 47–62.

Kruger, A. C., & Tomasello, M. (1986). Transactive discussions with peers and adults. *Developmental Psychology, 22,* 681–685.

Martin, L. M. W. (1985). The role of social interaction in children's problem solving. *The Quarterly Newsletter of the Laboratory of Comparative Human Cognition, 7,* 40–45.

Piaget, J. (1965). *The moral judgment of the child.* New York: Free Press.

Resnick, L. B., & Glaser, R. (1976). Problem solving and intelligence. In L. B. Resnick (Ed.), *The nature of intelligence.* Hillsdale, NJ: Erlbaum.

Rogoff, B., Malkin, C., & Gilbride, K. (1984). Interaction with babies as guidance in development. In J. V. Wertsch & B. Rogoff (Eds.), *Children's learning in the "Zone of Proximal Development": New Directions for Child Development, 23* (pp. 31–44). San Francisco: Jossey-Bass.

Saxe, G. B., Gearhart, M., & Guberman, S. R. (1984). The social organization of early number development. In J. V. Wertsch & B. Rogoff (Eds.), *Children's learning in the "Zone of Proximal Development": New Directions for Child Development, 23* (pp. 19–30). San Francisco: Jossey-Bass.

Sharan, S. (1980). Cooperative learning in small groups: Recent methods and effects on achievement, attitudes, and ethnic relations. *Review of Educational Research, 50,* 241–271.

Siegler, R. S. (1976). Three aspects of cognitive development. *Cognitive Psychology, 8,* 481–520.

Slavin, R. E. (1983). When does cooperative learning increase student achievement? *Psychological Bulletin, 94,* 429–445.

Tudge, J. (1985). The effect of social interaction on cognitive development: How creative is conflict? *The Quarterly Newsletter of the Laboratory of Comparative Human Cognition, 7,* 33–40.

Wertsch, J. V. (1984). The zone of proximal development: some conceptual issues. In B. Rogoff & J. V. Wertsch (Eds.), *Children's learning in the "Zone of Proximal Development": New Directions for Child Development, 23* (pp. 7–18). San Francisco: Jossey-Bass.

Youniss, J. (1980). *Parents and peers in social development.* Chicago: University of Chicago Press.

9

On the Cognitive Effects of Technology*

Gavriel Salomon
University of Arizona

Language makes us human, literacy makes us civilized (Olson, 1986), and technology makes us powerful. Powerful in what ways? Clearly, technology makes us powerful in many domains of life ranging from the physical to the intellectual, from the perceptual to the communicational. But does technology make our cognitive capacities more powerful? Differently put, technology is a function of human cognition; can cognitive functions be expected to be affected reciprocally by their own technological products? This chapter is a brief theoretical exploration of the possible ways in which technologies may interact with the mind, hence affect the mind's development.

There are many ways in which mind and technology interact and there are many ways in which the mind can be affected by technology (e.g., Bolter, 1984; Ellul, 1964; Goody, 1977). Most analyses of such effects are concerned more with sociocultural processes that span over long periods of time, as is the case with the study of how literacy affected Western institutions (e.g., Eisenstein, 1979) or the Western mind (e.g., McLuhan, 1962). Such analyses are concerned with the mind of the growing individual within a relatively short span of time only by implication. Indeed, it would be difficult to infer from analyses of the print's effects the kinds of cognitive changes that, say, Joachim, a ten-year old in the sixteenth century might have undergone. In this chapter I focus on ways in which technology, particularly recent developments in information technologies, might have on the mind of the individual.

But effects on what elements of the mind's functioning? Numerous alternatives come readily to mind: effects on the knowledge acquired, effects on the access to knowledge, improved facility with technology (literacy with technology's demands and possibilities), or effects on the organization of knowledge schemata. Here I discuss another class of cognitive elements, a class that entails what Perkins (1986) has called the *tactical components of intellectual performance*, or *thinking frames*. A thinking frame is "a representation intended to guide the process of thought, supporting, organizing, and catalyzing that process. . . . (The frame) organizes our thinking much as the frame of a viewfinder gives focus and direction to our composition as we snap photos" (Perkins, 1986, p. 7).

Note *The writing of this chapter was supported by a grant from the Spencer Foundation, given jointly to the author and to the late Tamar Globerson.

Thinking frames can be seen as occupying a midlevel between long-term on-togenetic developments of the kind studied by Piaget, and the very short-term changes of factual knowledge acquisition typical of school learning (Strauss, 1986). The former are apparently universal, basic, and concern very general cognitive structures, thus are not susceptible to cultural, let alone technological or instruction-al changes (Feldman, 1980); the latter are very limited in their applicability, highly situation- and experience-specific, often tied to the particulars of one's immediate social and instructional environment. Thinking frames, although not universal and widely applicable as Piagetian constructs, are of a more general nature than any bit of factual knowledge. They are, if you want, the levers that lean on the one hand on the "hardware' of a Piagetian-like fulcrum while on the other hand they operate on more particular objects—specific knowledge. The longer (read: more general) the lever, the greater a variety of objects that one can lift with it. Thinking frames entail such elements as thinking and learning strategies, the use of metacognitions, ways of viewing the world, and the mastery of specific processing skills (Resnick, 1986).

I have limited the discussion to one, albeit very wide and loosely defined class of cognitive elements—thinking frames or strategies—that can be affected by technol-ogy. This leads then to the question of the mechanisms involved in affecting that class. The problem is that we are dealing with cultural artifacts as possible sources of influence on an individual's mind. Cultural artifacts can be encountered in at least two distinct ways. They can be encountered as *cultural representations* whereby the representations, not the artifacts themselves, affect the individual's mind, and they can be encountered *directly*—when one watches television or interacts with computers; it is this direct experience that may affect the mind. To be sure, even in the latter case direct encounter is culturally mediated. Culture deter-mines the socially perceived status and nature of the technology so encountered, the tasks to be performed with it, and the values assigned to the encounter (Olson, 1986; see also Wertsch, chapter 4). Still, neither the nature of the effects nor the mechanisms accounting for them can be assumed to be the same for both cases.

This issue has recently been dealt with by two scholars. Sperber (1984) raised the question of how cultural representations become spread and the role that the cognitive psychology of the individual plays in the process. Olson (1986) presented a similar argument with respect to the more specific cognitive effects of print. Olson offers a single, though very interesting, mechanism to account for print's effects (I will discuss it below). Sperber, on the other hand, reaches the conclusion that a variety of mechanisms may account for what he calls the internalization of cultural representations. I concur with Sperber's position: There can be no single mecha-nism to account for how technology affects minds. Much may depend on the nature of the technology, the kinds of effects it can have potentially, on the social and psychological circumstances in which the technology is encountered and used, and on the individual's cognitive makeup.

Given the above, one can think of at least five kinds of effects of technology on those elements of cognition belonging to the class of thinking frames. These are: (a) the creation of metaphors that come to serve as "cognitive prisms" to examine and interpret other phenomena, (b) the stimulation of new distinctions and the consequent creation of new cognitive categories, (c) partnership with technology that empowers intellectual performance, (d) the cultivation of particular skills and the partial extinction of others, and (e) the internalization of technological symbolic modes and tools to serve as cognitive ones. These kinds of effect do not exhaust the range of possible ways in which technologies may impact on the tactical elements of thinking, but they represent a wide variety of such.

The variety of effects discussed here differ along three dimensions. The first dimension pertains to the source of effects, ranging from where the source is cultural representations of "defining technologies" to direct encounters with technology. The second dimension pertains to the role of the individual in producing the effect and it ranges from effects that are incidental, part of one's process of acculturation, to more deliberate ones where mindful engagement plays an important role. The third dimension pertains to how content-free or content-dependent the effect is. It ranges from effects that have a strong content component to effects which are more concerned with generalizable mental skills. These three dimensions are not independent of each other. In fact, they are highly intercorrelated. Thus, cultural reprentations of dominant technologies that do not require any direct experience with the actual technologies lead to the incidental adoption of such representations as content-laden metaphors. On the other hand, the internalization of symbol systems or tools requires direct, mindful encounters with the technology leading to the possible cultivation of realtively content-free modes of internal representation and information manipulation. In what follows I discuss each of these effects separately.

Creating Metaphors

The first kind of effect I wish to address does not concern technology itself but the effects of its cultural representation on individuals' ways of perceiving and interpreting the world. Bolter (1984) speaks of "defining technologies," such as the drop spindle and the potter's wheel in ancient Greece, the clock in medieval Europe later, the steam engine, and—today—the computer. These technologies assume such a role by virtue of "defining or redefining man's role in relation to nature" (p.13). Thus, adopted by philosophers, poets, and scientists, a novel and dominant technology is made to serve as a metaphor, a magnifying glass, by means of which seemingly disparate ideas in a culture are focused into one bright piercing ray. Thus, for example, Nicle Oresme, in the fourteenth century, stated that "the situation is much like that of a man making a clock and letting it run and continue its motion by itself. In this manner God allows the heavens to move continually . . . according to the established order" (quoted by Bolter, 1984, p. 27).

Why the clock and not, say, the moldboard plough? For the former, more than the latter—in its novel nature, shape, materials, and modes of operation—appeals to the mind as well as to the period's mode of thinking: the pleasing rotary motion of the spindle, the autonomy of the clock, the human intelligence-like nature of the computer. In short, a defining technology "develops links, metaphorical or otherwise, to a culture's science, philosophy, or literature; it is always available to serve as a metaphor, example, model, or symbol" (p.11).

How do such metaphors come to serve the individual and what cognitive functions do they serve? The process appears to be composed of two steps: the technology stimulates a single person's mind to create the metaphor and this, in turn, becomes what Sperber (1984) calls a cultural representation that becomes adopted by a great many individuals. These individuals do not have to be in daily contact with the technology in question (not even the inventor of the metaphor) to adopt it, but they have to be part of a larger community that frequently employs the metaphor. Why do individuals adopt it? Lakoff and Johnson (1981) suggest that metaphors are necessary for understanding most of what goes on in our world for they concretize and simplify otherwise abstract and complex phenomena. Metaphors like analogies and similes reframe the poorly understood and much too complex phenomena to make them fit already well organized and elaborate schemata. The universe is a poorly understood object, hardly at all comprehensible. But once defined as a clock the working of which can be seen and followed, the universe becomes familiar and rule-governed like the clock. In this sense such a metaphor is a mental tool, a prism (to use another metaphor) which can be applied to a variety of instances and yield them more comprehensible.

Metaphors function also to reorganize already acquired knowledge. As Olson and Bruner (1974) point out, it is a matter of second-order information processing whereby one uses an acquired metaphor to reexamine one's knowledge, reorganize it, and thus reinterpret it. Additionally, metaphors serve also to guide further exploration of novel phenomena. Once the mind is likened to a computer and its activities are described as "information processing" with input, output, frames, storage, retrieval paths, and the like, it becomes reasonable to ask about the size of the storage, whether processing is parallel or serial, and how "data"—that is declarative knowledge—is guided by a "program,"—that is, procedural knowledge. Indeed, as Lakoff and Johnson (1981) point out, there should be little wonder that once cast in such terms, the parallelism between mind and computer becomes confirmed.

Technology is, of course, not the only source for culturally shared and individually used metaphors. However, technology plays a unique role in this repsect: It offers sources of metaphors that daily nontechnological experiences cannot match. There is some mystique surrounding technology that sets it apart. For a metaphor to serve as a useful cognitive tool, not just a verbal token, it must entail a measure of novelty and surprise. Technology offers that.

Cultural metaphors are differently understood at different developmental levels —more literally by the younger child and less so by the older. However, at each level of its comprehension, a metaphor suggests a novel way of interpreting those elements of the world to which it pertains. Thus, the metaphor of water for electricity and of a water system for electric circuitry highlights (rightly or wrongly; see Gentner & Gentner, 1983) different aspects of electricity for different levels of understanding.

In sum, novel, outstanding, and dominant technologies ("defining technologies") lead a few individuals to use these technologies as metaphors to describe and explain daily phenomena. These metaphors turn into cultural representations and are adopted by others who need not have any direct contact with these technologies. The metaphors serve as assimilatory schemata for the acquisition and comprehension of new knowledge and for the reorganization of already acquired knowledge. It is not a newly acquired skill to process infromation with; it is a novel, culturally shared perspective to explore and interpret information. In this sense, metaphors may direct attention to particular components of a phenomenon at the expense of others: The computer metaphor of the mind excludes to an important extent considerations of such functions as volition, intention, and motivation (Gardner, 1985).

The Stimulation of New Cognitive Distinctions

A new technology often challenges scholars and even common users to answer questions that have not been raised before, and to make new distinctions. If humans are like a clock, are they just wound up by the Almighty and then left to run on their own? What does this mean in terms of predeterminism and of personal choice? If computers can "think" at least as well as humans do, what then distinguishes humans? (This question has led Searle [1983] to point out the importance of intentionality as distinguished from other cognitive-like functions, hence to set artificial and natural intelligence apart.) As Turkle (1984) writes, "The new machine that stands behind the flashing digital signal . . . is a machine that "thinks." It challenges our notions not only of time and distance, but of the mind" (p. 13).

Olson (1986), on the basis of Stock's (1983) discussion of literacy in the Middle Ages, develops the argument that one of the important consequences of literacy was the growing distinction between what is *said or written*, and what is *meant*, interpreted, added, and attributed. This distinction began as trial judges became more literate, thus distinguishing between dreams, prophecies, and visions (which were earlier admitted as evidence), and objective eyewitness and other independently verifiable accounts. This distinction then spread to other realms of society and, according to Olson, laid the foundation for the distinction between what is seen "out there" and how it is interpreted, a necessary foundation for modern science.

> That distinction . . . was invited by literacy because writing, in fact, split the comprehension process into two parts, that part preserved by text, the given, and that part, the interpretation, provided by the reader. Printing sharpened just this distinction. (Olson, 1986, p. 120)

Essentially, there is no need for direct contact with a technology or an individual to adopt a distinction first made by a few scholars or other creators of cultural representations. However, there are cases where it is the direct contact with technology that stimulates individuals to create new distinctions.

Olson finds that children conflate what is said and seen with what is meant and known. This changes at about the time they become relatively literate, initiated into the culture of text. Although the evidence for a link between children's literacy and their hermeneutic ability is indirect and possibly confounded with the effects of schooling, it is still an interesting case to consider. For we become aware of other distinctions that children come to make as a result of exposure to a technology that requires or at least invites these. For example, children who learn to program also learn to distinguish between an "error" (something bad and often irreversible) and a "bug" to be identified and "debugged" in steps.

Television, likewise, for its lifelike appearance coupled by its often less-than-plausible contents, seems to stimulate children's distinction between what is real and what is not (Kelly, 1981). Interestingly, Kelly found that although the distinction between reality and fiction takes the same developmental path for both televised and print materials, children make reality judgments based on a criterion of plausibility somewhat earlier with television, suggesting that exposure to the medium forces them to distinguish more clearly between presentation and *rep*resentation, and between what is and is not plausible despite lifelike appearance.

Turkle (1984) describes in vivid detail how children ranging in age from five to ten debate in great length whether computers (in the form of computer games) are alive and whether they can cheat. They are faced with a new object: It is not a live thing, but a mechanical toy which can cheat them. In another case the computerized toy cannot be turned off and continues to function on its own. New distinctions emerge: eight-year-olds reach the conclusion that that cheating involves awareness of cheating, and being alive entails intentionality. As Turkle points out, when children discuss computers they replace physical criteria by psychological ones to judge liveness. "Motion gives way to emotion" (p. 58). New technology leads to new distinctions that need to be made.

As with technology's effects through metaphor, its effects through the creation of new distinctions does not *require* one's direct contact with the technology. Distinctions can be stimulated in some individuals and then, provided they are functional, become culturally spread. However, as some of the examples above suggest, there is also a more direct path based on one's actual experience with a technology. Whereas the former path of making new distinctions is culturally bound and handed down to a relatively passive individual, distinctions made on the basis of first-hand experience are not necessarily shared, but require an active individual to make them. This is where one's tendency to be mindful or one's situationally stimulated mindfulness start to play an important role (Salomon & Globerson, 1987). The children described by Turkle, facing a curious gadget which they could not control, manifested, it appears, just such mindfulness. Many other children facing an otherwise smoothly functioning technology that can be taken for granted are less likely to invent a new distinction of the kind described by Turkle. I will discuss later on the possibility that technology's effects (or at least some of them) may not occur on their own but require active, mindful participation of the individual.

In sum, technology often stimulates, and in some cases requires the creation of new distinctions. Some of these become culturally shared and are, so to speak,

handed down to the individual; other distinctions are the result of one's direct
contact with the technology. As with metaphors, the creation of new distinctions
does not much alter one's mastery of cognitive skills but it affects the way one
perceives the world. I argued that the creation of new distinctions by the individual
facing technology requires mindfulness. When technology can be taken for granted
(as when it operates smoothly and in no novel ways), no novel distinctions are
called for and one can use it in a relatively mindless fashion.

Partnership that Empowers

So far I have described two ways through which technology can affect how
elements of one's world are perceived and interpreted. But some technologies are
not just something one is passively exposed to—directly or through cultural transmission; they are sets of tools with which one actively interacts. And concerning
computer technology, a technology that can transcend human cognition (Pea,
1985), one interacts within it in an *intellectual partnership*. As described by Perkins
(1985):

> The written word extended the reach of thought by helping us to circumvent low-level
> limitations of human short term memory. Information processing technologies might
> extend the reach of thought yet further by helping us circumvent low-level limitations
> of human computational ability, including not only computation with numbers but
> with words and images. (p. 14)

Pea (1985) offers an important constrast between an amplification metaphor of
technological (in this case—computer) effects and a cognitive-reorganizational one.
According to the amplification metaphor, technologies amplify our powers—
allowing us to accomplish tasks more efficiently and in less time. But the tasks
themselves remain essentially the same (see also Cole & Griffin, 1980). Such a
view guides, for example, the use of computers to more effectively impart the kind
of knowledge one traditionally teaches. In contrast, the reorganization metaphor
suggests that the partnership with computer tools affords the opportunity to engage
in new tasks and face new choice points that involve mental operations that could
not have been employed without it.

Indeed, it might be said that the real power of technology (read, in this case,
computers) is in its ability to redefine and fundamentally restructure *what* we do
(say, in using a sophisticated spreadsheet for budgeting purposes), *how* we do it,
and *when* we do it. *We come to use this technology as a tool to think with.* The
writer who uses a computerized *Writing Outliner* is now more "intelligent": The
qualitative nature of the writing activities he or she is engaged in, and more
importantly, the cognitive processes thus activated, are vastly different and more
powerful from those involved without that computerized tool. The budget planner
now does things he or she would have been quite unable to do before in terms of
manipulating clusters of variables and instantaneously testing out remote possibilities. The cognitive powers of the student who writes with the help of a comput-

erized *Idea Generator* have been qualitatively changed, as the student has been freed from carrying out a variety of menial or otherwise mundane operations. The user of such a technology is now free to engage in what may be called "higher-order cognitive thinking" without getting stuck in mechanical and rote activities. Moreover, the student can now pursue new *goals* which could not have been entertained beforehand: to design imaginary ecological "environments" or to test the wildest hypotheses in a computerized lab.

The partnership described here is akin in many important ways to that which can be achieved in a social setting where individuals pool their mental resources to jointly solve a problem, plan a strategy, or create a complex design (see, in this respect, the description by Brown and associates of "reciprocal teaching" in Chapter 7). Certain processes already mastered by some members of the social setting are exteriorized, allowing others to employ processes they could not employ when on their own. Here, though, the computer is the environment with which one interacts, making both the activity and its products more "intelligent."

Two issues of interest are involved here. One concerns a somewhat philosophical question: Where does the intelligence reside? The second concerns the cognitive effects on the *individual*. Concerning the "location" of the intelligence, one could argue in a Brunerian spirit that "intelligence is not a quality of the mind alone, but a product of the relation between mental structures and the tools of the intellect provided by the culture" (Pea, 1985, p. 168). Thus, the unit of analysis is not the individual but rather the partnership system of an individual working with an intellectual tool (or, in other cases, an individual working with a group). This, in itself, may have important ramifications with respect to the kind of tasks an individual can carry out, quite independently of the abilities that this individual already possesses.

The second issue is of a more developmental nature. While the individual's functional system of mental operations may be reorganized *during* the partnership with a computer that serves as a cognitive tool to think with, do any of the individual's cognitive capacities, specific or general, become altered as a *result* of that partnership? Assume that the kinds of mental operations that are activated during the partnership are within the individual's zone of proximal development (Vygotsky, 1978), do any of them become also cultivated? And do any of the elements of the exteriorized interaction become internalized to serve as elements in the individual's cognitive repertoire? To the extent that the partnership is within the individual's zone of proximal development, one would expect the activated operations to become internalized and to "become part of the child's independent developmental achievements" (Vygotsky, 1978, p. 90). Indeed, this is precisely the intention behind the arrangement of "reciprocal teaching" (Brown et al., Chapter 7): "In the course of repeated practice such . . . activities, first practiced socially, are gradually adopted as part of the learner's personal repertoire of learning strategies." Also for Pea (1985, p. 178), who describes the cognitive reorganizational function of partnership with cognitive computer tools, the ultimate question is "How can technologies for education serve not only as tools for thinking, but for helping thinking to develop?" To these kinds of effects I turn next.

The Cultivation of Skill

Most discussions and studies concerned with cognitive effects of technology have focused on the cultivation of requisite skills. Technology, as Ellul (1964) reminds us, is no more than a heap of raw stuff without skilled techniques to operate it and to attain with it the goals it was designed for. And these techniques need to be acquired. However, we are not concerned here with the acquisition of such technology-specific skill but with the cultivation of *transferable* skills which become employed during the partnership with a technology. Thus, for example, print, and the literacy it led to, were thought of as levers for the cultivation of abstract thinking, and television was studied as impairing children's development of imagination (Singer & Singer, 1981).

Based on a Vygotskian view, I wish to distinguish first between skill *cultivation* and skill *internalization*. Skill cultivation implies that some mental operation that is called upon by the use of a tool or symbol system becomes better mastered as a result of their use. It is not a set of procedures or modes of representation that have "gone underground," but rather a set of operations, the rudiments of which exist already in one's repertoire, whose improved mastery becomes stimulated and "stretched" by technology's demands: Coming to think in multivariate terms as a result of designing ecological "environments" with an ecological simulator (Mintz, 1987), acquiring an ability to be more explicit (Olson, 1985), or acquiring metacognitive strategies as a result of programming (Clements & Gullo, 1984). In the case of internalization, on the other hand, not the mastery of a skill has been improved but a whole tool or symbolic mode of representation has been mentally reconstructed and has become available for cognitive use. The difference can be illustrated as that between cultivating skills of analysis, required perhaps by the use of flow charts, and learning to think *in terms* of flow charts as a cognitive tool of representation. One of the differences between novices and experts is that the former can think *about*, say, a set of procedures, whereas the expert can think *in terms* of such (Bransford, Franks, Vye, & Sherwood, 1986).

How Could Technology Develop Transferable Skill?

For one thing, the technology has to be engaged and worked with. Unlike the preceeding two kinds of effect (creation of metaphors and the stimulation of new distinctions), skill cultivation cannot be attained without first-hand experience with the technology in question. Also, for a technology to affect the development of relevant skills it must demand mastery of these skills beyond the level already mastered without it. "User-friendly" technology that can be operated without any new skill being called upon may not cultivate any skills; the ones already mastered may suffice.

That much may be obvious. What is less obvious is the kind of first-hand mentally demanding experience that is required. For, as recent research on this question suggests, mere exposure, or even some inconsequential and poorly executed activity may not suffice (e.g., Salomon, 1979). Consider the findings of Scribner and Cole on the cognitive effects of the Vai literacy (1981), or the many studies on children's programming, which failed to show any measurable cognitive effects beyond some (usually poor) mastery of programming itself (Pea & Kurland, 1984).

Perkins and Salomon (1987) have developed a theory of transfer stimulated by the question of skill cultivation through, among other things, technological mediation. According to this theory, learning and transfer can take either one of two routes, or a combination thereof. One route, which we have termed the "low road," is characterized by much practice in a variety of situations leading to the near automatic (hence relatively mindless) mastery of the cognitions, skills, or behaviors acquired. These in turn become applied, quite mindlessly, to new situations which perceptually resemble the already practiced ones. As practice-accumulates, whatever has been learned is performed with greater ease, becomes increasingly less accessible to mindful inspection, and is increasingly under stimulus control.

The other route, termed the "high road," is characterized by relatively fast learning which is accompanied by much mindfulness through which the individual deliberately abstracts the essentials of the material and decontextualizes it. The abstractions, principles, or strategies that this process yields are then available for transfer which is also mindfully done. By mindfulness we mean the *metacognitively guided, deliberate, and focused employment of nonautomatic mental operations in the service of performing some task* (Salomon & Globerson, 1987). The attributes of such a behavior are the deliberate consideration of alternatives, while first responses are inhibited (Pascual-Leone, 1984); this is accompanied by the expenditure of mental effort, by focused attention to detail (Salomon & Sieber-Suppes, 1972), and—possibly of greatest importance—the employment of metacognitions (e.g., Brown, Bransford, Ferrara, & Campione, 1983; Resnick, 1986).

There appears to be a division of labor between the two roads. The low road of learning is important in processes of acculturation, habit formation, socialization, the establishment of self-image and general attitudes, and other cognitions and behaviors that cannot be taught explicitly in some abstractable way for they are neither disciplined nor based on logical deductions. Much of what we term "tacit knowledge," cultured behavior, or cognitive style is acquired in this way; it is incidental and practice intensive. Perhaps most importantly, the low road is the one taken when a newly acquired skill is called upon and develops-incrementally in very small steps. On the other hand, instruction, in its commonly known way, is usually concerned with disciplined knowledge and formal skills that can be explicated and which need to be mastered in a relatively short time. Instruction is thus designed to move the learner along the high road. Such learning applies, for example, to strategies the acquisition of which is (initially, at least) a matter of intention and reflective abstaction.

Skill cultivation could, of course, take either road, but one usually assumes that the cultivation of transferable skill via experience with some technology is an unnoticed and effortless side effect—that is, a low road phenomenon. However, using a skill repetitively for unimportant and routine tasks may not lead to even low road development that can transfer beyond its initial contect. As Scribner and Cole

(1981) point out, one possible reason for the failure of the Vai's literacy to show far transfer from their literacy skills to other cognitive tasks was that their literacy really served no important social function and, unlike literacy as we know it, was of little cultural consequence. However, the authors postulate that

> Whenever technological and economic conditions furnish many purposes to be served by literacy we would expect the skill systems involved . . . to become varied, complex, and widely applicable. (pp. 258–259)

A few hours of learning to program, cognitively powerful as programming may *potentially* be, do not even meet the basic requirements of low-roadedness: Achievements are usually poor, the activity itself is carried out in very small quantities, and it is socially inconsequential. If programming does affect transferable cognitive skills, as may perhaps be seen in expert programmers or in so-called hackers, then it surely is a result of a great many hours (some estimate over 5,000 hours) of programming by individuals for whom it is an important activity. It may well be the case, as our own research suggests (Salomon, 1979), that television's "language" features cultivate children's cognitions by means of the low road because of the many hours children spend televiewing. But where television is seen as a desirable source of information by mothers, and when it serves a socially valued focal point for children, it is handeled more mindfully and a higher road appears to be taken. The medium's effects are accordingly stronger. Indeed, a number of recent studies have shown that programming, when mindfully carried out (e.g., adults guide the children and provide externalized metacognitions), can lead to the cultivation of relevant and transferable cognitive skills and metacognitions (e.g., Clements & Gullo, 1984; Clements, 1987; Mayer, Dyck, & Vilberg, 1986). As the high, rather than the low road of learning was taken, not much experience was necessary to produce such effects.

Whether the high or the low road of transfer is taken, skill cultivation by technology has another side to it: the relative deemphasis and thus gradual extinction of skills that become unnecessary. The argument has been made, for example, that writing—the objective recording of knowledge earlier committed to memory — has made skills of memorization less needed, hence leading to the decline of their mastery. This could also be the case with, say, skills of arithmetic computation in an information age when hand calculations are simply not done any more, and, as Herbert Simon has pointed out, "knowing" becomes redefined as a verb pertaining to access rather than possession (Pea, 1985).

To summarize, the cultivation of transferable skills can take place when a technology is actively encountered, when the activity is mentally demanding, and when it is consequential. Given this, there are at least two ways that transferable skill can be cultivated: When the technology is continuously engaged in a variety of instances such that skills become relatively automated (low road effects), or when the technology-related activity is mindfully engaged, its constituent components reflected upon and generalization deliberately generated (high road effects). In this light, skills can become cultivated over the years without the individuals involved ever being aware of them, as could perhaps be the case with the cultivation of skills of explicitness by computer-related activities (Olson, 1985). Alternatively, skills can become developed over shorter time spans, as a result of mindfully encountering new technological demands; the few cases of programming effects appear to belong to the latter category.

The Internalization of Technology's Modes of Representation and Functioning

Münsterberg (1916/1976) has argued that film is the externalization of our associations and dreams. Similarly, artificial intelligence is conceived of as an attempt to explicitly simulate human thought processes. While such may be the case for insightful filmmakers and for cognitive scientists, for most others the process could be a reversed one. Involved in an intellectual partnership with a cognitive technology that entails demanding interactions, they may come to internalize some of its exteriorized representational modes and operations. Elaboration of this point requires a brief discussion of the nature of internalization, the nature of the candidates for internalization, and the conditions under which internalization can take place.

On the Nature of Internalization

The concept of internalization appears to imply the establishment, by whatever process, of a mental representation or set of internal procedures that, in many important ways, serve as counterparts to the external, communicationally used tools, procedures, or symbol systems (Vygotsky, 1978). However, as Wertsch and Stone (1985) point out, Vygotsky entertains two somewhat contradictory views of that relationship between external (tool) and internal (sign). On the one hand he argues that internal processes retain certain attributes of their external sources, but on the other hand he argues that "internalization transforms the process itself and changes its structure and functions" (Wertch & Stone, 1985, p. 163). I wish to argue that these two mechanisms describe skill internalization (implying some isomophism between the external and its cognitive counterpart) and skill cultivation, respectively. In this light, we would expect to find at least a modicum of structural and functional resemblance between the external tool and its internal counterpart when internalization is involved (Diaz, 1986; see also Brown et al., chapter 7).

This, in turn, suggests one possible way to distinguish between skill cultivation and internalization on the basis of their results: Skills that have been cultivated bear no resemblance to and are not isomorphous with the external agents that have "stretched" them, whereas skills that have been internalized do. Thus, for example, one would not expect any isomorphism between the demand for hypothesis-testing in a computerized simulation and the actual processes the child employs. But one would expect at least some measure of isomorphism between the kind of conceptual-spatial map a child can create and observe using the *Learning Tool* (Kozma & Van Roekel, 1986), and the way the child comes to represent conceptual fields to him or herself. Although both cases may be within the child's zone of proximal development, hence, produce cognitive change, only the latter shows internalization of an explicit component in the interaction. It fulfills a number of conditions that make it a candidate for internalization, as discussed in the next section.

The Nature of the Internalized

Not every element in a social interaction or in one's interaction with a computer tool is an equally reasonable candidate for interaction. To be a candidate, a number of nonobvious conditions need to be met. For something to be internalized and come to serve a cognitive function it must somehow pertain to and be made of the same (or similar) "stuff" the mind is using and manipulating: modes of symbolic representation, operations, and metaoperations. And to be internalized and serve as a cognitive tool, that "something" needs to fit the learner's ontogenetic level of development. That is, the symbolic modes, the operations, or the metaoperations encountered during interaction with a technology that serves as a cognitive tool should be such that they could potentially be reconstructed and then carried out in the learner's mind. They should thus be congruent with the learner's knowledge base, intuitions, and abilities.

But why should a learner engage in the process of internalizing a new mode of representation or strategy? The answer is similar to the reasons for the adoption of culturally based metaphors, because that mode of representation or strategy comes to serve a novel and cognitively useful function for the individual. It may be the case that children internalize social speech, but would they do the same with, say, the Morse Code? The answer, it appears, is clear. While speech, once internalized, serves important self-regulatory functions, the Morse Code, being a secondary symbol system, does nothing of the kind. It serves no new and important function that language, on which it is based, does not accomplish already. Indeed, past research (Salomon, 1979) concerning the internalization of filmic symbolic modes of representation and manipulation systematically shows that only learners who do not yet master the relevant, counterpart skills are the ones to show evidence of internalization. For them, interaction with the filmic code supplants a mode of representation or an operation they do not master yet. The others, more skilled learners, often fail to show internalization since the elements they interact with do not serve any new function for them. Some of them even manifest signs of cognitive interference.

Another condition is that the candidate for internalization be such that the user could assimilate it into his or her existing schemata. For if internalization means cognitive reconstruction then this implies that the requisite skills and knowledge are already available. There is little chance that a very young learner will be able to use the *learning tool*, mentioned above, as a cognitive tool to create cognitive maps with if he or she has not yet acquired the ability to think in multivariate terms. But a somewhat older learner could. Put differently, a tool or representational mode could be internalized if its functions fall within what Vygotsky has called the zone of proximal development. This implies that the tool or the mode of representation is sufficiently simple to allow its cognitive reconstruction. But compatibility with the users' cognitive apparatus and simplicity may not be enough. Both the abacus and a pocket calculator are tools. But while the abacus can be internalized (Hatano, Miyake, & Binks, 1977) the calculator apparently cannot.

Indeed, another important condition is that the technological candidate for internalization be explicit in its operations. Programs such as spreadsheets (particularly when they are ''intelligent'') could not be internalized because much of what they accomplish is carried out ''implicitly'' *for* the users but not *with* them. A tool that is a candidate for internalization ought to show what it is that has been carried out such that the user could emulate the procedure and reconstruct it in his or her mind. One cannot reconstruct or emulate procedures that are carried out in hiding.

Recently we (Tamar Globerson, Eva Guterman, and I) have developed a computerized *Reading Aid* through which seventh graders are provided with externalized, reading-related metacognitions (Salomon, Globerson, & Guterman, 1989). Children interacted with this tool, while others interacted with control versions: a version that presented content, test-like questions that accompanied the texts, or one that presented the texts with no explicit guidance of any kind. The results were very consistent. First, the children interacting with the *Reading Aid* showed clear evidence of internalizing the metacognitions. Second, they showed dramatic improvements in reading comprehension later on. Third, that improvement was totally accounted for by the internalized metagcognitions. And last, similar improvements were manifested *a month later* in the quality of the essays they were asked to write. Also this improvement was accounted for by the internalized metacognitions. No such changes were evident in the other groups.

These findings highlight three important points. They show that the interaction with a computerized tool can lead to the internalization of activity-related metacognitions which are within the learners' zone of proximal development; they show that the explicit modeling of the metacognitions to be internalized may be a crucial attribute, and that the internalization of such metacognitions affects subsequent performance, in the absence of the external guidance. Moreover, it appears that these internalized metacognitions are also transferred to another class of activities—writing.

Conditions for Internalization

Assume that the conditions described above are all met. Still, not all experiences with a technological tool lead to its actual internalization. There are obvious conditions that need to be met—such as active interaction and learner control—without which even the best of tools would not be internalized. Additionally, the two-road theory of Perkins and Salomon (1987), mentioned earlier, appears to apply here as it applies to skill cultivation. Continuous and varied experience with an intelligent, explicit tool or mode of representation may lead to its internalization in the fashion typical of the low road of learning. Learners may not even be aware of the fact that they start using artificial intelligence in their thinking. This may indeed be the way media's modes of representation—the linearity of print, television's figural and spatial transformations—have gradually affected cognitions in the real world. But such learning takes a very long time. It is also limited in the range of new instances to which it can be applied.

More often than not, however, we'd want to make learners come to think in terms of an intelligent tool or in terms of some contrived images in a relatively short time, not just leave it to be an eventual side effect of tool use. We'd also want to see them apply that cognitive tool to a variety of instances, an indication that what has been internalized is indeed a cognitive tool of some generalizability. Thus, we'd want them to take the high road of mindful learning and abstraction. Addressing the role of conscious reflection, or intellectualization, a state akin to mindful abstraction, Vygotsky goes as far as arguing that it is a necessary condition for internalization (Wertsch, Chapter 4).

We have good reason to believe that when users of a computer tool or mode of representation are mindful of its nature and functions (hence the importance of explicitness of a tool's functions and operations) they are more likely to reconstruct it in their own congition and use it as a cognitive tool. We have found in our past research that the internalization effects that can be produced under controlled experimental conditions, where learners are more mindful of the process, are far stronger than the ones that are "naturally" produced on their own, where learners are more mindless (Salomon, 1979). This implies that tool users become not only proficient, but that they learn to use the tool while mindfully considering its functions and observable procedures. Without this mindful consideration of how the tool works, its potential internalization is left to the long and tedious low road of slow acquisition.

The study with the *Reading Aid* clearly showed that when learners' mindfulness is aroused (as was indeed the case in the study), internalization takes place. Another study of ours (Zellermayer, Salomon, Globerson, & Givon, in press) was based on a computerized tool we called the *Writing Aid*. It resembled in important ways the *Reading Aid* inasmuch as it accompanied youngsters' writing on a word processor with writing-related metacognitions. Results were not as dramatic as in the reading tool study (mainly because the youngsters failed to master typing). Still, there was clear evidence to show that the internalization of the writing-related metacognitions was mediated by the learners' mindfulness—the volitional effort they expended in answering the metacognitive questions presented to them during writing. The more mindful learners also showed improved writing ability, itself mediated by the internalization of the metacognitions.

In sum, the computer can serve as a cognitive tool, an environment to intellectually interact with. When the tool's operations meet a number of conditions—particularly ontogenetic appropriateness and explicitness, and when learners are sufficiently mindful of the process, they can internalize the tool's operations and modes of presentation. They create cognitive counterparts to the ones encountered in the partner-like interaction with the tool. Thus, they show not only improved performance *with* the tool but also *subsequent* cognitive changes that *result* from this partnership. Improved performance with a tool appears to preceed more lasting changes that become evident in the absence of the tool. What starts out as a joint intelligence gradually becomes the person's.

Technology's Effects as Related to Development

So far, I have outlined five ways in which technology can affect the individual's mind. Granting that such effects can and possibly do take place, one faces the question of how such effects relate to cogntive development. For, after all, a person's mind can be affected by numerous cultural and social factors, ranging from culture's institutions (e.g., schooling) to culture's norms and mores, which would not qualify as developmental. Moreover, culture's effects—in this case, technology—may be limited and shaped by development without affecting development reciprocally. And to qualify as "developmental" such effects would need to alter in some significant way an individual's course of cognitive deveopment which would not have taken place in the absence of the technology or its cultural representation.

To answer this question, however, one would need to address first a preceding question: How profound and cognitively significant are technology's cognitive effects? For if its effects, the kinds described in this paper, are of marginal cognitive consequences, then their developmental impact might be exceedingly limited from the very outset. One can speak here of two levels of effects, levels which have been labeled by Perkins (1985) as the first- and the second-order "fingertip effect." First-order fingertip effects pertain to the straightforward performance capabilities afforded by technology: faster commotion, easier computation, faster communication, easier access to larger and better organized bodies of data. The second-order fingertip effects pertain to "deeper and more wide-ranging reprecussions on society, personality and thought" (p. 11)—that is, they pertain to lasting effects on what has been called here "thinking frames" or the levers of thinking: outlooks, skills, strategies, and the like. As it has been argued by Olson (e.g., 1986), print has not only allowed us to examine an argument long after it has been made, but it provided us a medium in which we can think, thus affecting new modes of logical and combinational thinking.

It needs to be recognized, however, that technology can and often has no more than the first-order cognitive fingertip effect. As argued by Perkins (1985) and Salomon (1985), technology may afford the opportunities for second-order cognitive fingertip effects, but the opportunities thus afforded may not be taken in actuality. Databases may carry a message that classification and cross-classification are powerful intellectual tools, potentially serving as tools-to-be-internalized, but this does not assure their actual internalization and employment as cognitive tools. Assuming that in many cases the potential for second-order cognitive effects is there, the answer to the question of how significant, profound, or "deep" the actual effect are, lies less with the technology and more with the individual using it within a social context.

Indeed, for relatively immediate cognitive effects to take place, much may depend on how mindfully (Salomon & Globerson, 1987) an individual handles the technology and its cognitive challenges. Case (1985), summarizing his theory of stage transitions which, according to Piaget, involve the integration of two or more structures, points out that such integration requires active attention to the structures.

On the other hand, low-road engagement, which does not involve much deliberate and effortful attention to the technology and the way it operates, can lead to cognitive effects only if much, varied, and extensive practice is provided (Perkins, 1985; Salomon & Perkins, 1989). Such is more characteristic of long-term societal effects than of short-term individual ones.

Moreover, one's mindful engagement with technology—contemplating the application of a new metaphor, thinking of whether computers can cheat, considering new relations between unrelated phenomena when engaged in an intellectual partneship with a computer tool, or internalizing a tool's "intelligence"—greatly depends on the social context in which this engagement takes place. Some social contexts emphasize the benefits of the first-order fingertip effects, as when computer drill and practice activities are carried out to get them over with, or when tool-operation is carried out within a context that demands task efficiency. Other contexts, richer with exploratory possibilities and encouragement, invite more mindful engagement and reflection (Globerson, 1988; see also Wertsch, Chapter 4), facilitating second-order fingertip effects. It appears, then, that the cognitive significance of technology's effects is very much an individual-in-social-context affair, not something that can be determined ahead of time by examination of the technology in and of itself.

This brings me back to my initial question. Assume that the effects under consideration are "deep" and lasting, how do they relate to cognitive development? The answer depends on how development is conceived of. Traditionally, cognitive development is conceived of as orderly, age-related, sequential, universal, spontaneous and biologically based (e.g., Feldman, 1980; Strauss, 1986). A "deep" or genuine developmental change would, accordingly, involve a cognitive structural change that is—a change in the relations among structures or among a structure's elements, not just a change in the content, avaliability, or accessibility of the elements themselves (Globerson, 1985). When development is seen in this way, it is doubtful that the kinds of effects I have discussed in this chapter would qualify as "developmental." Technology's effects may be constrained by development but not affect basic cognitive structures reciprocally. Put in terms of the metaphor I have used in the beginning of this chapter, the fulcrum (basic structures) can affect the acquisition of a new cognitive lever (skills and strategies) through interaction with external agents, but influences on the lever do not affect the fulcrum on which it leans

However, when seen from Vygotskian or Brunerian points of view, points of view that take school, tool, and cultural symbol systems-related learning as affecting development, a somewhat different conclusion can be entertained. Seen in this way, the effects of technology do not determine the course of development but they realize its potential by providing it with representational and tool-like means and by "stretching" it thorugh internalization. Moreover, it is quite possible that small cognitive changes, microgenetic ones, gradually accumulate to pave the way for more qualitative ones (Cole & Griffin, 1980). Thus, the impact of technology is to be judged for its developmental impact not as discrete small-scale effects but as a sequence of gradual changes on a relatively longer scale of time. In such a sequence, structures that are intially socially or tool-based, can gradually become instruments for self-regulation (Case, 1985; Brown et al., Chapter 7; Wertsch, Chapter 4) which in turn enable new modes of interaction with the technology.

Two implications follow from this point of view. First, it might well be the case that since mindful attention to technology's functioning is so crucial, and since a child's attentional capacity grows with age (Pascual-Leone, 1984), that the developmental impact of technology (or for that matter, culture in general) becomes increasingly more significant with age (Case, 1985). Second, not all of the effects I have mentioned here, profound as they may potentially be, carry the same developmental weight. Not every "thinking frame"—metaphor, constructed distinction, or skill—is acquired at the appropriate ontogenetically appropriate level. Moreover, it can be mastered, it can be internalized, yet not necessarily become interwoven with other "frames" and structures. Whether it does may depend not only on the nature of the impacting agent or the nature of the effect per se, but also on other cognitive, developmental, and social factors the specific nature of which we still have to study.

References

Bolter, J. D. (1984). *Turing's man*. New York: Simon & Schuster.

Bransford, J. D., Franks, J. J., Vye, N. J., & Sherwood, R. D. (1986). *New approaches to instruction: Because wisdom can't be told*. Paper presented at the conference on Similarity and Analogy, University of Illinois, Urbana, IL.

Brown, A. L., Bransford, J. D., Ferrara, R. A., & Campione, J. C. (1983). *Learning, remembering and understanding*. In P. H. Mussen (Ed.), *Handbook of child psychology* (4th ed. Vol. 3, pp. 77–166), New York: Wiley.

Case, R. (1985). *Intellectual development: Birth to adulthood*. New York: Academic Press.

Clements, D. H. (1987). *Componential employment and development in Logo programming environments*. Paper presented at the Biennial Meeting of the Society for Research in Child Development, Baltimore, MD.

Clements, D. H., & Gullo, D. F. (1984). Effects of computer programming on young children's cognition. *Journal of Educational Psychology, 76*, 1051–1058.

Cole, M., & Griffin, P. (1980). Cultural amplifiers reconsidered. In D. R. Olson (Ed.), *The social foundations of language and thought: Essays in honor of J. S. Bruner*. New York: Norton.

Diaz, R. (1986). The union of thought and language in children's private speech. *Laboratory of Comparative Human Cognition, 8*, 90–97.

Eisenstein, E. (1979). *The printing press as an agent of change*. Cambridge, England: Cambridge University Press.

Ellul, J. (1964). *The technological society*. London: Random House.

Feldman, D. H. (1980). *Beyond universals in cognitive development*. Norwood, NJ: Ablex.

Gardner, H. (1985). *The mind's new science*. New York: Basic Books.

Gentner, D., & Gentner, D. R. (1983). Flowing waters and teeming crowds: Mental models of electricity. In D. Gentner & A. L. Steves (Eds.), *Mental models*. Hillsdale, NJ: Erlbaum.

Globerson, T. (1985). When do structural changes undelie behavioral changes? In I. Levin (Ed.), *Stage and structure: Reopening the debate*. Norwood, NJ: Ablex.

Globerson, T. (1988). *How do make connections among different situations? Local and global constructions*. Paper presented at the Annual Meeting of the American Educational Research Association, New Orleans, LA.

Goody, J. (1977). The domestication of the savage mind. In P. Horton & R. Finnegan (Eds.), *Modes of thought*. London, England: Cambridge University Press.

Hatano, G., Miyake, Y., & Binks, M. G. (1977). Performance of expert abacus operations. *Cognition 5*, 5–12.

Kelly, H. (1981). Reasoning about realities: Children's evaluation of television and books. In H. Kelly & H. Gardner (Eds.), *Viewing children through television*. San Francisco: Jossey-Bass.

Kozma, R. B., & Van Roekel, J. (1986). *Learning tool*. Ann Arbor, MI: Arboworks, Inc.

Lakoff, G., & Johnson, M. (1981). The metaphorical structure. In D. A. Norman (Ed.), *Perspective on cognitive science*. Norwood, NJ: Ablex.

Mayer, R. E., Dyck, J. L., & Vilberg, G. (1986). Learning to program and learning to think: What's the connection? *Communication of the ACM, 29*, 605–610.

Mcluhan, M. (1962). *The Gutenberg galaxy*. Toronto: University of Toronto Press.

Mintz, R. (1987). *Computer simulation as an instructional tool for the teaching of ecological systems*. Doctoral dissertation, Tel Aviv University, Israel.

Munsterberg, H. (1970). *The film: A psychological study*. New York: Dover (original: 1916).

Olson, D. R. (1985). Computers as tools of the intellect. *Educational Researcher, 14*, 5–8.

Olson, D. R. (1986). *Intelligence and literacy: The relationships between intelligence and the technologies of representation and communication*. In R. J. Sternberg & R. K. Wagner (Eds.), *Practical intelligence*. Cambridge, England: Cambridge University Press.

Olson, D. R., & Bruner, J. R. (1974). Learning through experience and learning through media. In D. R. Olson (Ed.), *Media and symbols: The forms of expression, communication and education* (73rd Yearbook of the National Society for the Study of Education). Chicago: University of Chicago Press.

Pascual-Leone, J. (1984). *Attention, dialectic and mental effort: Toward an organismic theory of life stages*. In L. M. Common, F. A. Richards, & C. Armon (Eds.), *Beyond formal operations*. New York: Preager. (pp. 182–215).

Pea, R. D. (1985). Beyond amplification: Using the computer to reorganize mental functioning. *Educational Psychologist, 20*, 167–182.

Pea, R. D., & Kurland, D. M. (1984). On the cognitive effects of learning computer programming. *New Ideas in Psychology, 2*, 137–168.

Perkins, D. (1985). The fingertip effect: How information processing technology shapes thinking. *Educational Researcher, 14*, 11–17.

Perkins, D. (1986). Thinking frames: A model for teaching thinking. In J. Baron & R. Sternberg (Eds.), *Teaching thinking skills: Theory and practice* (pp. 285–304). New York: Freeman.

Perkins, D., & Salomon, G. (1987). Transfer and teaching thinking. In D. Perkins, J. Lockhead, & J. Bishop (Eds.), *Thinking: The second intenational conference*. Hillsdale, NJ: Erlbaum.

Resnick, L. B. (1986). *Education and the learning to think* (Special Report for the Commission on Behavioral and Social Science and Education.) Washington, DC: National Research Council.

Salomon, G. (1979). *Interaction of media cognition and learning*. San Francisco: Jossey-Bass.

Salomon, G. (1985). Information technologies: What you see is not (always) what you get. *Educational Psychologist, 20*, 207–217.

Salomon, G. (1988). AI in reverse: Computer tools that turn cognitive. *Journal of Educational Computing Research, 4*, 123–139.

Salomon, G., & Globerson, T. (1987). Skill may not be enough: The role of mindfulness in learning and transfer. *International Journal of Educational Research, 11*, 623–637.

Salomon G., Globerson, T., & Gutterman, E. (1989). The computer as a zone of proximal development. *Journal of Educational Psychology, 81*, 620–627.

Salomon, G., & Perkins, D. N. (1989). Rocky roads to transfer. *Educational psychologists, 24*, 113–142.

Salomon, G., & Sieber-Suppes, J. (1972). Learning to generate subjective response uncertainty. *Journal of Personality and Social Psychology, 23*, 163–174.

Scribner, S., & Cole, M. (1981). *The pscychology of literacy*. Cambridge, MA: Harvard University Press.

Searle, J. R. (1983). *Intentionality: An essay in the philosophy of mind*. Cambridge, England: Cambridge University Press.

Singer, J. L., & Singer, D. G. (1981). *Television, imagination and aggression: A study of preschoolers.* Hillsdale, NJ: Erlbaum.

Sperber, D. (1984). Anthropology and psychology: Towards an epistemology of representations (Malinowski Memorial Lecture). *Man, 20,* 1–17.

Stock, B. (1983). *The implications of literacy.* Princeton, NJ: Princeton University Press.

Strauss, S. (1986). Educational-developmental psychology and school learning. In L. Liben & D. H. Feldman (Eds.), *Development and learning: Convergence or conflict?* Hillsdale, NJ: Erlbaum.

Turkle, S. (1984). *The second self: Computers and the human spirit.* New York: Simon and Schuster.

Vygotsky, L. S. (1978). *Mind in society: The development of higher psychological processes.* Cambridge, MA: Harvard University Press.

Wertsch, J. V., & Stone, C. A. (1985). The concept of internalization in Vygotsky's account of the genesis of higher mental functions. In J. V. Wertsch (Ed.), *Culture, communication and cognition: Vygotskian perspectives.* New York: Cambridge University Press.

Zellermayer, M., Salomon, G., Globerson, T., & Givon, H. (in press). Enhancing writing-related metacognitions through a computerized writing-partner. *American Educational Research Journal.*

Author Index

Subject Index